# A Grounded Theory of Decision-Making under Uncertainty and Complexity

Eurico Lopes

# A Grounded Theory of Decision-Making under Uncertainty and Complexity

## Decision-making

VDM Verlag Dr. Müller

## Impressum/Imprint (nur für Deutschland/ only for Germany)

Bibliografische Information der Deutschen Nationalbibliothek: Die Deutsche Nationalbibliothek verzeichnet diese Publikation in der Deutschen Nationalbibliografie; detaillierte bibliografische Daten sind im Internet über http://dnb.d-nb.de abrufbar.

Alle in diesem Buch genannten Marken und Produktnamen unterliegen warenzeichen-, marken- oder patentrechtlichem Schutz bzw. sind Warenzeichen oder eingetragene Warenzeichen der jeweiligen Inhaber. Die Wiedergabe von Marken, Produktnamen, Gebrauchsnamen, Handelsnamen, Warenbezeichnungen u.s.w. in diesem Werk berechtigt auch ohne besondere Kennzeichnung nicht zu der Annahme, dass solche Namen im Sinne der Warenzeichen- und Markenschutzgesetzgebung als frei zu betrachten wären und daher von jedermann benutzt werden dürften.

Coverbild: www.purestockx.com

Verlag: VDM Verlag Dr. Müller Aktiengesellschaft & Co. KG
Dudweiler Landstr. 99, 66123 Saarbrücken, Deutschland
Telefon +49 681 9100-698, Telefax +49 681 9100-988, Email: info@vdm-verlag.de
Zugl.: Leeds Metropolitan University, Uk

Herstellung in Deutschland:
Schaltungsdienst Lange o.H.G., Berlin
Books on Demand GmbH, Norderstedt
Reha GmbH, Saarbrücken
Amazon Distribution GmbH, Leipzig
ISBN: 978-3-639-24768-8

## Imprint (only for USA, GB)

Bibliographic information published by the Deutsche Nationalbibliothek: The Deutsche Nationalbibliothek lists this publication in the Deutsche Nationalbibliografie; detailed bibliographic data are available in the Internet at http://dnb.d-nb.de .

Any brand names and product names mentioned in this book are subject to trademark, brand or patent protection and are trademarks or registered trademarks of their respective holders. The use of brand names, product names, common names, trade names, product descriptions etc. even without a particular marking in this works is in no way to be construed to mean that such names may be regarded as unrestricted in respect of trademark and brand protection legislation and could thus be used by anyone.

Cover image: www.purestockx.com

Publisher:
VDM Verlag Dr. Müller Aktiengesellschaft & Co. KG
Dudweiler Landstr. 99, 66123 Saarbrücken, Germany
Phone +49 681 9100-698, Fax +49 681 9100-988, Email: info@vdm-publishing.com

# Dedication

To my lovely children

Joana, João, Mimi, Joe

and my dear wife

Arminda

# Acknowledgements

There are some people who I would like to acknowledge for their contribution in some way to this book.

I would like to thank my supervisor, Professor Antony Bryant from Leeds Metropolitan University for his support, recommendations and critical help during the writing of this book.

I am indebted to all those participants in the interviews of this research, especially Eng. Belmiro Azevedo (SONAE) who also referred other participants and gave me the permission to record an interview, and also to José Mourinho (Chelsea F.C.) for his time and participation - to them I present my gratitude.

I would also like to sincerely thank Clare Horner, my proof reader, who, although pregnant and with other commitments, was always helpful and always delivered work on time.

I would like to express my immense gratitude to my dear wife Arminda who always gave me time, help and support despite the heavy work burdens and pressures she was under herself. She provided much empathy, encouragement, help and love for me throughout my working on this book.

I also want to thank my daughter Joana for her support and every day assistance, and for the interesting issues she herself brought to the family.

For my son João, I would like to express my gratitude for his patience and co-operation in coming to the UK, and studying here, leaving his friends behind. Despite this uprooting and our lack of attention due to studying commitments, I am proud of his achievements in the UK.

To my daughter Mimi, the best English Teacher in the world, thank you for your help and for having adapted so well to your new environment, and for being so lovely.

To my baby Jomi, my constant companion and guardian, who was himself an additional project to my book, for me he is the cherry on the top of the cake.

And finally to my father, may he rest in peace.

# Table of Contents

# List of Figures

# Diagrams

# Tables

# Glossary of Terms

ANT    Actor-Network Theory

BPR    Business Process Reengineering

CRM    Customer Relationship Management

CST    Critical System Thinking

D-M    Decision-Making

EAI    Enterprise Architecture Integration

ERP    Enterprise Resource Planning

EUT    Expected Utility Theory

GTDM    Grounded Theory of Decision Making under uncertainty

GTM    Grounded Theory Methodology

HAS    Human Activity Systems

IS    Information Systems

LEUT    Local Expected Utility Theory

OOM    Object Oriented Modelling

PMM    Probabilistic Mental Models

RDEU    Rank-Dependent Expected Utility Theory

RUP    Rational Unified Process

SCM    Supply Chain Management

SOSM    System of Systems Methodologies

SSM    Soft System Methodology

TNNC    Two-person Non-zero-sum Non-cooperative Game

TZNC    Two-person Zero-sum Non-cooperative Game

# Chapter 1   Introduction

## 1.1. Book Context

### 1.1.1. Aims and Objectives

This book presents a research study of how decision-making (D-M) under uncertainty and complexity is experienced from the accounts of a discrete set of decision-makers, under Grounded Theory Methodology (GTM) and complemented with Actor-Network Theory (ANT) guidelines. Grounded characteristics of decision-making under uncertainty and complexity are a phenomenon which explicate and explore factors that characterize the process of D-M derived from a qualitative research approach.

Furthermore it will be shown how decision-makers under uncertainty define a learning story together with the construction of a social-web, where they gather information, and construct the human elements that provide the ways to calculate decision knowledge using a mix of systems tools and human interactional techniques in order to reconstruct reality. D-M under uncertainty has an impact on learning (new knowledge) and on the decision-maker's professional composure (self), in terms of experience controlled risk behaviour, and the amount of knowledge, satisfying the decision-maker. But it also affects the directly surrounding social-web, who sometimes only understand the full impact after the decision has been made and effects are visible, permitting reflection about the decision rationality. Uncertainty is a common category in all the interviews. Human interaction and understanding are important clues to deal with uncertainty.

The practical research was conducted and data was gathered from three sets of interviews corresponding to three stages of research; in the first set in-depth interviews were kept open to the collection perspectives around which further data collection

1

could be focused. The second set of interviews corresponds to an enlargement of the professional background of D-M. Finally the third set of interviews was directed by the constructed concepts from the previous sets, involving a strategic selection of informants and more structured interview protocols.

During the time the researcher was researching, he developed a theoretical sensitivity through adopting the Grounded Theory Method, and through theorizing with Grounded Theory about the nature of D-M. As Charmaz states *"we cannot assume to know our categories in advance, much less have them contained in our beginning research question"* (Charmaz, 2006, p.100). Following Charmaz's thoughts, the researcher focused on the role of learning in D-M under uncertainty and developed the following GTM research questions.

The data analysis' results permitted to design three frameworks: a conceptual framework which is the outcome of the application of GTM; the ANT network or process framework which is the result of ANT method and the behavioural framework being the connection of the former and the second one.

### 1.1.2. GTM Research Questions

- How is a process of learning in D-M under uncertain and complex contexts mobilized?

- What are the organizational/managerial mechanisms which facilitate the process of learning in D-M under uncertain and complex contexts?

- What is the contribution of learning to D-M in uncertain and complex contexts?

## 1.2. Book development summary

This book explains D-M under uncertainty and complexity, through the use of GTM. Glaser and Strauss explain *"Generating a theory from data means that most hypotheses and concepts not only come from the data, but are systematically worked out in relation to the data during the course of the research"* (Glaser and Strauss, 1967, pp. 6). For this end, hypotheses of a research study under Grounded Theory Methodology are created during the development of the research analysis as a consequence of applying GTM to the research study. Hypotheses should come forward during the research work, and help the researcher look for meaning and understand special emergent topics in the data analysis and construction, which appear during the research development. In general, within research methodologies, research questions and hypotheses are established at the outset of the research. In GTM, a general context is questioned, from where the research work under GTM will develop research questions and hypotheses, accompanying the research analysis. GTM is a process where both data and questions are created by the researcher, in order to create meaning, constructing a Grounded Theory that explains the subject of the research. A more detailed explanation about the ontology and epistemology adopted in this book is given in chapter 3.3.

The author used open-ended unstructured interviews and, under GTM, conducted a deep analysis through qualitative data that were drawn from a first set of interview sources. Initially the researcher was trying to answer research questions within a first group of interview participants. The author had an idea that decision-makers under uncertainty and complexity followed a model, an external and explicit representation of part of reality as they see it. Through this supposition, the following three questions were posed: 'Are decision-makers using complexity theory? Are decision-makers making some sort of risk evaluation? Are decision-makers using Decision Support Systems or other tools to help?'

Modelling techniques were also a first goal: what are they, how are they used, how are they applied in the organization and how they improve the knowledge of the decision-maker. This first stage helped the author to recognize the qualitative and social nature of the research context, moving away from quantitative and modelling fields, such as Prescriptive Decision Theory, First Order Systems Thinking and also Complexity Theory in areas of modelling agents. A detailed explanation about this modelling stage is given in chapter 2. However, from this first group a common pattern appeared sustaining the existence of a learning process during D-M. Aiming to research this new and revealing learning process during D-M under uncertainty and complexity, a second round of interviews was undertaken using a second set of professional informants. This was particularly beneficial in theory generation as it provided multiple perspectives on this issue and supplied more information on emerging concepts, allowing for cross-checking substantiation of grounded constructs (Glaser and Strauss, 1967).

Then a new stage of analysis that corresponded to another deep exploration of data, led to the finding of patterns. In this process new data was constructed, simultaneously with theory building. This involved a constant data reanalysis and comparison to permit starting to build the theory.

The use of Actor-Network Theory concepts such as *inscriptions, translations* and *punctualisations*, used as non-human and human constructs, provided another path of the data analysis, and helped the grounded categories' reshaping. It also offered an enhanced overview explanation of an ANT network. However, this ANT network is not used as normal ANT networks, from where firstly a network's structure is built and subsequently their ramifications and content are found. In the current research, the network is revealed from these ramifications and through the use of GTM categories, which created a sustained bottom up ANT network.

This mix of qualitative data helped the author to formulate his major themes on D-M under uncertainty and complexity: "Calculating Decision Knowledge", "Decision-maker Learning Story", "Impact of Learning on the decision-maker professional composure" and "Uncertainty" that sustain the Grounded Theory of Decision Making under uncertainty (GTDM). To consolidate the research findings a further stage of interviews, adding a new informant-participant, verification with two previous interviewees and with public exposition and discussion. A detailed explanation of the research stages is given in chapter 5.


## 1.3. Theoretical perspective


D-M under uncertainty has been associated with two positions (Bazerman, 2006) related with the study of prescriptive models where the prescriptive decision scientist develops methods for making optimal decisions, for example mathematical models to help a decision maker act more rationally. The other position is related to the study of descriptive models where the author considers the bounded ways in which decisions are actually made.

- For the current research a Learning process under uncertainty explains how rationality, a constructed reality is formed in order to facilitate D-M.

The classical models of rationality are associated with Bernoulli (1713), Jevons (1871) and Von Neumann and Morgenstern (1944) who suggest that we reach decisions in accordance with an underlying structure that enables us to function predictably and systematically. Furthermore, choice under uncertainty is the heart of decision theory following the work of De Moivre, Blaise Pascal (1623-1662) and Thomas Bayes (1702-1761) that stands for the Expected Utility Theory (EUT) from Neumann and Morgenstern (1944). The expected utility is an expectation in terms of probability theory, "*It is what the decision-maker expects at the time of decision-making*" (Chacko, 1991, pp.156). Measuring the expected value is the central problem to decision theory, by which the rationality of human decision making is measured. To this end several types of measures were adopted: Objective, Subjective and Subjectively Derived Objective measures. One important characteristic to all measures is the diversity of terms used to assess a concept which is contextually and socially dependent: *credibility, pessimism, optimism, confidence, confirmation, acceptance, belief, preference* and *surprise* (see chapter 4.2). It is always possible to introduce more terms, getting *verbal*-probabilistic propositions and with no prior evidence we have no reason to choose one form rather than another.

- Consequently, this research study was supposed to consider how verbalizations and dialogue stand for interactional constructs in a social-context under which an uncertain reality is re-framed and reconstructed to define rationality for D-M. However, measuring and other *verbal*-probabilistic propositions are not important, as it will be shown, being substituted by the grounded proposition "Calculating Decision Knowledge" for D-M under uncertainty and the individual's risk behaviour which must be seen conjointly with the directly surrounding social-web.

In terms of descriptive decision theory, Simon (1945, 1957 and 1982) first discussed D-M as programmed and non-programmed to cover routine versus complex decisions. He also considers that D-M processes are generally bounded by rules, norms and institutions. His concept of "*satisficing behaviour*" postulates, "*an organism would choose the first object that satisfies its aspiration level-instead of the intractable sequence of taking the time to survey all possible alternatives*" (Simon quoted in Gigerenzer and Goldstein, 1996, pp. 651). Kahneman and Tversky (1979) discovered behavioural patterns that make our decisions deviate from the classical models of rationality. They argue that emotions often destroy the self-control that is essential for rational D-M and decision-makers are often unable to understand fully what they are dealing with. They also argue that 'people' are not risk-averse, but loss-averse; *"it is not so much that people hate uncertainty, but rather, they hate losing"* (Tversky, 1990, pp.75).

- Furthermore this research study will show how pleasure, working hard, family/partner and confidence counts in bounding decision-makers under uncertainty. It will also show how bounded rationality is resolved within the directly surrounding social-web under the decision context.

Using the systems thinking literature field there is some evidence of the learning process in D-M under uncertainty, the focus of the present research. This learning evidence is used in the second order systems thinking, mainly by Checkland (1981) with Soft System Methodology and Wenger (1998) with Communities of Practice: Learning is a process of negotiated meaning, between participants. From the organizations literature: Argyris (1994) refers to double feedback organizational learning and Ackoff's (1994) focus on interactive planning.

- Learning is mainly related with a formation of reality, i.e. how the uncertain and complex context is understandable; how meaning is formed through social interaction to frame a system where change happens instead of an approach of finding only solutions.

Organizations are social contexts, human activity systems (HAS), which change over time. Social interaction creates stability and instability, predictability and unpredictability, creation and destruction at the same time. This means managers, as decisions makers, will have to make decisions under conditions of uncertainty, and social complexity.

- This research study will show that decision-makers have a common understanding about uncertainty, which is a permanently vague contextual reality that has not a unique solution, and is better treated through human interaction and understanding. The world moves and more uncertainty become visible, requiring more decisions, where emotional behaviour has a part in this process.

This research study will provide three results in the form of frameworks, respectively a situational framework, a process framework and a behavioural framework.

## 1.4. Limitations and key assumptions

The current research of D-M under uncertainty and complexity assumptions points to the development of theory grounded on the living experience of the interviewees who have offered their knowledge and experience of D-M under uncertainty and complexity.

The resulting grounded theory intends to be a basic type of theory, according to Gregor "*a theory for analyzing, describing and classifying dimensions and characteristics of individuals participants and situations, by summarizing the commonalities found in open interviews and observations*" (Gregor, 2006, pp.263). Supported by actor-network theory, an understanding of objects and material systems as co-agents of human intentional actors is given as an extension to the basic theory.

There are two main limitations to this research. The first relates to gathering data about D-M under the research context. The choice of interviewees was extremely demanding on research resources because some decision processes typically span periods of years; therefore the author is obliged to rely on the traces of completed decision-process in the minds of those people who carried it out. The second one is related to the interview sample. Those who advocate the logic of quantitative research could ask for a representative sample of the population under research. As Charmaz argues "*the error of this advice lies in assuming that qualitative research aims for generalization although this strategy may be useful for initial sampling, it does not fit the logic of grounded theory and can result in the researcher collecting unnecessary and conceptually thin data*" (Charmaz 2006, pp.101) and as will be shown, grounded categories have been theoretic saturated with nine interviews. The tenth and final interview was used to verify results.

## 1.5. Ethical and Privacy issues

The ethical and privacy issues of the research under development are mainly based on deontological and professional codes of conduct, since data is gathered using individual interviews. Inherent rights of the volunteer participants are considered with privacy, respect, equal treatment and informed consent. The work is guided by the Policy, Procedures and Guidance Research Ethics of the Leeds Metropolitan University as explained in chapter 3 - Research Methodology.

## 1.6. Book outline

To fulfil the GTM guidelines, answer the GTM developed research questions and make a contribution to knowledge with the resulting Grounded Theory of Decision Making under uncertainty and complexity, this book is organized into seven chapters, as follows.

A brief note about the book' organisation must be made: Chapter two 'Initial Research' is the chapter that explains the initial goals of this research and some of the literature review presented in this chapter only serves as background information to support the author's argument that information modelling or complexity systems were not the best approach to follow. Chapter three 'Research Methodology' is where the author justifies the methodology chosen and the reasons to pursue it. Chapter four 'Literature Review' contains the sources for explanation that the author used to consolidate knowledge and to justify some of the options taken. Chapter five 'Research Conceptual Development – Data Analysis' is the one that presents a detailed data analysis following grounded theory and actor-network theory. In chapter six, 'decision making under uncertainty', the results of data analysis are stated.

**Chapter 2 – Initial Research**

- This chapter presents the initial author's goals on decision support systems within information systems. A literature review was made concerning Soft Systems Methodology (SSM). An initial case study is briefly presented. Later, the author decided to merge other concepts found in literature such as complexity and uncertainty which are explained in this chapter. The reasons to discard the initial methodology proposed and to follow Grounded Theory methodology are presented.

## Chapter 3 – Research Methodology

- Chapter three introduces the research methodology of the study D-M under uncertainty and complexity. The choice for a qualitative approach is justified in this chapter and the epistemological and ontological approach of the research is exposed. An overview of Grounded Theory and Actor-Network Theory is given as well as the conciliation between both theories' methods used in this research study. The research process under the guideline of GTM is explained. Finally, the ethical and privacy issues under which the research was developed are discussed.

## Chapter 4 - Literature Review

- This chapter provides a Literature Review covering Decision Theory, Systems Thinking and Organizations, literature fields that GTM practice compelled the author to find answers and confirmation of research questions that address the context under investigation.

## Chapter 5 – Research Conceptual Development - Data Analysis

- This chapter reports the research stages, data collection and research analysis using Grounded Theory Methodology and Actor-Network Theory. The development of the theoretical sensitivity using GTM will be shown starting with open interviews, gathering data, constructing tentative ideas about categories in the data and then examining these ideas through further empirical inquiry to write memos, develop categories and finally enhance with Actor Network Theory. The theoretical development of categories: interviews transcription, coding, memos, categories and main categories are described. An explanation of ANT analysis developed along the research practice is also described. Finally, two interviews are included as an example of the work the author did during this research.

## Chapter 6 - Decision Making under Uncertainty - Frameworks

- This chapter explains the development and verification of the Grounded Theory of Decision Making. Firstly an explanation of the set of definitions that are at the basis of the current research, such as Knowledge, Information, Experience and Facts is given. Secondly, a discussion of the independent categories found in all the interviews is made. Subsequently, the resulting developed main categories of D-M under Uncertainty are presented, explaining a conceptual framework, an ANT Network and the enhancement provided by ANT over the conceptual framework. Then the Grounded Theory of Decision Making under uncertainty is explained. A comparative analysis with theories analysed in Chapter 4 - Literature Review is then included, and finally the verification of the theory, with reference to a supplementary interview showing the categories' theoretical saturation and the validity of independent categories is explained. The complementary interview is discussed and it is revealed how this corroborates the theory. A final confirmation and presentation of the theory to two interviewees and a small group is then discussed. A brief critique of the used methodology is presented.

**Chapter 7 – Conclusion**

• This chapter provides an overview of the research. The main contributions the research makes to the ongoing task of elucidating how D-M under uncertainty and complexity works are presented. The research questions are answered and the heuristic use for the theory is exposed. Finally, limitations and directions for future research are presented.

## 1.7. Summary

This chapter introduces the research context, aims, objectives of the investigation and research questions. Then a research development is described, exposing the initial research and how GTM has influenced the research questions. A theoretical background is shown in order to situate the literature context of the research study. Research limitations, ethical issues and key assumptions are summarised. Finally, a book outline, which gives a perspective of the current research work and the organization of this book, is made.

# Chapter 2   Initial Research

## 2.1. Introduction

This chapter summarizes the initial research centred on Decision Support Systems through an Information Systems view.

Initially the author was interested in understanding how decision support systems worked within information systems. With this in mind, a literature review was made concerning Soft Systems Methodology (SSM) (Checkland, 1993), and a draft of an initial case study is presented. As the research continued, the author decided to merge other concepts found in literature such as complexity and uncertainty. At this stage, some research questions were designed and interviews were made. Then, when trying to find the answers to those questions, the author realised that the methodology he was following would not help to reach the goal. So, the necessity to discard the initial methodology was evident and a new one, Grounded Theory Methodology, was considered to suit the research purpose.

However, for background information, the acquired knowledge is presented to explain and support the reasons for the discarding of the first ideas.

## 2.2. Information Systems Approach

In the area of Information systems there are some development methodologies (RUP, ICONIX, XP) and development frameworks such as the Zachman Framework (Sowa and Zachman, 1992). Information systems also have some guidelines to project management and life-cycle control (Richardson and Ives, 2004). In addition, Business Process Reengineering (BPR) provides a set of business rules, undertaken as a typical process carried out by organizations. Software components (Herzum and Sims 2000),

11

Business objects (Bolloju, 2004) or Model Driven Architecture (Frankel et al., 2003) seem like the artefacts to implement these issues. Some enterprises offer a set of well-defined implementation processes for vertical markets, since they traverse the whole organization – Enterprise Resource Planning (ERP). This is just a problem of getting people working with a new system, and some tedious work to parameterize the system on the new organization (see ERP failures in Soh et al., 2000; Vogt, 2002; Martinsons, 2004). Enterprise Application Integration (EAI) also offers a wide range of technical solutions, integrating old applications with new ones, providing web accessibility and portals (Lee et al, 2003), and even more web-services providing on line communications facilities with the external organization (Casati et al, 2003).

In this chapter, modelling thinking is presented, following Pidd (2003) and Decision Support Systems (Turban and Aronson, 2001). The author describes SSM giving an historical overview and then he will use a case study summary to demonstrate these ideas.

## 2.3. A brief overview of Soft Systems Methodology

Enterprise Modelling has its roots in the 1970s with Soft Systems Methodology (SSM), involving the entire organization and being sensitive to political and social contexts for organizational change. The 1980s knowledge-based approaches are used where knowledge representation schemes build executable domain models, capturing static and dynamic aspects of the domain. In the 1990s, teleological approaches appeared: requirements were really just goals, and modelling was for goal hierarchies. The focus is on the "why" question, rather than "what/how", using scenarios as concrete examples of how goals can be satisfied (Nuseibeh and Easterbrook, 2000; Evernden and Evernden, 2003).

. SSM is used wherever there is a symptom but not a clear-cut problem, or a clear-cut solution. It is used in responding to symptoms when the underlying problem is not yet understood. The intention is not to design an information system, but to help and to ensure that the human activity systems (HAS) has been considered, and that the information systems to be specified are those that support the business activities needed to implement the strategy (Malcolm, 2004, pp. 5).

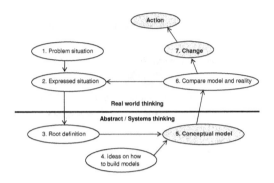

**Fig. 1. 1** – Checkland SSM stages (adapted from Malcolm, 2004)

SSM, regarded as a whole, uses system ideas to formulate basic mental acts of four kinds (Checkland, 1993, pp. 17):

- Perceiving (stage 1 & 2). Expressing the problem;

- Predicating (stage 3 & 4). Root definition and Conceptual modelling;

- Comparing (stage 5). Centre of SSM. The rich picture, root definition of relevant system and conceptual model give the analyst the wherewithal to understand the problem situation and to discuss possible changes and thereby action to improve the problem situation (Malcolm, 2004);

- Deciding on action (stage 6).

The output of the methodology is thus very different from the output of hard systems engineering: it leads to a decision to take certain actions, knowing that this will not lead to the problem being solved but to a changed situation. This is a direct consequence of the nature of the concept HAS. We attribute meaning to human activity (domain-type) and our attributions are meaningful in terms of a particular image of the world. The methodology teases out such world-images (domain-objects) and examines their implications (Checkland, 1993, pp.18).

This might focus the conceptual model (stage 5) providing routes to an embedded system, with the organization as whole: HAS and the dynamic provided by the action to be taken under some decision support by who is enabled to take such decisions. Citing Robey and Markus (1998) in Kangas "*Social science research has traditionally focused upon how organisations behave and think*" (Kangas, 2003). Weick argues that "*thinking is inseparably linked to action*: *'managers behave thinkingly'...*" (Weick, 1984 in Kangas 2003, pp. 222)".

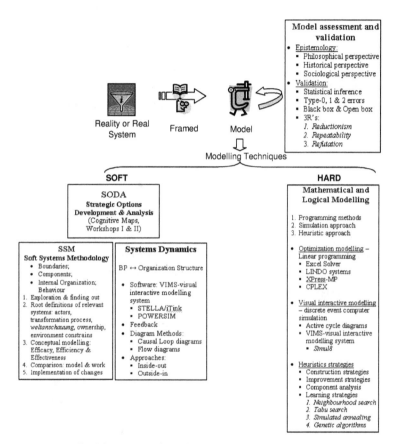

**Fig. 1. 2** – A resume of Modelling Techniques as seen in Pidd (2003)

Citing Bryant *"crossing the boundary between "analysis/observation"* and *"participant/experiencing"* (Bryant, 2000, pp.13) constrains full understanding. Understanding the practices of others does not mean to understand fully the complex system, although some systems approaches and other operational research methods do indeed stress becoming one of the *"problem owners or problem-context owners"*. But it is surely important for human-centred attempts to gain insight into the knowledge practices of others. Accordingly, with Vanhoenacker *et al "systems theory as a language can be used to describe all sorts of phenomena... means that a model, stated in systems terms, need to be created'* (Vanhoenacker *et al*, 1999, pp. 26). If we are able to do such thing, with the embedded capacity to provide an overview of the state aligned conditions, we are able to take better and supported actions, or at least ones aligned with the organization.

A summary of modelling techniques, following Pidd (2003) is presented in figure 1.2. Within this diagram both soft and hard methodologies can be found. The former are usually used during the earlier stages of the life cycle, when uncertainty about goals and strategies within the organisation exists. The latter are used when uncertainties and ambiguities have been solved, as Bennett *et al* (2002, pp. 568) state.

## 2.4. Initial case study

The author collaborated in an enterprise, from June 2003 until March 2004, within which he was asked to suggest the most advanced production system, to help with D-M in conditions of uncertainty. A production engineer believed that a new system would improve the production's planning and create more planning certainties. The enterprise has around 400 employees and an annual return of 20 million Euros. Their base operations focus on production in the apparel industry, producing goods for other brands in the men's fashion market in Europe, USA and Canada. The author endeavoured to understand why they needed such an application. A series of interviews and group discussions with staff members were made. The obtained data produced a series of UML diagrams with rich pictures to represent business rules. At stage 5 (page 13) some root definitions and some conceptual models were defined and made. The author had meetings with the board of administration and production engineering to reveal to them that if they were running at full production capacity, a new system, even understood by those that worked in planning and production, would not help D-M in uncertain and complex conditions. Some discussion occurred around the problems that would emerge from the scope of planning and production. For the author, the situation was that they were facing a new dynamic of the business strategy.

All the hard work had been done, providing support to make a decision, whether to build or buy a new system. Following SSM, conflict areas had been located, from the shop's demand and production. A new human behaviour dynamic and new types of interaction had happened in a new way of dealing with new business rules. At present, this enterprise has branched out and is now running their brand and some new stores.

This initial case study was thought to be a source of data for the present research. However the author understood in his consultancy that Small Medium Enterprises are difficult to model and to apply some of the well-known business rules to. The business types, the enterprise dimension, the inexistence of a cluster of mid-level executives are some of the impediments to understanding D-M under uncertainty. These sort of enterprises are described and implemented in vertical markets with ERP, CRM and SCM.

Citing Venkatraman (1989) in Kangas (2003) *"the new challenge for strategists is how best to reconceptualise the role of IT in business, how to identify the applications relevant to their particular strategic context, and how to reconfigure the business to not only fully exploit the available IT capabilities but also to differentiate their operations from competitors"* (pp. 126–127).

Subsequently, the author realised that the decision-maker would probably decide by considering other factors beside the implementation of new tools to support the business. Based on this impression, he started searching for new information in literature and opportunities for a new kind of interaction with decision-makers in conditions of uncertainty. This motivated him to carry on the investigation and to discard this initial case study as a source for data collection and analysis.

## 2.5. Complexity

Complexity refers to situations that are confused in two ways: one is related to the external view, where boundaries are not clearly defined, and the relations with their external context do not have a particular behaviour pattern. The interactions between the elements are not visible, and so D-M is made difficult by the inherent environment. The other refers to the internal view, where the number of elements is large and their structure is intricate. This amount of unstructured elements contributes to the impossibility to draw a structure, to observe behavioural patterns that may be manageable in order to make a decision.

Typically, complexity in terms of Decision Theory represents the bounded rationality of the decision-maker. Complexity can also be used to describe situations where the dynamic interactions between the elements in the context do not provide the means to evaluate a probability measure due to the absence of patterns.

In other fields, complexity is understood as a measure. For example in computational theory, complexity represents the number of steps that it takes to resolve a function. In information theory, it is described as descriptive complexity or algorithmic entropy and is a measure of a string that represents the length of the shortest binary programme which outputs that string. In information processing, complexity measures the total number of properties transmitted by an object and detected by an observer. In physical systems, complexity measures the probability of the state vector of the system. In mathematics, complexity is not a measure but the study of finite semi-groups and automata. In biology the term irreducible complexity is used as an argument against the theory of biological evolution.

Complexity is part of our environment, and many scientific fields have dealt with the study of designated complex systems, founded in complexity and chaos theory from the systems thinking world like Ashby (1959), von Bertalanffy (1968), Churchman (1970) and Weick (1977). Arthur (1999) states *"Complex systems are systems in process, systems that constantly evolve and unfold over time"* (Arthur 1999, pp.1). Concepts of command-and-control, explicit rules and algorithms over complex systems, according to Bryant (2006) *"must be contrasted with strategies that assume that there is no final answer upon which to arrive at a definitive and calculated solution"* (Bryant, 2006, pp.151). Complex adaptive systems are special cases of complex systems. They are complex in that they are diverse and made up of multiple interconnected elements and adaptive in that they have the capacity to change. A complex adaptive system consists of a large number of agents, differenced from one other, but each of which behaves to the same set of rules. These rules require agents to adjust their behaviour to that of other agents that interact and adapt to each other. Stacey (2003) argues that they display the capacity of spontaneous evolution to new forms: *"The whole is always evolving, never completed, finished"* (Stacey, 2003, pp. 268).

These systems ideas, with the application of mathematical and modelling techniques of complex systems, have been used in the study of D-M situations: Financial Markets (Peters, 1991), Production and Inventory Scheduling (Morley, 1995); Allen's (1998) search for equilibrium in fishing fleets, assuming bounded rational D-M; and Levy (1994) simulates a model that can be used to guide decisions concerning production location, sourcing and optimum inventory levels. Levy argues that complex systems must be understood as a whole to aid D-M. Levy points out that human systems are not deterministic and he uses simple rules as guidelines that may influence decisions. He recognizes the impossibility of long-term prediction. Instead of asking how managers are actually now proceeding in the absence of forecast, Levy states they should foresee a number of scenarios and set simple guidelines. Marion (1999) uses fitness landscapes to develop a model of the microcomputer industry, which exemplifies organisational complexity development. Marion follows an evolutionary neo-Darwinian perspective that the genes of an organisation are a blueprint that determines the biological structure of that organism. Meme from Marion are: ideas, concepts, beliefs, scientific theories, ideologies, fads, fashion the blueprint for social and organisational structure which are able to produce the content of culture (shared understanding of how things should be). Kurtz and Snowden (2003) propose the Cynefin Framework into the use of narrative and complexity theory in organizational knowledge exchange, decision-making, strategy and policy-making.

In the presented examples, they are more than models for D-M. Complexity is modelled by a system, and this model gives an explanation for the behaviour of the system under research. However, decision-makers may be making strategic choices, changing simple rules and managing boundaries. They cannot therefore know the long-term outcome of the choices they are making. Even Levy (1994) recognizes the long-term predictions are not possible and states that decision-makers should foresee scenarios and set simple guidelines.


## 2.6. Uncertainty


Uncertainty has played an important role during human history in how people make the best decisions, *"some basis is on quantification and numbers, determined by patterns of the past, and others on more subjective degrees of belief about the uncertain future"* (Bernstein, 1996, pp.6).

Decisions are influenced by uncertainty in a wide variety of fields, where the goal is to reduce uncertainty with a set of applied techniques. In fields such as social sciences, policy-making, risk analysis, economics, management, physical sciences and engineering, uncertainty has been the subject of research and used to develop reducing techniques. A selection of distinct viewpoints to indicate the different approaches to the topic is here presented.

Classical Economic theory assumes that the decision-maker will make decisions with full knowledge of what the outcome of their decision will be; there is no space for uncertainty. Knight states "*Uncertainty must be taken in a sense radically distinct from the familiar notion of risk, from which it has never been properly separated*" (Knight, 1964 quoted in Bernstein 1996, pp.219). Bernstein argues that "*the prevalence of surprise in the world of business is evidence that uncertainty is more likely to prevail than mathematical probability*" (Bernstein, 1996, pp. 220-1). Uncertainty is also classified as ambiguity, when fundamental uncertainty is associated with an event which cannot be imagined or may occur in the future. Ambiguity is defined as uncertainty about probability (Yates and Stone, 1992).

Systems Analysis simplifies uncertainty into risks and treats uncertainty as ignorance. In the domain of Physical Sciences, uncertainty is primarily related to error analysis, which represents the difference between a measured value and the actual value. Heisenberg, with the Principle of Uncertainty introduces the quantum structure of matter itself pointing out that is impossible to determine with unlimited precision the position and movement of a particle simultaneously. In Engineering, certainty is achieved through observation, and uncertainty is that which is removed by observation. The Engineering field deals with uncertainty classifying it as the difference between a model and the reality.

For the Management field, uncertainty is that which disappears when we become certain. Measures of uncertainty are simply abstract measures, divorced from choice. They depend on the specified knowledge from the decision-maker, determined by observing possible choices at determined conditions.

## 2.7. Research Questions

After the first stage of literature review, the author designed the presented research questions:

- Are decision-makers using complexity theories under uncertainty and complexity?

- Are decision-makers making some sort of risk evaluation to help D-M under uncertainty and complexity?

- Are decision-makers using Decision Support Systems or other tools to help D-M under uncertainty and complexity?

To answer these questions, a set of interviews was made for decision-makers, as will be shown in the next section.


## 2.8. Research Methodology


In order to continue the research, the author decided to interview some decision-makers from the business world. The author established contacts with some enterprises and in an open-interview style, collected data that could establish the premises for answering the research questions.

For this end, a set of heterogeneous participants in the business and management field, from small to very large organizations, were interviewed. The author used open interviews ask the decision-makers how they have achieved decisions under uncertainty. The choice for open interviews was in order to understand the premises and the processes that they may have used to make a decision. With open interviews, informants are only questioned in general terms about the subject, allowing them to recount their experiences. However, other approaches may be used: for example, following decision-makers during the experience of D-M under uncertainty and then taking notes and observing them. This approach proved to be difficult, because some decisions take time to be made. Also, the availability of informants to allow such an intimate approach, proved to be very difficult in the business world. Therefore, the author used open-interviews, to keep the studied subjects as "open" as possible from early on.

The author's choice was firstly in the business field, asking those who had the availability and interest in the research topic to participate. At this point, the first interviewee (01-Dinefer) accepted to be interviewed, which provided the first experience of conducting open interviews under the research topic. In addition, the author decided to establish contact with the largest private Portuguese enterprise (02-Sonae), a business whose decisions create change, in business terms, in Portugal. Following the interview to request participation, the contact agreed to help, referring future participants to the author, including a Professor from the London Business School (04-LBS) and a Banker from Goldman Sachs (05-Goldman), in London. They were not an initial choice or target of the author, but came through the kind opportunity of the second interviewee and their availability and willingness to participate. The remaining participant in this first group was a choice of the author, chosen for three reasons: proximity, availability and also the enterprise being run by unknown business decision management rules, the Leeds Metropolitan University Vice-Chancellor (03-Leedsmet).

With this first group of interviews, laborious and detailed work was carried out, working with the initial research questions. A decision-maker uses modelling techniques, to explore which of them are used, how they are used, how are they applied in the organization and how they help the decision-maker. The author was testing the research questions but simultaneously searching for new hypotheses that could be researched with this group of interview participants that may lead to further empirical inquiry.

## 2.9. Learning focus

Initially the author was inspecting the hypothesis that decision-makers under uncertainty and complexity build a model, an external and explicit representation of part of reality as seen by the decision-maker. The answer to this question was surprising. Referring to the author's hypothesis, based on his professional experience in the computer system engineering field and reinforced by the initial literature review, the author was expecting answers that supported a calculated way of thinking or risk evaluation technique. Following an open-interview format, no direct questions were asked, giving the interviewees the possibility to speak freely whilst also revealing their feelings about their experience. In this way, the interviewees' accounts are subject to reconstruction without any preconceived questionnaire or other research strategy. After each interview, the author perceived that D-M under uncertainty and complexity was more a social process than a question of using mathematical procedures. Each interviewee did not relate any objectively observed natural world, he did not recount any formulated hypothesis that he had previously tested against obtained quantified data. Each interviewee revealed how he became involved in a social interaction and what were they perceived for. This is in accordance with a constructivist position where every explanation people put forward of any phenomena is a socially constructed account, not a straightforward description of reality (Gergen, 1985, quoted in Robson, 2002).

The task to find answers was then a work of serendipity from the interviews, data, readings and a recurring return to the interviews.

From these experiences the author interpreted and constructed meaning that sustains a central concept of *Learning*, which guides the D-M in an uncertain and complex context. This interpretation was not something that is there waiting to be observed and measured. That reality was hidden and has to be constructed in order to have existence, it is not something that is offered as material substance or has been asked for. Rejecting and failing to create meaning through described experiences creates a momentum for meaningful construction of these hypotheses. There now follows the first interpretations, impressions that the author sensed that uphold this *Learning* concept.

From the first impressions and analysis of the first interview (01-Dinefer), modelling techniques from the system thinking world were not used, not because they weren't asked, but because they did not keep the interviewee's D-M process going. This fact was not present, even if attempting to link with Strategic Management or other techniques. The link does not work and the recounted experiences did not fit, sustained hypotheses were empty, and nothing made sense at this first analysis.

Furthermore, in the second analysis work over the 02-Sonae interview, the analysis gave the author a new horizon. Modelling techniques and risk evaluation were not the decision-maker support. The interviewee knew risk evaluation and game theory, however, as he argued, these techniques were not the substance that guided D-M under-uncertainty. It was not a question of risk evaluation or use of supportive tools. At that time, the author perceived from the 02-Sonae interview that learning is indirect; it is a process that, from the interviewee's words it provides meaning around the central concept of Learning.

The author did a third analysis after interviewing an expert from the London Business School but the results of this interview did not give new insight for the research. The method was: the author based their assumptions on suggested theories by the interviewee and he supposed that they could fit with the recounted experiences. The results were mainly that the research of a qualitative nature could be carried out and that the concept of learning stated by the interviewee guided D-M: "*I think there are connections between the way people learn and the way they take decisions*". However the idea that learning is a process under D-M under uncertainty and complexity was not clearly sustained by common literature found in the field.

The central idea from the 05-Goldman interview was the need to learn having confidence to solve problems, to create a social relationship with professional colleagues based in daily meetings and be supported by the use of information and communications technology. A central idea of *Learning* to decide fast and later adjust decisions if necessary also evolved.

| Initial research questions<br>Are decision-maker's | | | | |
|---|---|---|---|---|
| | using complexity theory? | making some sort of risk evaluation? | using Decision Support Systems or other tools to help? | Sensed, Interpreted and Constructed Meaning |
| 01-Dinefer | No | No | Yes, but he does not understand them "*It is that I do not perceive anything of that. There are things I do not know that they had become there.*" | Decisions under uncertainty are not found in this premises, in information systems |
| 02-SONAE | No, but he believes in natural evolution | Yes, but it has no impact how he decides, in his words | Yes, scenarios and game theory, but he does not feel confident with them, it his a personal position, assuming risk | Decisions under uncertainty depend on the personal confidence and risk taking behaviour and not in alternative tools |
| 03-Leedsmet | No, but organization history and values are important | Yes, some statistics, but in his words they do not count | Yes, managerial and statistical packages which does not account for a decision under uncertainty. "*It is not a financial model with lot of consultants, statistics and so on... it is much more about living the values*" | Decisions under uncertainty are more about the living values of the decision-maker. |
| 04-LBS | No. "*I don't see how complexity theory helps*" | No. "*...managers don't reduce uncertainty objectively... they reduce the perception of uncertainty*". | No | Decisions under uncertainty are a question of how a personal manager reduces the perception of uncertainty |
| 05-Goldman | No | Yes, but not a way to reduce uncertainty. Decisions must be prompt in great uncertainty context, no time for reducing uncertainty | Yes, mainly to support organizational communications between bankers and the market and as a living report from successful and failed cases | Decisions under uncertainty must be prompted and not much time to reduce uncertainty |

Table 2. 1 – Analysis summary of initial research questions

The Leeds Metropolitan University (03-Leedsmet) interview also offered fundamental ideas around the learning concept and need for a social network which becomes more consistent. In the interviewee's words "*opposition or disagreement is not a bad thing, it is good, it is learning*", "*I think too many managers in universities spent time with computers and charts... it is much more about living the values, expressing the spirit of what the University should be*", "*I don't think I need a huge amount of statistical modelling to reach a decision, because often a decision is all about the human interaction".* This is also a rejection of hypothesis, from where systems and modelling strategies should be important. Table 2.1 shows a summary analysis of how the author interpreted and made a construction of meaning from the interviewees' accounted experiences. So, it became clear in the researcher's mind, that decisions under uncertainty are not based on initial hypotheses. Decisions under uncertainty depend on risk taking behaviour or are more about the living values of the decision-maker. Decisions under uncertainty are a question of how a personal decision-maker reduces the perception of uncertainty, but conversely decisions under uncertainty must be prompted and with not much time to reduce uncertainty.

From the answers obtained, a commonality that unites all the related experiences started to surface. Every one seemed to be embedded in a learning experience. What should be investigated was the structuring of the context, construction of meaning, and the search for knowledge that guides the decision maker further in the process of D-M.

Then another problem materialised – the literature does not make references to this *learning* process, and even fewer references exist of *Learning under Uncertainty*. This provides a justification of the research focus, the core of the research. All the subsequent research work drew on the premise of this focus, and tried to understand how it works, what processes are involved and properties surrounding them. Table 2.2 presents some examples of sample phrases from each interview and created meaning.

| Interview | Extracts Interview | Sensed, Interpreted and Constructed Meaning |
|---|---|---|
| 01-Dinefer | *"People know that the direction is for there, but not the way! Let us say that the way become walking, experience."*  *"The reactivity of whom is in this process all has to be very great; therefore if people will not have capacity to answer to the necessities, in this case of the customers, but sometimes this can not be only customers... It can be fans, can be the proper family, it can be whatsoever, depending the type of organization, what we need is find out to react"* | Learn with experience Sense other needs, and Learn to be capable to answer them |
| 02-SONAE | *"We at SONAE assume a risk taker position and when we have much uncertainty we go to the challenge and when it arrives exactly at the dark room, where we become lost. Before this, it goes trying... and the limit is basically to never back the company."* | Trying, going to the challenge and learning how to became out successfully |
| 03-Leedsmet | *"We have to look at the history institution, personal dynamics, or students want to do"*  *"opposition or disagreement is not a bad thing, it is good, it is learning"* | Sense and learn the organization history and values. Learn also with disagreements |
| 04-LBS | *"I think there are connections between the way people learn and the way they take decisions"*  *"...learning value decisions ..."* | Making decisions is a Learning process |
| 05-Goldman | *"Here we have to learn to decide extraordinarily fast and always under conditions of great uncertainty. This is different from European organizations where we try first to reduce uncertainty and then take a decision"* | Learn to observe and be prompted to decide, not delaying reducing uncertainty |

**Table 2. 2** – Sample phrases from each interview and created meaning

## 2.10. A new approach using Qualitative Research

It was understood that learning and social network will be a potential approach under a qualitative research type.

Bryman (1993) describes qualitative research as an approach that concerns the social world, and looks to explain and analyze the culture and behaviour of individuals, from the point of view of these being studied. Eldabi *et al* (2002) believes qualitative research provides a systematic, empirical strategy for answering questions about people in their own bounded social context, also the direct and in-depth knowledge of a research setting is necessary to achieve contextual understanding. The advantage of viewing behaviour in its social setting seems to provide a greater depth of understanding, allowing greater flexibility. Strauss and Corbin (1990) claim that qualitative methods can give the intricate details of phenomena that are not easy to express with quantitative methods, also qualitative data are data represented by words not numbers. There is growing recognition, within these disciplines, that qualitative research techniques are needed to capture holistic real-world answers to real world problems in a way that is not possible in a quantitative context (Neuman, 1991; Tesch, 1990). Qualitative methods produce a wealth of detailed data on a small number of individuals (Patton, 1991). Glaser and Strauss (1967) focus on qualitative research, which is usually the most "adequate" and "efficient" way to obtain the type of information required, and to contend with the difficulties of an empirical situation.

Despite these strengths, qualitative research also shows some weakness, related with qualitative samples, and there is no systemic or statistical approach, usually working with small samples of people (Miles and Huberman, 1994). Eldabi *et al* (2002) claim that qualitative approaches to research take a less planned approach with more preference towards judgmental and expert knowledge rather than hard data. Quantitative research has been criticized for scratching the outside of people's attitudes and feelings, where the complexity of the human soul is lost through the counting of numbers (Wright and Crimp 2000). In other words it describes the general characteristics of a population, and ignores the details of each particular element studied (Hyde, 2000). Blalock focus his criticisms on the deductive nature of quantitative processes and the preoccupation which researchers supporting quantitative process have with statistical analysis, to the detriment of quality data production. He claims that this narrow approach forces researchers to work within theory rather than challenge or extend it (Blalock, 1991).

Minchiello *et al* (1990) distinguish qualitative from quantitative research into two main areas: Conceptual and Methodological.

| | Qualitative | Quantitative |
|---|---|---|
| Conceptual | Concerned with understanding human behaviour from the informant's perspective. | Concerned with discovering facts about social phenomena. |
| Methodological | Assumes a dynamic and negotiated reality. | Assumes a fixed and measurable reality. |
| | Data are collected through participant observation and interviews. | Data are collected through measuring things. |
| | Data are analyzed by themes from descriptions by informants. | Data are analyzed through numerical comparisons and statistical inferences. |
| | Data are reported in the language of the informant. | Data are reported through statistical analysis. |

**Table 2. 3** – Distinguishing qualitative from quantitative research in two main areas[1]

According to Eldabi *et al* (2002), qualitative research emphasizes getting close to the subject(s) of study; an experience which is a good way to understanding social behaviours. Thus, the aim of qualitative data is to describe social reality from the perspective of the subject, not the observer. Therefore, qualitative research has the advantage of viewing behaviour in its social location, providing greater depth of understanding and allowing greater flexibility. Stake (1994) stated that researchers use qualitative research to expand and generalize theories rather than to establish the frequency with which an event is likely to happen.

### 2.10.1. Qualitative methods

Qualitative research typically relies on the following methods for gathering information: Participant Observation, Non-participant Observation, Field Notes, Reflexive Journals, Structured Interviews, Unstructured Interviews and Analysis of documents and materials. Myers (2009) refers to qualitative data sources which include observation and participant observation (fieldwork), interviews and questionnaires, documents and texts, and the researcher's impressions and reactions. Myers (2009) deems that qualitative methods are action research, case study research and ethnography.

---

[1] Conceptual and Methodological, Adapted from Minchiello *et al.*,1990, pp.5

In a brief summary there follows the description of some of the qualitative research methods and the justification for the choice the author adopted.

**Observation** - Observational techniques are methods by which a researcher gathers data mainly with the objective of studying behaviours. They provide the opportunity to collect data on a wide range of behaviours, and to capture a great variety of interactions, for example. One of the goals is to observe activities and understand the context within which they were developed. There are two types of observation techniques: participant observation and direct observation. In the former, the researcher is required to become a participant in the culture or context being observed and become accepted as a natural part of the culture. In the latter, a direct observer does not normally try to become a participant in the context. The researcher is watching rather than taking part. It also concerns observing certain sampled situations or people rather than trying to become immersed in the entire context.

The term "**case study**" has multiple meanings. It can be used to describe a unit of analysis (e.g. a case study of a particular organisation) or to describe a research method. Yin defines the case study research method as "*an empirical inquiry that investigates a contemporary phenomenon within its real-life context; when the boundaries between phenomenon and context are not clearly evident; and in which multiple sources of evidence are used*" (Yin, 1984, pp. 23).

The author did not use the case study method to build upon theory, or to produce new theory, or to dispute or challenge theory, because it would be necessary to explain a situation, to provide a basis to apply solutions to situations, to explore, or to describe an object or phenomenon. At the beginning of this research, the author was interested in understanding D-M under uncertainty and he only knew that answers could arrive from people who decided under uncertainty. So, asking questions to enterprise or institutions' leaders would be more interesting.

**Action research** is action oriented and participative to achieve a change. The change occurs as understanding occurs. For Cormack (1991, pp.155) action research "*is a way of doing research and working on solving a problem at the same time*". The method was developed to allow the author and participants to work together to analyse social systems with a view to changing them. In other words, to achieve specific goals. So, the author did not know what kind of goals he would achieve and he knew that he would not contribute to decision making, mainly because of the different author skills, background, experiences and knowledge within the variety of areas of the interviewees. This was the main reason to abandon the idea of using this research method.

Wilson and McLean (1994) consider that the questionnaire is a useful instrument for collecting survey information, providing structured, often numerical data, being able to be administered without the presence of the researcher. This method was not considered by the research since it did not fit with the author's initial ideas.

After considering the presented methods, the author believed that interviews and note taking were the qualitative methods that suited this research because the author's goals were to understand how decision makers decided under uncertainty. Therefore, following GTM, even though the data may come from many sources, a common source beside observation and case study, is interviews, which the author considered more suitable in consideration of the hypothesis he had in dialoguing with experts from different backgrounds and professions.

The participants in this research were people who work in specific environments that have ethical procedures to follow and it was thus difficult for the author to get permission to be a participant or direct observer within the participants' environment, for example to fly and observe pilots, to participate in decision making meetings, or to assist doctors in action.

So the choice of the **open-ended unstructured interviews'** method was thought to be the most appropriate method since it involved direct interaction between the author and the research participants. The author had some initial guiding questions or core concepts to ask about, but there was no formally structured plan. The interviewer was free to move the conversation in any direction of interest that came up. Although the author interacted with the participant asking questions, asking for detail, and asking for clarification, the participant was not forced to follow any direction.

Benbasat *et al* (1987) showed that the goals of the researcher and the nature of the research topic influence the choice of a strategy.

## 2.10.2. Justification for GTM Utilization

The research methodology followed was GTM (Glaser and Strauss, 1967) to generate a descriptive and explanatory theory of D-M under uncertainty and complexity. This approach was adopted here for many reasons.

This initial research helped to support that D-M under uncertainty is not just a question of modelling an information system to help the decision process. GTM could help to explore further the utilization of IS and its relationship to D-M. The author decided to use GTM to investigate the phenomenon (D-M) within real-life contexts, especially when the boundaries between phenomenon and contexts are not clear. Neither happened concerning a clear definition, in this research, between the practices of IS and D-M under uncertainty experiences.

In addition, GTM presents a single, unified, systematic method of analysis; the previous interviews' data can be kept as well as the accounted experiences, but now the data can be analysed under a new framework for example, by using line by line coding. Also, GTM includes processes such as open coding and selective coding, axial coding or theoretical coding; not as other structural analysis methods or qualitative methods, which often rely upon the application of general principles. According to Charmaz (2003), the major strength of GTM is that it provides tools for analyzing processes that make it easier for the researcher to follow specific steps to develop the concepts, categories, hypotheses and theory.

A GT approach allows a degree of flexibility in both the selection of instances for inclusion in the sample and the analysis of the data, both of which are appropriate to the investigation of new topics, and new ideas as D-M under uncertainty issues in real companies; it also permits to discover the factors that influence D-M application in the context and to determine the extent of its application. This was done by using GTM that includes orderly procedures for selecting the sample and continues the analysis and comparison process, which has helped the researcher to make continuous modifications within the data.

Additionally, the GT approach includes the means of developing theoretical propositions from data which should increase the researcher's confidence in the area of theorizing. The author was looking for generating data about this new topic rather than evaluating or assessing something that had already been found, as previous experiences have shown.

GTM thus allowed the author to enter the field of research without any specific concepts to be tested, especially when the author did not have sufficient support from the interviews and adequate literature about the stage of D-M application in the uncertain context. The author started his research without any representative samples by interviewing people in companies without developing any specific hypothesis about D-M under uncertainty. Surveys or structured or semi-structured interviews could not initially be used because there were no specific themes. In addition, the formulation of questions and design were not possible, nor was hypotheses formulation.

## 2.11. Summary

This chapter firstly presents an empirical approach design to be followed by the author. Also a literature review concerned with Soft Systems Methodology (SSM) (Checkland, 1993) is presented. To support SSM and the D-M, an initial case study was briefly described. Finally, the reasons for the discard of the initial methodology and the justifications to use a Qualitative Research approach and the choice for Grounded Theory Methodology are cited.

# Chapter 3   Research Methodology

## 3.1. Introduction

The research method approach used in this book is qualitative research that makes use of the Grounded Theory Method (GTM) (Glaser and Strauss, 1967; Charmaz, 2006) to offer an explanatory theory of D-M under uncertainty and complexity. Then, Actor-Network Theory (Law, 1992; Callon, 1999; Law and Hassard, 1999) is used to help the development of the grounded categories and improve and enhance the obtained results.

The choice of a qualitative approach is justified in this chapter and the philosophical approach of the research is explained. An overview of Grounded Theory and Actor-Network Theory is given as well as the conciliation between both methods used in this research study. The research process under the guideline of GTM is explained. Finally, the ethical and privacy issues under which the research was developed are described.

## 3.2. The choice of Qualitative Research

Grounded Theory is used to generate data which have been created through interaction within a systematic researcher's interpretative view, which organizes and reduces the data and gathers them into themes, which in turn provide descriptions, categories, hypotheses, models and finally theory (a detailed explanation is given in chapter 5). This process of data analysis is classified as qualitative research and as Miles and Huberman state "*manages words, language, and the meanings these imply*" (Miles and Huberman, 1994 quoted in Walker *et al*, 2006, pp. 549) and is not a statistical evaluation of events, as Stake (1994) states - researchers use qualitative research to expand and generalize theories rather than establish the frequency with which an event is likely to happen.

GTM aims to understand phenomena through the meanings that people assign to them (Boland 1985, 1991; Deetz 1996; Orlikowski and Baroudi 1991). It is used for an interpretation and construction of meaning beneath which D-M under uncertainty and complexity stand. The context, where the decision-process develops, is uncertain and complex, furthermore the decision-maker is reconstructing reality, reshaping his knowledge in order to make a decision. Assumptions of a quantitative nature of this process are not available and not yet formed, only suppositions which have representations under a hypothetical measure of risk probability, or *"assumptions of certainty as guides to decision-making"* exist (Knight and Keynes quoted in Newman, 1988, p. 1336). Reality and its perceived meaning are under construction, which will be interpreted and made visible by the decision-maker in order to decide.

Thus, the aim of qualitative information adopted in this research using GTM is to describe the social reality from the outlook of the decision-maker, and to enable the researcher to construct a classification of specific dimensions that characterizes and explains the decision-maker experience. This is done by constructing and summarizing the commonalities found in a discrete group of decision-makers who have been participating in this research study. More specifically, the researcher used open-ended unstructured interviews and conducted an in-depth analysis through qualitative data that were drawn from a first set of interviews. Then, through a sensitive analysis of the data rich interviews, themes, concepts and categories were generated. The researcher inspected the decision-maker models that they may use to comprehend and to handle the context of uncertainty and complexity under which a decision occurs. In doing so, the researcher was inspecting how the decision-makers frame reality, how they use modelling techniques from the system thinking world.

The author has adopted a constructivist position as stated by Charmaz *"we are part of the world we study and the data we collect"* (Charmaz, 2006, pp. 10) in opposition to an objectivist grounded theory in the positivist tradition sense, which assumes data represent objective facts about a knowable world. Quoting Charmaz *"For Objectivist Grounded Theory the data already exists in the world; the research finds them and discovers theory from them"* (Charmaz, 2006, pp.131). Furthermore, the current research stands in a constructivist perspective, investigating how our knowledge of reality is formed and gained through social constructions such as language, consciousness, shared meanings, documents, tools, and other artefacts that guide D-M under uncertainty and complexity.

Finally, using Actor Network Theory, concepts such as *inscriptions, translations* and *punctualisations*, are used as non-human constructs that help the development of the grounded categories researched as well as offering an enhanced overview explanation.

## 3.3. Research Paradigm

Some philosophical issues emerged from the present research, posing questions about the underlying assumptions and whether they fit with the research claims. The field of D-M according to Bazerman can be divided into two parts:

- *"Study of prescriptive models: the prescriptive decision scientist develops methods for making optimal decisions and*

- *Study of descriptive models: the descriptive decision researchers consider the bounded ways in which decisions are actually made"* (Bazerman, 2006, pp.6-7).

Prescriptive models are mathematical models that help a decision maker act more rationally, about which Bernstein argues *"the concept of rational behaviour, measurement always dominates intuition: rational people make choices on the basis of information rather than on the basis of whim, emotion, or habit"* (Bernstein, 1996, pp. 246). In the field of Prescriptive Decision Theory, decision-makers are rational people, whose behaviour could be ruled under a mathematical description when information is available, and *"in classical economics, buyers and sellers, and workers and capitalists, always have all the information they need... Business managers regularly extrapolate from the past to the future but often fail to recognize when conditions are beginning to change from poor to better or from better to worse. They tend to identify turning points only after the fact happened"* (Bernstein, 2006, pp.220). It could be pointed out that some of the most apparently prescriptive mathematical models allow users to detect areas in which uncertainties in data values are particularly critical. For example, sensitivity analysis serves this purpose and is an approach applicable to many types of model, while the concept of the "value of perfect information" can be used in more specific instances. For example sensitivity analysis can be used to help develop a particular model. If the response to the model is reasonable from an intuitive or theoretical perspective, then the model users may have some qualitative behaviour of the model even if the quantitative precision or accuracy is unknown (Frey and Patil, 2002). However, the difficulty of the forecasting process extends beyond the impossibility of applying mathematical propositions to forecasting the future.

According to the current research, information is not completely available in the reality in which decisions are made, because the context is uncertain and complex. This means that reality is under construction and information is not formally available, in a prescriptive narrow sense. The knowledge of that reality is constructed in order to understand what sustains D-M under uncertainty and complexity. This approach is justified because the most important decisions we make usually occur under complex, confusing, indicting, or frightening conditions and according to Bernstein with "*Not much time to consult the laws of probability... Life is not a game it often comes trailing Kenneth Arrow's clouds of vagueness*" (Bernstein, 1996, pp.269).

Conversely, D-M is said to be a psychological construct (Tversky and Kahneman, 1982) and according to Barnard "*decisions depend on personal or psychological factors and require interaction and communication*" (Barnard, 1938 quoted in Rowe and Boulgarides, 1992, pp. 16). This means that although we can never "*see*" a decision, it is possible to infer from observable behaviour that a decision has been made. Descriptive analyses of D-M suggest that decision makers "*adopt a variety of strategies for dealing with their limited ability to process complex information*" (Montgomery and Svenson, 1989, quoted in Yates and Stone, 1992, pp.293). These descriptive models sustain the idea that decision-makers reach decisions in accordance with an underlying structure that make them predictable. For this end, Pitz states that "*behavioural decision theory usually provides a descriptive account of people's behaviour, seeking to explain observed decisions in terms of general psychological principles*" (Pitz, 1992, pp. 285). However, either decision-makers' decisions were irrational or the expected utility theory wrong (EUT). A large number of experiments have been conducted that when faced with similar choice problems, a substantial number of subjects usually violate the EUT. These paradoxical observations are known as Allais paradoxes (Biswas 1997, pp.4-5) where either a rational decision-maker could make irrational decisions, or the expected value theory is wrong. Additionally, several non-expected utilities were theorized, proposing alternative theories of D-M behaviour under uncertainty (see Chapter 4.3). Furthermore, a centred research study should focus on the psychological patterns observed in decision-makers under uncertainty and complexity, analysing cognitive difficulties and other emotional patterns in psychological terms. The most influential research on how decision-makers manage risk and uncertainty under psychological terms has been conducted by two psychologists Daniel Kahneman and Amos Tversky, developing Prospected Theory (see Chapter 4.3). Despite this type of research, focused on psychological inconsistencies, myopias, bounds and other forms of distortion throughout the process of D-M, another outlook is suggested by Bernstein *"perhaps people are not non-rational... and the problem is with the model of rationality rather than with us human beings"* (Bernstein, 1996, pp.265). This is to say, the reality under such model of rationality has to be reconstructed according to other assumptions, other social constructs which may give a new meaning. Chase *et al.* (1998) also make a statement that the classical definition of rationality also has problems:

- No single conception of probability is shared by all statisticians and philosophers – and probability is one amongst other measurement attempts of uncertainty;

- Definition of rationality is its blindness to content and context – where rationality stands for the construction of reality, by the social decision-makers involved in the process. The social decision-makers stand in an assumption of others' behaviours, but with their own reality, making judgments and inferences;

- It makes unrealistic demands of the mind - In the real world, matters are more complicated than the simple content-blind norms tested in most laboratory problems assume. Quoting Chase *et al* (1998) *"In many situations, a rational model cannot even be specified because the problem space is unbounded. Expecting people's inferences to conform to classical rational norms in such complex environments requires believing that the human mind is a Laplacean demon: a supercalculator with unlimited time, knowledge, and computational power"* (Chase *et al.* 1998, pp.207).

Given then this attention to this definition of rationality, and how we construct meaning to content and context, Steir states *"there are two main perspectives how an individual perceives reality: the cognitive perspective where a decision-maker perceives an objective reality and will act on that perceived reality and the constructivist perspective where the decision-maker acts on the basis of perceptions built up through past experience and in so doing selects, or enacts, an environment"* (Steir, 1991 quoted in Stacey, 2003, pp.9).

Referring to research paradigms, independent of positivist or constructivist research, all paradigms respond to three basic questions (Guba, 1990) and more clearly – whatever one's research approach the following need to be clarified:

- *"What is the nature of reality? A question of ontology;*

- *What is the nature of the relationship between the knower (inquirer) and the known (knowledge)? A question of epistemology;*

- *How should the inquirer go about finding out knowledge? A question of methodology"* (Guba, 1990, pp. 18 quoted in Shaw, 1999, pp. 44).

The ontological problems arise from the definition of reality. In this research, the attempt to define what reality is, in terms of uncertainty, where many issues are not taken-for-granted, was difficult. Generally, positivism is interested in causality and explanations, in contrast with human subjects, expectations or systems that are produced through human interaction in D-M. As Orlikowski and Baroudi state *"Positivist researchers tend to ignore the fact that people think and act, that people are active makers of their physical and social reality...Such studies serve primarily to test theory, in an attempt to increase predictive understanding of phenomena"* (Orlikowski and Baroudi 1991, pp.5 quoted in Klein and Meyers, 1999, pp.73). A position for constructivist studies, according to Klein and Meyers states *"Interpretive researchers insist that any observable organizational patterns are constantly changing because organizations are not static and that the relationships between people, organizations, and technology are not fixed but constantly changing. As a consequence, interpretive research seeks to understand a moving target"* (Klein and Meyers, 1999, pp.73) and not to test a cause-effect positivist relationship theory. So when we act, we also change reality, and this movement, this dynamic of change creates the work of a constructivist approach which, as Holstein and Gubrium state, *"is the interactional procedures of knowledge production – the how of meaning making – centre stage"* (Holstein and Gubrium, 1995 quoted in Shaw, 1999, pp. 147). This living experience should be interpreted to create meaning about the experience of D-M under uncertainty and complexity.

The methodological problem is closely associated with a definition of knowledge. This research will seek to clarify the process of learning under uncertainty, a process of calculating knowledge, a disambiguation process from an initial imperfect knowledge state, K, to a later state with knowledge, K,' constructing meaning and interacting with a social-web directly related with the uncertain context, where the D-M occurs. Thus a definitive position for knowledge is needed. For Davenport and Prusak (1998) knowledge is viewed as a framework for evaluating and incorporating new experiences and information, "*This framework originates in the mind of the knower and it is formed by past experiences, current values and beliefs*" (Davenport and Prusak, 1998 quoted in Stacey, 2003, pp.163). Knowledge is equated with the notion of mental models. According to Habermas (1984), Popper (1986) and Gregor "*there are three different worlds to support a knowledge existence: the objective world of actual and possible states of affairs, the subjective world of personal experiences and beliefs, and the social world of normatively regulated social relations*" (Gregor, 2006, pp. 615). Under these definitions, and knowing that a constructivist research approach was adopted, knowledge should be referred to the social world, the constructed regulated social relations based on the participants' experience in search for their objectives that guide D-M under uncertainty and complexity.

So, in summary, for the current research a constructivist position to "*What is the nature of reality?*" was then followed. The reality which sustains D-M under complexity and uncertainty is volatile, something that needs to be constructed and interpreted for a decision to be made possible. That reality has been experienced by the researcher's participants and then interpreted by the author, supported by the research methodology.

The epistemological question "*What is the nature of the relationship between the knower (inquirer) and the known (knowledge)?*" is answered with observable organizational patterns that are constantly changing. Organizations are not static and the relationships between people, organizations, and technology are not fixed but constantly changing. This is particularly the case in the current research, where the reality frame is uncertain and complex, meaning D-M is a question about how to build social networks, to find answers that help and support a decision.

The answer to "*How should the inquirer go about finding out knowledge?*", a question of methodology, was resolved by following Grounded Theory Methodology, to understand and construct the reality that supports the living experience of the decision-maker. This presupposes an involvement in data collection and analysis constructing analytic codes and categories from data, making comparisons during each stage of the analysis to stand theory development on each step of data collection and analysis. Writing memos to elaborate categories, specify their properties, define relationships between categories, identify gaps and make sampling aimed toward theory construction, not for population representativeness, occurred (Charmaz, 2006, pp.5-6).

## 3.4. Methodology

The research methodology followed is GTM (Glaser and Strauss, 1967; Charmaz, 2006) which aims to develop a theory grounded in empirical data obtained in the research context. GTM puts forward a detailed approach for collecting and analyzing material with the aim of developing systematic theories, in this case being concerned with D-M associated with complexity and uncertainty. The data was obtained from a variety of sources such as interviews, journals and other documents that provide a public description of the participant's experience. Grounded theory lends itself to the analysis of qualitative data; also, the emphasis of the method is not just on the way data are collected, but also on how they are analyzed at the same time as they are gathered. So, grounded theory serves as a 'rigorous, orderly guide' (Glaser, 1978) to the development of hypotheses that have their genesis in the observed world as opposed to being derived from deductive reasoning; in other words, not from hypotheses developed from existing theories. GTM represents an alternative to the logic-deductive approach to theory development, where hypotheses are, typically, formulated away from the field and then empirically verified. In grounded theory, concepts are derived from empirical data, linked and, if necessary, modified through constant comparison with other data. Therefore, the method incorporates deduction and verification in the same process (Charmaz, 2006).

The role of Actor-Network-Theory is to serve as a complement, an enhancement to the theory developed. The use of ANT concepts, the research process, and the structuring of ideas was aided with concepts such as how *inscription* and *translation* can explain the D-M relations between non-humans things and humans, and how the ANT concept of *punctualisation* can be applied to the D-M process.

### 3.4.1. Grounded Theory

According to Glaser (1978), GTM requires an understanding of related theory and empirical work in order to enhance theoretical sensitivity. Strauss and Corbin (1990) say that *"good science"*, or good theory is formed during this relationship of creativeness and the skills acquired through exercise. It is also significant to define grounded theory (GT) as opposed to GTM i.e. the method as opposed to the theory. Strauss and Corbin (1994) describe grounded theory as a set of relationships that offer a reasonable explanation of the phenomenon under study, explicitly, the theory that is grounded in data which are systematically gathered and analyzed. The theory develops during the research process itself and is a product of the continuous relationship between analysis and data collection (Glaser and Strauss, 1967; Glaser, 1978; Charmaz, 2006).

A Grounded Theory, it is argued, is a theory derived from the experience it represents and meets four central principles: fit, understanding, generality and control (Strauss and Corbin 1990). Fit demands that the theory fits the working data. Understanding entails that the theory be clear for those involved in the research study. Generality demands that the theory is valid in a variety of circumstances. The theory should grant control with regard to D-M. Grounded theory makes available a systematic method connecting several stages which is used to ground the theory, relating it to the realism of the phenomenon of D-M under uncertainty and complexity in the study's context (Scott, 1996).

As stated by Charmaz *"grounded theory methods consist of systematic, yet flexible guidelines for collecting and analysing qualitative data to construct theories 'grounded' in the data themselves"* (Charmaz, 2006, pp.2). Bryant states about Grounded Theory that it *"is a way of how to discover theory from data systematically obtained and analysed in social research"* (Bryant, 2002, pp.28). For this end Strauss and Corbin state *"The research does not begin with a preconceived theory in mind, rather the researcher begins with an area of study and allows the theory to emerge from the data"* (Strauss and Corbin 1998, pp.12 quoted in Bryant, 2002, pp. 31).

According to Scott (1996), GTM provides a systematic method involving several stages from sustaining the theory to relating it to the reality of the phenomenon under consideration. Thus, GT is derived from the phenomenon under research, conflicting with the hypothesis deductive method, where theories are generated from a repeated cycle of testing and refined from a previously constructed hypothesis. In GT research the theory emerges from the organized assessment of the experience, associated with the researcher's development of categories and consequently advances towards theory construction. For that purpose another stage engages the researcher, a stage to explore data, find patterns and suggest possible hypotheses. This stage is an interpretation in the experimental research and it does not match prior theories. Within this process, data is collected, simultaneously with theory structuring, which involves a learning loop, or in any case a reverse and forward direction linking theory and the study.

Thus Grounded Theory frames this research in the main aspects of its development. This involved starting with a selection of research participants provided a relational involvement with them. This has led to the discarding of the researcher's initial hypothesis and the initial ideas for further empirical enquiry. Then analytic codes and categories were constructed, that have provided further hypotheses, and then engaged in a new process of enquiry and analysis with the research participants until data categories have been saturated. Categories were then organised into memos and their relationships consolidated, followed by the gathering of new data toward validation and theory construction. Finally, a comparative literature review was conducted. Thus grounded theory methods consist of systematic, yet flexible guidelines for collecting and analysing qualitative data to construct theories grounded in the data themselves. The author followed Charmaz (2006) constructivist GTM, a detailed research stages explanation is in chapter 5.

### 3.4.2. Actor Network Theory

Actor-network theory (ANT) is a social science approach for describing and explaining social, organisational, scientific and technological structures, processes and events. Thus it is useful for describing the context network of the decision-processes taken by decision-makers in conditions of uncertainty and complexity. It assumes that all the components of such structures (whether these are human or otherwise) form a network of relations that can be mapped and described in the same terms or vocabulary. It was developed by Michel Callon, Bruno Latour and John Law (Law, 1992; Callon, 1999; Law and Hassard, 1999).

According to Tatnall and Gilding Actor-network theory *"extends ethnography to allow an analysis of both humans and technology by using a single register to analyse both, so avoiding the need to consider one as a context for the other"* (Tatnall and Gilding, 1999, pp. 963). This characteristic helps the researcher to not think in terms of human/non-human binaries and the different discourse with which each may be aligned. An actor-network analysis of D-M may well be described as ethnography since people and artefacts are conceptualised in terms of socio-technical networks (decision-makers and social-context).

However, D-M in a context of uncertainty and complexity is a challenge for the Actor-network theory because D-M introduces a separation between what is intangible (information which is inert, passive and classified as non-human) and human agents who are active and capable of making complicated decisions. The actors involved are characterized by very specific and highly demanding competencies: they are calculators, know and pursue their own interests, and make informed decisions. This challenge arises in conciliation between Grounded Theory's commitment to a constructivist perspective of reality and the passive and inert properties associated to non-human objects in ANT i.e. conciliating D-M constructivist grounded theory and the passive orderly view of ANT. This conciliation was resolved by the researcher by strategically using ANT objects as auxiliary constructs to develop GT categories which are representations precluded by ANT objects.

To sustain this approach, through a comparison between D-M in uncertain and complex contexts with Callon's (1999, pp.183) paper "Actor-Network Theory – the market test" a question is posed: Is Actor-network theory of any use to the research for understanding D-M? A decision-maker decides in a context, surrounded by an intricate network of interest, where he captures information to take informed decisions, when possible. Those decisions also reshape the network as a result of the decision action, influencing the decision but also trying to *satisficing* the decision maker, as Newell and Simon states *"The individual decision maker uses a number of problem solving shortcuts – instead of maximizing, not looking too far ahead, reducing a complex environment to a series of simplified conceptual 'models"* (Newell and Simon, 1972 quoted in Mintzberg *et al.* 1976, pp. 247). D-M in the context of uncertainty and complexity is a continuous constructivist social system, where both decision-maker and social network are involved in the decision-process, reshaping the network as a result. This reshaping is a consequence of the learning process, which should be positive or less positive. Certainly the decision-maker learns from previous experience, and in the next opportunity, the network should look different from the biased previous experience and as a consequence of the decision process, which also affects it. According to Bernstein *"Decisions, once made, create a new environment with no opportunity to replay the old"* (Bernstein, 1996, pp.228) and as it will be shown in chapter 6.3.4, once made a decision under uncertainty, the decision-maker changes his social context, his knowledge, as Keynes' prescribed *"as we make decisions we do change de world"* (John M. Keynes quoted in Bernstein, 1996, pp. 230).

Continuing this comparative analysis and according with Callon "Actor-Network Theory – the market test" a question is posed - how can decision-makers take decisions *"when no stable information on the future exists"*? (Callon 1999, pp.184) i.e. in uncertain and complex contexts.

A decision-maker, research participant, uses two approaches:

1. Callon proposes *"Interacting and exchanging information as it is produced"* (Callon 1999, pp.184). This is an uninterrupted social interaction involving many different actors (human and/or non-human) in order to help the decision-maker;

2. With a "focal point" or strategic view. Callon proposes *"that the agents share common knowledge which guarantees their coordination. The nature of this knowledge is highly variable. It may pertain to a shared culture, rules, procedures, routines or conventions which guarantee the adjustments and predictability of behaviour... rules, conventions or cultural devices do not govern behaviour completely since they imply irreducible margins of interpretation"* (Callon 1999, pp.185). These margins of interpretation are removed through a process of interaction, negotiation and involvement, the realm beginning, a constructed reality emerges, from where a D-M process stands.

For this end, the researcher firstly consolidates the construction of GTM categories. Then, at a final stage the constructs developed from using GTM are then enhanced and elaborated through, again, the use of Actor-Network Theory. Being more specific, using Actor-Network Theory, terminology was investigated in how *inscription* and *translation* explains the D-M non-human associations, and how the ANT concept of *punctualisation* is applied to the D-M process, providing the construction of conciliated categories:

- *Inscription* refers to the way technical artefacts embody patterns of use. In decision terms what are the meaning and the role of the objects at hand in the decision-process;

- *Translation*, stability and social order are continually negotiated as a social process of aligning interests. In D-M terms, translation is the process the decision-maker works out to make the decision;

- *Punctualisations* or black boxes' is used to deal with bounded rationality. Quoting Law "*We do not cope with endless network ramification. Much of the time we are not even in a position to detect network complexities. So it is something much simpler – a working television, a well-managed bank or a healthy body - comes, for a time, to mask the networks that produce it*" (Law 1992, pp.385). In other terms, *punctualisations* are used to analyze how decision-makers simplify the context helping them to think; how simplifications help in the D-M process; and how to make inferences about the context in D-M process.

In addition, explanations follow from tenets that decision-makers can work out in their decisions, because they are entangled in a web of relations and connections that "*contain their world*" (Callon, 1999, pp.185). These tenets raise a solution to the decision learning process which will be a coordinated social world construction in a situation of radical uncertainty and complexity. This is in accordance with Callon's ANT market-test paper, which states "*The only possible solution is that provided by the network; not a network connecting entities which are already there, but a network which configures ontologies*" (Callon, 1999, pp.185). Ontologies are related to the knowledge (existing in the social-network) and knowing (need to reconstruct uncertain context). These ontologies are commitments and agreements with respect to the social-network context, built for decision-maker shared knowledge with and among actors, which constructs meaning, a *social rationality* in order to achieve D-M:

- The decision-makers, their dimensions, and what they are and do, all depend on the type of the relations in which they are involved. For example, interests, projects, expectations, preferences and, the most important, a social network, where they may ask for more information, for help, to sense the unknown, depend on the relationships between the decision-makers and the other actors. The flow, the circulation, the connections provide an ANT network result.

This ANT network is a result from categories obtained from GTM. However, the ANT network is not used as normal ANT networks. A structure was not built firstly followed by their ramifications and content. In the current research, the root is deeper since the network is revealed from these ramifications; through the use of GTM categories, created as a sustained bottom up ANT network. This provides a D-M social network structure from where a decision-maker founds his decision.

## 3.5. The Research Process

The Grounded Theory Method was followed to develop a grounded theory of D-M under uncertainty and complexity. Next follows a description of the theoretical procedures that were adopted during data collection and analysis. A brief explanation of how ANT objects are used is also included. The practical procedures will be described in detail in chapter 5.

### 3.5.1. Data Sources

The main technique which has been used for collecting the data for this research were interviews. Interviews were face-to-face, in-depth, open-ended and also recorded. The recording of interviews allowed the author to write memos and to be more open to what is being said during his interviews.

Quoting Charmaz "*Interviews are retrospective accounts subject to reconstruction in view of present exigencies and purposes*" Charmaz (2006, pp.142). For this end, observation is a powerful and reliable method, however as Mintzberg *et al* argue "*interviews are extremely demanding of research resources because strategic decision processes typically spans periods of years; therefore the researcher is obliged to rely heavily on interviewing*" (Mintzberg *et al*,1976, pp.250). So, the author decided the best way was to interview a set of participant decision-makers, asking them how they have achieved decisions, recalling their memories on previous decision experiences or actual experience, if they are or have been involved in any particular decision under complexity and uncertainty. Then the author meticulously followed GTM guidelines.

For this end, they were interviewed as a heterogeneous set of informants, starting with business management activities such as the chief executive office from small to very large organizations. A second set of professional informants that were available to participate in the research were used, aiming at generalization. This is particularly beneficial in theory generation as it provides multiple perspectives on an issue, supplies more information on emerging concepts, allows for cross-checking and yields stronger substantiation of constructs (Glaser and Strauss, 1967). Finally, a third set of participants were interviewed in order to saturate categories and to evaluate the resulted theory. In this set two of the initial interviewees were interviewed again aiming to confirm results with them (interviews detail is shown chapter 5).

Using the data provided by the interviews, new data was generated, as a consequence of the GTM process. This new data was then interpreted and associated with Actor-Network Theory objects, providing an auxiliary and important source of meaning in the research study. Practical details of this process are explained in chapter 5.

## 3.5.2. Interviews

There were three sets of interviews corresponding to three stages of research; in the first set of this research in-depth interviews were kept open to the collection of interesting responses and perspectives around which further data collection could be focused. Open-ended interview questions were chosen because they have the potential to generate rich and detailed accounts of the individual's D-M experience. It was flexible enough to allow the discussion to lead into ideas which may not have been considered prior to the research but may be relevant to the research subject. In open-ended interviews it is important to be calm, to build up a relationship between the interviewer and the interviewee so that questioning does not cause any preconceived notion in responses. In addition, it gives the interviewees the chance to talk freely about behaviours, beliefs, events and perceptions in relation to the research topic. Overall, the research data is created and grounded in these lived experiences of D-M, which are now exposed and explained.

The second set of interviews corresponds to an enlargement of the professional background of D-M. This is particularly valuable in theory generation as it provides multiple perspectives on the research study. This second set is related to the emerging concepts from the first set, involving a more heterogeneous selection of informants. For this end Glaser and Strauss' position was borne in mind *"The researcher must remember that he is an active sampler of theoretically relevant data, not an ethnographer trying to get the fullest data on a group, with or without a pre planned research design"* (Glaser and Strauss, 1967, pp.59). However, the main tool that was used for collecting the core data for this set again involved unstructured open-end interviews. This aims to enlarge the scope of initial categories, searching for new ideas that could generate hypotheses and be tested again with the new data. From literature review, initial expectations were not sustained which caused a feeling of weakness in the author. Therefore, a new process of literature review was initiated, which was in accordance with GTM procedures.

Finally the third set of interviews was directed by the emerging concepts from the previous sets, involving a strategic selection of informants and interview protocols were more structured (Glaser and Strauss, 1967; Charmaz, 2006). For this end, two of the initial interviewees were interviewed again and a new professional informant was added, aiming to saturate data and sustain the resulted theory.

All the interviews were open without a specific structure or questions. The author had chosen appropriate informants, who could provide him with the right information more relevant to D-M in an uncertain and complex topic. However, the author did not use them to provide the research with pre-fixed information or ideas, which could misrepresent the research's grounded categories. The author chose research participants according to their expertise and relevant professional experience. As an example, the author chose CEOs from the professional business field initially because he thought they could provide him with better information than other people, especially because they can be expected to have a clear picture about the topic under research and their decisions shape the overall organization.

### 3.5.3. Sample

Grounded Theory is the discovery of theory from data methodically obtained and analysed in social research and then further used to generate a theory. Glaser and Strauss explain *"Generating a theory from data means that most of the hypotheses and concepts not only come from the data, but are systematically worked out in relation to the data during the course of the research"* (Glaser and Strauss, 1967, pp. 6).

Furthermore, the author while trying to discover theory *"cannot state at the outset of his research how many groups he will sample during the entire study; he can only count up the groups at the end"* (Glaser and Strauss, 1967, pp.61). So, to sustain the research claims using GTM principles, the sample used in this study did not follow the principles of statistical sampling.

The criterion for judging when to stop sampling the different groups of interviews is the category's theoretical saturation. Saturation means that no additional data are found whereby the author can develop further properties of the category. *"As he sees similar instances over and over again, the researcher becomes empirically confident that a category is saturated"* (Glaser and Strauss, 1967, pp. 61). The researcher, who wishes to generate theory, cannot state beforehand *"how many groups he will study"* (Glaser and Strauss, 1967, pp.74). Glaser and Strauss (1967) argued that sampling is determined by the type of coding procedures to be used, as well as by theoretical sensitivity. GTM research will sample until no new or relevant data appears, until all elements of the theoretical concept are covered and until the relationships between categories have been validated.

In GTM, sampling begins by talking, collecting information, from those informants who are most likely to provide initial information. This information will be analyzed and interpreted, which should help to identify temporary descriptive concepts and direct the researcher in identifying the next steps, samples and outline of data. This process is called theoretical sampling, according to Charmaz (2006), which is a strategy of determining what data will be collected next, where they will be found and for what theoretical purpose, and this changes in the course of the research (a detailed explanation is given next chapter 5.2 – Research Stages).

Therefore, initially the author searched for business management D-M activities from small to very big organizations. He went to organizations in his social contacts, looking for D-M in uncertain and complex practices, and the most likely informants such as the chief executive office were interviewed, in search of information. Theoretical concepts were identified and hypotheses started to develop in a later stage. Further interviewees were involved in order to collect more data to reinforce the findings for validity issues. According to *"The Principle of Interaction between the Researchers and the Subjects"* (Klein and Myers, 1999) a critical reflection on how the research materials were socially constructed through the interaction between the researchers and participants is required. As Klein and Myers argue *"in social research the 'data' are not just sitting there waiting to be gathered, like rocks on the seashore"* (Klein and

Myers, 1999, pp.74). Furthermore, sampling in this case, is not a question of statistical inference.

GTM challenges the value of a representative sample. Those who advocate quantitative research could ask for a representation sample of the population under research. As Charmaz argues *"the error of this advice lies in assuming that qualitative research aims for generalization"* (Charmaz, 2006, pp.101). The resulting Grounded Theory of D-M under uncertainty and complexity is an Explanation Theory in Gregor (2006) terms. There is no lower or upper sample limit size, but sampling in the beginning of the study has to cover a broad range of events, apart from of their evident importance to the research study. For this end, initially Portuguese and English informants where interviewed from small to very big enterprises, CEOs and experts on organizations. Later, the sampling process was an arduous task that progressed according to the theoretical importance of the characteristic of the items sampled and the completeness of the theoretical framework (Glaser, 1998). Thus, grounded theory allows, and to a certain extent mandates, the relationship of sampling, data collection and analysis, from the initial phase throughout the entire research process (Strauss, 1987). In other words, collecting, versus sampling, and analysis occur simultaneously.

The first interviews were those individuals whose decisions under uncertainty and complexity shape overall organizations, either positively or negatively. These informants are the principal actors in the process of D-M under uncertainty and complexity in organizational terms. An auxiliary informant agreed to participate, offering his professional expertise in Organizational Change to the research study. The next stage consisted of general activities of heterogeneous professional expertises. An extra interview was produced with the purpose to expand to areas not yet covered, to ensure saturation as well as validation. A final stage of interviews occurred representing a return to the initial sample, in order to confirm and validate results.

### 3.5.4. The Analysis of Data

Interviews were transcribed and research analysis broke down the data into distinct units of meaning. The process started with the open coding of data that guides the sampling process in many directions until core variables, which were constantly sensed in the data, were found. Quoting Charmaz *"Coding is the pivotal link between collecting data and developing an emergent theory to explain these data. Through coding, you define what is happening in the data and begin to grapple with what it means*" (Charmaz, 2006, pp.46). Despite using computer facilities, such as NVivo, the author preferred Charmaz's method because it is more direct, facilitates the creation of codes with an open mind, and is not preoccupied with a process of standardized codes that will be used to provide an axial cross verification, in which selective result could be hard to define and eventually not be relevant. During this process, each interview was analyzed individually and then compared to previously collected data with a vision to identify categories that embraced similarities and differences between interviews. The first set of interviews was coded more than once, depending on the author's ideas at the time.

When core variables were reached, sampling became more selective and focused on the central subject to the emerging theory. The overall process was complemented with memo writing. Next, the author searched for similarities and discrepancies judging actions within the data under analysis, in order to review new data and compare it with core variables. An essential and critical stage in the GTM analysis is the origin of concepts and subsequently categories. A cycle of going over and returning to, memos, notes (and worksheets also used in the research), merging codes occurred in an attempt to find emerging new concepts as well as categories. This process is the heart of GTM, how data is analysed, and not how data are collected. Quoting Walker and Myrick "*At the core of grounded theory..., is the data analysis process in which the researcher engages to generate theory from the data*" (Walker and Myrick, 2006, pp. 548).

The discovered categories were not based on the persons that provide the data. After all, the research is not intended to design a psychological picture of decision-makers, but the actions taken by decision-makers in contexts of uncertainty and complexity. What are the common patterns, experiences, relations and actions taken in these particular situations? Regarding this, Charmaz argues "*The development of theoretical sensitivity was conducted by focusing the coding process on actions and processes, not in the individual*" (Charmaz, 2006, pp.136). The categories result from people's objectives and actions rather than being linked to certain individuals. The result specifies the conditions showing conceptual relationships and forecast consequences, with a resulting Grounded Theory, rather than making explicit theoretical propositions. Theoretical sensitivity refers to the individual's immersion into the research subject and relates to understanding the meaning and refinement of data. Furthermore, theoretical sensitivity has been described by Glaser (1978) as the process of developing insight, which the author brings to the research situation. Such insight was conceptual rather than concrete; it is often referred to as the creative aspect of GT and involves the researcher working in the area to obtain experience and expertise (Glaser and Strauss, 1967). A detailed account on developing theoretical sensitivity is explained in chapter 5.4.

The second set of interviewees, focussed on the emerging concepts from the first stage, involved a strategic selection of interviews (Charmaz, 2006). However, the strategic selection of interview participants veered away from management business to research in heterogeneous professional contexts, pursuing unexpected paths suggested by the theoretical sensitivity developed by the researcher throughout the research process. At this stage, the author became more familiar with the topic, especially after he analyzed the initial interviews.

Furthermore, the author utilised a stage of a deep exploration of data, finding patterns that suggest reasonable hypotheses. This reasoning stage occurs at a point at which an observation in the empirical research data does not match with prior theories, underlying the search for new fitting theories to an empirical observation, which is called "theory matching" (Dubois and Gadde, 2002 quoted in Kovács and Spens, 2005, pp. 138). In this process new data is constructed, simultaneously with theory building. This involved a learning loop, a 'go and come back' to data and memos, between theory and the research study. For this end a creative process of "theory matching starts in an attempt to find a new matching framework or to extend the theory used prior to this observation" (Dubois and Gadde, 2002 quoted in Kovács and Spens, 2005, pp. 139). This reasoning research stage can only start out with a "surprise" (Kovács and Spens, 2005, pp. 139). Quoting Bryant "Assuming that there is an element of 'surprisal' in the information" (Bryant, 2006, pp.49) then the research process is guided within this 'surprisal' element, which leads to the formation of new hypotheses and theories. This stage of reasoning, which reflects theorizing within the ground data, establishes a common pattern which aggregates the results.

Finally, using a third set of interviews, two of the initial interviewees were interviewed again and a new professional informant was added, aiming to saturate data and sustain hypotheses. The reason for interviewing two previous participants for a second time is linked to the need for confirmation of ideas, to see what they have to say. Albas and Albas develop a method of inspection and eventually refine their categories; "They explain their major categories to certain participants they have studied and then inquire whether and to what extent these categories fit each *participant experience"* (Albas and Albas, 1988 quoted in Charmaz, 2006, pp. 111). Alasuutari presents his interpretation to the participants and pushes for a dialogue about it; *"He gained confirmation of his view then pushed further later in the same conversation"* (Alasuutari, 1996 quoted in Charmaz, 2006, pp. 112).

Actor Network Theory objects provide the means to understand non-humans or inanimate objects and humans as systems of human intentional activity, in the research context of D-M. ANT objects: *inscription, translation* and *punctualisations* were used throughout the interview analysis, during the process of theoretical sensitivity. These ANT objects have been sensed and then assigned values corresponding to patterns of use. In a final stage of individual analysis of each interview, they are used to make a deeper understanding of the categories, providing an embellishment of each informant's analysis in order to explore non-human things, how systems are used and how complexity is reduced. Practical details are given in chapter 5.8.

## 3.6. Ethical and Privacy issues

The ethical and privacy issues of the research under development are mainly based on deontological and professional codes of conduct, since data was gathered using individual interviews. Inherent rights of the volunteer participants have been considered with privacy, respect, equal treatment and informed consent. The work was guided by the Policy, Procedures and Guidance Research Ethics of the Leeds Metropolitan University. For this end *"Research endeavour must abide by standards of professionalism and honesty; our efforts must strive to earn the respect and trust of both research participants and the public at large"* (Ruane, 2005, pp.16).

With informed consent each potential interviewee was adequately informed of the aims, methods and goals of the research. An abstract of the work and a author interviewer's resume was distributed previously by e-mail or by hand. The supervisor was always included in all the e-mails sent, so in this way the participants were aware of how to make complaints or ask further questions. Before each interview, their locality and availability was taken into consideration. A comprehensive and appropriate explanation to the participant was given. Each participant was informed that they were free to withdraw consent at any time, without any adverse implications.

The interviews were recorded, always with the consent of the participant. They were transcribed and the interviewees have the right to review the transcripts of their participation, which was facilitated by sending them a copy for revision and comments of the interview.

Confidentiality or privacy applies in two ways: first when the participant wants to grant his or her anonymity. In this research personal names are not used. The other is related with the organization to which the participant belongs. Further citations on the organization require authorization. Since the research is motivated by D-M from decision-makers, the sample of interviewees were authorised by them. All the collected data is maintained and kept private by the author of this research.

## 3.7. Summary

In conducting this research study a considerable amount of time and attention was devoted to the issue of methodology because the author sees this as the foundation on which the credibility of the research stands. This belief is reinforced by the lack of universally accepted methodologies in research into D-M. GTM was primarily used because it allowed D-M under complexity and uncertainty to be examined in a holistic manner within a real life situation. ANT was used as an enhancement to grounded categories, giving an understanding of non-human things and humans as systems of human intentional process.

# Chapter 4   Literature Review

## 4.1. Introduction

This chapter summarizes a literature background review regarding D-M under uncertainty and complexity. According to Grounded Theory Methodology (GTM), researchers should enter the field with a completely open mind or with very little knowledge of the problem under investigation. However Charmaz argues *"We construct our grounded theories through our past and present involvements and interactions with people, perspectives, and research practices"* (Charmaz, 2006, pp.10). This is true of this research because, at the beginning, the author chose relevant literature for his research regarding Decision Support Systems and Complexity Theory, fields related to his background studies and also professional and personal interests. However, after the initial fieldwork the author could determine the relevant literature according to the emerging concepts, their categories and properties from the field.

Under GTM guidelines, the author conducted a deep analysis through qualitative data that were drawn from a first set of interview sources. This first stage helped the author to recognize the qualitative and social nature of the research context, moving away from his initial ideas, and consequently to new literature review areas, mainly Descriptive Decision Theory and also $2^{nd}$ Order Systems Thinking. Then, through a sensitive analysis of the rich data obtained from the interviews, themes, concepts and categories were generated, under GTM guidelines. This mix of qualitative data helped the author focus on the role of learning in D-M under uncertainty. Subsequently, this data founded the next stage of interviews, used, mainly, to consolidate and confirm the research findings. A detailed explanation of the research stages is given in following chapter 5.

After this introductory research note, this chapter will first make a general introduction to prescriptive and descriptive decision theories. An introduction to

Systems Thinking then follows, providing a general overview of decision making in this context. Finally a literature review on learning theories is presented.

## 4.2. Prescriptive Decision Theory

Prescriptive or Normative Decision Theory is concerned with how decision-makers make decisions, and how optimal decisions can be reached. Von Neumann and Morgenstern (1944) lay great stress also on uncertainty on the Expected Utility Theory (EUT). In expected utility theory, each alternative is assigned a weighted average of its utility values under different states, and the probabilities of these states are used as weights. According to Chacko *"Decision-making depends not only on the outcome, but also on the attitude: the preparedness to accept [adverse] outcome"* (Chacko, 1991, pp. 156). The expected utility hypothesis of an agent facing uncertainty is a calculus in each possible state choice constructing a weighted average. The weights are the decision-maker's estimate of the probability of each state. The expected utility is thus an expectation in terms of probability theory. To determine utility according to this method, the decision maker must rank their preferences according to the outcomes of various decision options. Furthermore Chacko states regarding utility *"What is the cost of surprise?... Utility is the potential significance of or satisfaction from goods... It is what the decision-maker expects at the time of decision-making"* (Chacko, 1991, pp.156).

Measuring the expected value is the central problem for decision theory, by which the rationality of human D-M is measured. According to White this measure, *"depends on the person itself"* (White, 2006, pp.53). The problem stands in finding a real measure, which represents a determinant choice in the domain of uncertainty. For this end, White (2006) states that there are three types of measures of probability: Objective, Subjective and Subjectively Derived Objective measures (White, 2006, pp. 53).

According to the expected utility theory, an individual should rank uncertain prospects according to the expected utilities from the prospects. If we do not know exactly the specific utility function defined on the space of outcomes, we cannot predict how the individual is going to rank the prospects. So the *"expected utility theory does not work satisfactorily when the objective probabilities are not clearly defined"* (Biswas, 1997, pp.108). Thus, with regard to constraints imposed by expected utility theory on measurement uncertainty, we can conclude that measurement uncertainty has to be represented by a probability distribution. Consequently, measuring the expected value, the central problem for decision theory, by which the rationality of human D-M is measured "*it must depend on the person itself*" (White, 2006, pp. 53).

Other efforts in rational D-M came from Game Theory, which covers a substantial part of the process of D-M under uncertainty. Game Theory is a branch of applied mathematics and economics and has drawn attention from computer scientists because of its use in artificial intelligence, providing a fertile ground for computer simulation. The foundation of Games Theory began in the 17th century with James Waldegrave providing a strategic solution to a card game, although "*the inventor of game theory was John von Neumann in the 20th century*" (McMillan, 1992, pp.4). In a game we are concerned with a group of players, each maximizing his pay-off. Each player has to consider the possible reactions of other players to his moves in deciding his own move. He does not know the moves of his opponents with certainty, but he has to make a decision about his move with some rationality. This search for a rational decision is D-M under uncertainty. The uncertainty is introduced by considering what others might do – who will also be using these ideas. Biswas argues "*the acceptability of any of these solutions depends on the notion of fairness or equity prevailing in the society (the group of players), but people differ in their perceptions of fairness in real-life social situation*" (Biswas 1997, pp.174).

Games are of two-types: cooperative, where the players share their strategies, and non-cooperative where each player chooses his strategy independently. The *Nash Equilibrium* is defined as a strategic combination of the players such that, given the strategies of other players, a player cannot be better off by choosing another strategy. The strategy solution of a non-cooperative game may not exist. Some non-cooperative games have gained some relevance and have been used to explore real-life contexts: Two-person Zero-sum Non-cooperative Game (TZNC), which is essentially a betting game where the loss of one is the gain of another and it is a game where each player has two strategies. It has been used to study strategies and the analysis of market share (Biswas, 1997); Two-person Non-zero-sum Non-cooperative Game (TNNC) describes a situation in which the interacting players aggregate gains and losses which are either less than or more than zero, for example Cooperation is usually analysed in game theory by means of a non-zero-sum game called the "Prisoner's Dilemma" (Axelrod, 1984); The Battle of the Sexes Game is used to complement TNNC games and is based on the idea of cooperation despite conflicting preferences, where the opponents (in this case boy and girl) choose to cooperate or not, based on their knowledge of each other. Finally the Cournot game of duopoly is an example of the

*Nash equilibrium* with two opponents. It has been regarded as a fundamental contribution to microeconomic analysis (Biswas 1997).

Games also are used to analyse collective or group decisions. In this type of game the strategy is either cooperation or non-cooperation (Bernstein 1996). The chosen one is obtained in terms of maximising a pay-off matrix in terms of an expected utility. Some examples are: Cooperative bargaining games where the main problem resides in knowing the share of each play-off from cooperation where they can cooperate or ignore each other to choose strategies; *N*-person cooperative games with transferable or non-transferable utility where a scheme for the distribution of pay-offs among the members of the group is assumed. The members of the group can make coalitions.

Evolutionary Games are another type of game where the emphasis is not on optimisations but stability of behaviour. For decision theory they provide a set up for studying the evolution of a group of individuals with limited knowledge (bounded rationality). The concept of common knowledge central in game theory is a special kind of knowledge for a group of agents. Aumann and Brandenburger argue *"We note that the belief system[2] itself may always be considered common knowledge among the players"* (Aumann and Brandenburger, 1995, pp. 1175).

Games against Nature are another type of game in D-M theory. They are basically one-person games in the sense that only one player is actively making a decision and the decision is being taken under ignorance. In this circumstance there are four major criteria which have been suggested in the literature: The principle of insufficient reason which states if a decision-maker has to take a decision under complete ignorance, he will assign equal probability to all states; The *maximin* criterion where a decision-maker should select the strategy which maximizes his minimum pay-off; The *minimax* regret criterion stated by Savage (1951) which is based on the idea of *regret*. A regret is a measure of loss when making a particular choice. The decision-maker builds a pay-off matrix and a regret matrix. From the regret matrix he will choose the minimum expected value. Finally the Pessimism-Optimism Index, suggested by Hurwicz (1951) where a pessimism-optimism index is constructed from a pay-off matrix, from where the strategy with the highest value is chosen. The game against nature is temporally static, but a more complicated variant exists to deal with a multi-period decision problem. One example is the portfolio problem, where the decision-maker is completely ignorant of the future rates of return. One suggestion in the literature is that the person should allocate the *"fund myopically"* (Biswas, 1997,

---

[2] *"Belief systems are primarily a convenient framework to enable us – the analysts – to discuss the things we want to discuss: actions, payoffs, beliefs, rationality, equilibrium, and so on"* (Aumann and Brandenburger, 1995, pp. 1175)

pp.191). This means *"He should look at the current rates of return or the rates in the immediate past and put his money in the security yielding the higher rate. If the rates are equal he should divide his investment equally between the two securities"* (Biswas, 1997, pp.191).

As a summary, games are a branch of applied mathematics and economics and there are several types of games, providing a perception of real-life situations. This perception involves the players gathering and interpreting information similar to that of real life. Games are representations of simulated worlds from where a decision-maker manipulates and observes behaviours in order to get information to make a decision and the information is used in some manner to produce clarity or reduce uncertainty. Game theory is also a collection of rigorous models attempting to understand and explain situations in which decision-makers must interact with one another. It offers a rich source of both behavioural tasks and data, in addition to well-specified models for the investigation of social exchange. However, it is considered difficult to apply game theory independently of other modelling techniques which is the reason why the author decided not to follow this method for research and also because the conditions for game theory application within enterprises were not easy to create.

Furthermore, a question is posed - why does a decision-maker, apparently, act irrationally? Or non-rationally? The answer may be found in Newell and Simon's (1972) theory of Bounded Rationality. There is a cost of obtaining and processing all the information. Biswas states *"calculating the expected utility function and the expected utility for each lottery is a lengthy procedure and people are likely to use their intuitions"* (Biswas, 1997, pp.6). Tversky and Koehler believe that *"probability judgements are attached not to events but to descriptions of events... the judged probability of an event depends upon the explicitness of its description"* (Tversky and Koehler, 1994, pp. 548 quoted in Bernstein, pp.279). Knight and Keynes both distrusted the laws of mathematical probability or assumptions of certainty as guides to D-M, despising the *"mean statistical view of life"* (Bernstein, 1996, pp.223). If a person, apparently, acts irrationally, according to Simon he did not evaluate all the possibilities, because there are too many, and he was bounded, or he just simply decided because he found a choice that satisfied him – one could ask if this is an irrational act. It is perhaps non-rational. Following prescriptive decision theory, we should also specify some expected value based on *satisfaction*, or could ask if it is only a question of misunderstanding, constructed reality as Tversky and Koehler suggest about probability. Biswas argues the irrationality of a decision act is due to a lengthy procedure and how people use their intuition. It seems *time* and other resources constrain the decision-maker's behaviour, 'probably' he tends to become bored and makes decisions based on previous experience and intuition – it could be asked if this is irrationality, or if we have to produce an expected utility value of *time*, since in our days, time is money. Or we can argue that the reality where rational decisions are produced is irrational, complex or uncertain that turns a pure rational decision process into an inadequate one. According to Chase *et al* (1998) the classical definition of rationality also has problems *"No single conception of probability is shared by all statisticians and philosophers"* (Chase, 1998, pp. 207) (a detailed explanation is given in chapter 3.3 Research Paradigm).

In summary, when decision-makers model reality, or use mathematical equations to describe reality, other problems emerge related to an understanding of their behaviours in terms of D-M context. This seems to be related to the understanding of a common reality context, from where actors participate in the construction of the information that stands for that uncertain context, i.e. re-defining the context in order to reach D-M. Those who have not participated in this re-definition and change of context do not understand it, and consequently the decision-maker's action is labelled as irrational behaviour. This may be related to *"The Principle of Multiple Interpretations"* from Klein and Myers which requires participation and *"sensitivity to possible differences in interpretations among the participants as are typically expressed in multiple narratives or stories of the same sequence of events under study"* (Klein and Myers, 1999, pp. 77).

## 4.3. Descriptive Decision Theory

In most of the traditional literature dealing with risk and uncertainty, decision-makers are classified as risk averse or a risk taker (Biswas, 1997). A 'person' is risk averse if he never accepts a fair revenue; a 'person' is called a risk taker if he always accepts a fair bet and a 'person' is risk neutral if always indifferent between accepting a fair bet and rejecting it. A fair bet is interpreted as an uncertain prospect whose expected yield is zero. Generally a 'person' is assumed risk averse.

The main problems associated with the rational behaviour of the decision maker guide the descriptive decision theories. They are based on what is termed the *Allais paradox*, where either the rational decision-maker could make irrational decisions, or the expected value theory is wrong. Consequently, non-expected utilities were theorized, and alternative theories of behaviour D-M under uncertainty were proposed, creating a separation between subjective and objective probabilities. This separation provides the basis for a discussion about the epistemological interpretation of probability. Biswas writes "*Probability is a psychological state of a person, at a particular point of time, conceiving it as quantitative representation of a state of partial knowledge*" (Biswas 1997, pp. 61). So, in a different personal state, the 'probability' quantity has a different representation, varying from person to person and time to time. Ramsey and de Finetti argue: "*Probability is always subjective and 'personal' in character. There is nothing called objective probability. The laws of probability follow from the logical consistency of the thought process*" (Ramsey, 1926 and de Finetti, 1974 quoted in Biswas, 1997, pp.61). White complements this discussion with knowledge: "*whether we use objective measures or subjective measures, subjectivity must enter into their derivation. Such measures must depend on the knowledge content, of the individual*" (White, 2006, pp.64). Einhorm argues "*Knowledge is difficult to achieve because of the inductive way in which we learn from experience*" (Einhorm, 1982, pp. 282).

Other research directions are represented by Kahneman and Tversky (1982). Their work tries to show that people rely on a limited number of heuristic principles which reduce the complex task of assessing probabilities and predicting values to simpler decision operations. They focus on emotions and bounded rationality, following Simon (1965, 1982).

Rowe and Boulgarides (1992) propose a cognitive decision model founded on the perceptual and cognitive aspects of decision making based on the individual's cognitive complexity and values. Their cognitive decision model has four phases: the process starts with a *stimulus* or need to which the decision maker responds. The information taken depends on individual perception. A tentative choice is made after the decision-maker examines the implications of a decision (*cognition*). Next, the decision-maker manoeuvres for position to accommodate power centres, which depend on his *personality*, i.e. those attributes that affect the manner of interaction with others: attitudes, needs, values, beliefs, and drives. At the last phase is *leadership*, a generic process, from where the manager's vision, ability to influence others, to assert and share power to achieve goals is crucial to gaining acceptance for a decision. Values have a central role in the decision-maker's style.

Gigerenzer and Goldstein (1996) state that cognitive mechanisms capable of successful performance in the real world do not need to satisfy the classical norms of rational inference, since humans and animals make inferences about the world under limited time and knowledge. They propose the Probabilistic Mental Models theory

(PMM). This theory assumes that inferences about unknown states of the world are based on probability cues. It accounts for choice and confidence. This theory tries to replace classical rationality axioms with simple, plausible psychological mechanisms of inference, mechanisms that a mind can actually carry out under limited time and knowledge and that could have possibly arisen through evolution. It is like a 'guessing' probabilistic model.

Thaler (2000) follows Simon's work on the field of behavioural decision research. Thaler suggests that D-M is bounded in two ways, not precisely captured by the concept of bounded rationality:

- our *willpower* is bounded; such that we tend to give greater weight to present concerns than to future concerns. As a result our temporary motivations are often inconsistent with our long-term interest in a variety of ways, such as the common failure to save for retirement;

- our *self-interest* is bounded; unlike the stereotypical economic actor, we care about the outcome of others (Thaler, 2000, quoted in Bazerman, 2006, pp.7).

Bazerman (2006) introduces other bounds such as bounded *ethicality* and bounded *awareness* as psychological barriers to recognizing conflicts of interest. Bounded ethicality refers to the notion that our ethics are limited in ways we are not even aware of ourselves. The concept of bounded awareness refers to the category of failures, or ways in which we fail to notice obvious and important information that is available to us.

According to the literature reviewed as mentioned previously, the author has not found any studies to inform the process of learning in D-M. We have Simon with the "*satisficing* action" and other bounds that influence the way a decision-maker behaves. From Kahneman and Tversky we have emotions and risk behaviour. Rowe and Boulgarides offer a framework where values play a central part on the decision style. Gigerenzer and Goldstein with their probabilistic mental model try to justify a 'guessing' theory of probability cues. Thaler and Bazerman add more bounds to our rationality. There are several other limitations to the mechanistic sequential model of decision-maker behaviour; there might be influence from culture, religion, education, morality etc. Bernstein argues "*The heart of our difficulty is sampling. We use shortcuts that lead us to erroneous perceptions, or we interpret small samples as representative of what larger samples would show*" (Bernstein, 1996, pp. 271).

Further research has to be done in the way we sense things and how we learn under uncertainty: if there exists a difference from initial imperfect knowledge $K$ to a later state with knowledge $K'$ where the D-M occurs, then it will occur under a process of learning. Does this process of learning under uncertainty and complexity guide the decision-maker? The decision-process under uncertainty and complexity is an unconscious (or clue, or intuition, or guess) decision if the decision-maker does not learn. Or as Gigerenzer and Goldstein (1996) argue, humans as animals and other organisms make inductive inferences when deciding about the world under limited time and knowledge. But inductive inference is learning, is sensing the context, is recognizing by looking, is interpreting by communicating, is understanding by listening (asking and dialoguing), is interacting in surrounding social-web reality where decision-makers are embedded. According to Kaplan and Maxwell "*our knowledge of reality is gained only through social constructions such as language, consciousness, shared meanings, documents, tools, and other artefacts*" (Kaplan and Maxwell 1994 quoted in Klein and Myers, 1999, pp.69).

A concluding point should be made. Mintzberg *et al* (1976) 'Recognition' phase, similar to Simon's (1965) 'Intelligence' offers a perspective that could support a possible existence of a Learning process: "*In recognition, problems and opportunities are identified in the vagueness streams of ambiguous, largely verbal data that decision makers receive*" (Mintzberg, *et al*, 1976, pp.254). This means uncertainty can also mean a vague stream of ambiguity which acquires meaning (or is less ambiguous – by adding knowledge) through a process based on dialogue, or 'verbal data'. This means knowledge is acquired through a process of socialization, and in doing this process, participants are learning that they are also changing the context, since it becomes (possibly) less vague and ambiguous. Argyris argues "*the source of learning is socialization*" (Argyris, 1994, pp.198). For Argyris learning is the detection and correction of error. An error is any mismatch between intentions and what actually happens: "*behind this view of learning is a view of human nature and organizations*" (Argyris, 1994, pp.132). The decision is made and the reality is constructed, even only in the mind of decision maker through a process of learning.

## 4.4. Systems Approach

The present research aims to study the mechanism of D-M under uncertainty and complexity, particularly investigating a learning process. The research study is to understand the multiple social constructions of meaning and knowledge to construct the 'reality' where decisions are made. Following Argyris *"human beings design their intentions and their actions – they are designing systems. Organizations design their strategies and they design the implementations of the strategy"* (Argyris, 1994, pp.132). Organizations do not perform the actions that produce the learning; it is individuals acting as agents of organizations who produce the behaviour that leads to learning.

From the point of system thinking, in the Middle Ages people in the West thought that the world and themselves were created by God. Unlike other creatures, humans were believed to have souls, enabling them to choose whether to obey the laws of God or not. Knowledge of God's creation was thought of as divine revelation to be found in the Holy Scriptures. People thought in this way for hundreds of years until the Scientific Revolution, leading to the Age of Enlightenment (Stacey, 2003). Since the times of Newton, Bacon and Descartes, scientists have tended to understand the natural world in terms of machine-like regularity in which given inputs are translated through absolutely fixed laws into given outputs. This way of reasoning and understanding was imported into economics and social sciences and some schools of psychology (Arthur, 1999). Quoting Stacey *"Such a belief is realistic if cause-and-effect links are of the Newtonian type, for them the future of a given system can be predicated over the long term and its future can be controlled by someone (Nature is driven by laws)"* (Stacey, 2003, pp.228).

The Scientific Revolution was a movement of thought in which the individual scientist objectively observes nature, formulates hypotheses and then tests against quantified data. These laws were understood to take the form of universal, deterministic, linear 'if-then' causal links. Copernicus and others worked in the early sixteenth century, observing and measuring the movement of the planets and putting forward theories on the laws governing their movement. Galileo, Newton and Leibniz took this work up in the seventeenth century. In addition, the philosophers Bacon and Descartes articulated the way in which people were coming to experience themselves as individuals with minds. By the end of the seventeenth century, the scientific method was established with a highly individualist way of thinking about nature and ourselves. The consequence of this Scientific Revolution extends until the present, and occidental culture is grounded in this way of thinking.

Kant postulated a dualism: on the one hand there was reality, which he called *noumenal*, and on the other hand, there was the appearance of reality as sensations, the *phenomenal*. Kant's thinking provoked many controversies and has continued to have a major impact on the evolution of Western thought to the present time in the form of systems thinking. The idealist view of systems promotes the understanding of systems as mental constructs. To qualify as a system such mental constructs must constitute meaningful wholes produced by interacting ideas, beliefs, habits and values. *"A system can be defined as a set of elements standing in interrelations"* (von Bertalanffy, 1968).

The system model is an enclosed world where interrelations and behaviour are used where an outside observer with their social-actors participate in the construction of the lack of partial information that stands for that uncertain context. The participants in the system model construction understand it because they made part of the reality re-construction through the model. Those who did not participate will have a different reality's interpretation within the model. To reach D-M, the system's context is modelled (reframed) and re-defined. In Kant's terms the appearance of reality as sensations, is the *'phenomenal'*. The literature commonly refers to two main schools of systems thinking:

- First order system thinking which occurred in the first wave of the twentieth century. In first-order systems thinking, reality is assumed to be deterministic. It departs from mechanistic and reductionist approaches in that they stress dynamic interaction between parts of a system. There is a separation of the observer from the observed. Main examples of first-order system thinking are: *General Systems Thinking* (Boulding, 1956; von Bertalanffy, 1968) – the central concept is homeostasis, which means systems with a self-regulating tendency to move towards a state of order and stability, or adapted equilibrium; *Cybernetics* (Ashby, 1956; Beer, 1979; Wiener, 1948) – Cybernetic systems are self-regulating, goal directed systems adapting to their environment. They form the basics of strategic choice management; *Systems Dynamics* (Forrester, 1958; Godwin, 1951; Philips, 1950; Tustin, 1953) – Where mathematical models are constructed of how the system changes states over time. The system is not self-regulating but self-influencing.

- Second-order system thinking is built on the understanding that human beings determine the world they experience. Von Foerster (1984) argues that we are part of the universe and whenever we act we are changing both ourselves and the universe. Bateson (1972) explores how the observer could be and must be included in the system being observed. It addresses the paradox of the observing participant eliminating and redrawing boundaries and changing levels of description, reframing the uncertain context, in order to have a constructed common understanding. Main examples of second-order system thinking are Soft System Methodology (SSM) from Checkland (1981); Critical System

Thinking (CST) from Midgley (2000); System of Systems Methodologies (SOSM) from Jackson (2000) and Communities of Practice (Wenger, 1998).

Checkland (1981) and Checkland and Scholes (1990) developed the SSM as a way of probing alternative worldviews. SSM uses specific models of systems to explicate these world-views in specific situations, rather than trying to identify the truth about the nature of systems. Checkland is not explaining how people actually go about dealing with life in organisations. Instead he presents prescriptions for dealing more effectively with problematic situations. This is prescribing rather than describing. Checkland is critical of a positivist engineering view of systems since they take a realist perspective, regarding the world as actually consisting of systems having an objective existence. Checkland proposes that systems are the mental constructs of observers. The aim of the methodology is to integrate multiple viewpoints of free participants in order to assist them to predict and control the changes to their systems in vague situations in which there are no agreed goals. SSM moves from a paradigm of goal seeking and optimisation (as in first order systems thinking) to a paradigm of learning, understood as the maintaining and development of relationships. *"SSM regarded as a whole, is a learning system which uses system ideas to formulate basic mental acts"* (Checkland, 1983, pp.17). SSM output is learning which leads to a decision to take certain actions, knowing that this will lead not to the problem being solved but to a changed situation and new learning. This is a direct consequence of the nature of the concept of human activity systems - the construction of a common understanding and meaning that stands for reality.

The main problem of systems thinking is derived from building a boundary, a surrounding line reframing the context. In this way system thinking frames reality and system thinkers postulate the context separated from another one, by a boundary - for one context there is always an inside and an outside. It is then essentially a choice to include or exclude other incidents that may participate in the construction of reality under analysis. This may be caused by a need for focus – hard system thinking needs a problem, something real, visible and understandable that works as a focus, and then in a systematic manner, using specific methodologies frames, manages the problem, trying to find solutions to resolve it. In another way, second order systems thinking, fundamentally from Checkland and Wenger, is where a learning process comes to appear as a result of negotiated meaning between participants. The idea of human systems as systems of meaning is closely linked to an emphasis on participation. Human systems are best understood as systems of meaning (ideas, concepts, and values) and for the present research, learning. In the realist position of hard system thinkers, people are taken to be parts of a real system, while in the constructivist position the system is thought of as a mental construct of the people involved. System thinking needs the realm, the soul of the thing, and then works with it, constructing meaning.

The interaction between decision makers, as social human beings, provides the construction of meaning in developing ideas, mental models which represent a simplified complex reality. So learning should be a process of finding meaning, by social interaction, which should be represented by simplified models, which represent a personal knowledge view.

Learning is also a process of negotiation and socialization (Dalbello *et al* 2003). In the interaction among interpersonal situations people work to find a mutually acceptable solution to an issue and they learn in common or different ways and humans are essentially social creatures, and it is through learning that they become socialized.

In summary, once a human being designs systems, they design their intentions and actions. Historically, systems thinking were faced in different perspectives since the Middle Ages, when it had a religious base, until the scientific revolution when scientists thought to understand the natural world in terms of machine-like: cause/effect. Later, with the scientific method a new way of thinking about nature and ourselves was established. Kant's ideas incited controversies: reality/appearance of reality. Systems were also viewed as mental constructs.

Two schools of system thinking are referred to in the literature: first order system thinking and second-order system thinking. In the former, reality is assumed to be deterministic. In the latter, human beings determine the world they experience. SSM is a way to explain different worldviews. Learning is a negotiation process within the interaction between decision makers.

## 4.5. Learning Theories

Learning theories are attempts to describe how people learn. From the literature there are three main learning theories, Behaviourism, Cognitivism, and Constructivism (Learning Theories Knowledgebase, 2008):

- Behaviourism is an approach to psychology where learning is a result of conditioning behaviour. This behaviour may result either in reinforcement, which increases the likelihood of that behaviour occurring again; or punishment, which decreases the likelihood of the same behaviour recurring in the future. In behaviourism, "*a learner is essentially passive, responding to environmental stimuli. The learner starts off as a clean slate (i.e. tabula rasa) and behavior is shaped through positive reinforcement or negative reinforcement*" (Learning Theories Knowledgebase, 2008).

- Cognitivism expands behaviourism accepting that mental states are appropriate to analyse and subject to examination to understand mental function. Humans are assumed to act on the basis of representations of their environment that are processed in their brains. Learning is a process of developing more and more accurate representations of external, pre-given reality. "*Cognitivism uses the metaphor of the mind as computer: information comes in, is processed, and leads to certain outcomes*" (Learning Theories Knowledgebase, 2008).

- Constructivism views learning as a process in which the learner constructs or builds new ideas or concepts based upon current and past knowledge. Constructivist learning involves constructing one's own knowledge from one's own experiences. This should be the most appropriate learning theory for the present research, since uncertainty is not known; this should be sensed and learned with the experience, since "*Learners continuously test these hypotheses through social negotiation. Each person has a different interpretation and construction of knowledge process. The learner is not a blank slate (tabula rasa) but brings past experiences and cultural factors to a situation*" (Learning Theories Knowledgebase, 2008).

As recommended by grounded theory methodology, during data analysis the author found it necessary to re-consult the literature to find information about learning under uncertainty.

Following is an overview of learning under uncertainty in specific fields where uncertainty has been addressed in the context of learning.

Bligh (2001) states a constructivist position in teaching to know what to teach, but also to know what students know and think. He proposes an approach using uncertainty to guide students in thinking and behaving to produce medical decisions. Bligh proposes "*expressing uncertainty is the best way of learning and teaching because it allows exploration of the cognitive processes involved in clinical decision making*" (Bligh, 2001, pp.2). This is related with how students (doctors in training) apply the information they obtain from clinical experience and investigations, to perform a diagnosis. Bordage states "*Knowing more about what students are thinking when they are presenting a case to you, or about what they are thinking after a lecture will enable teachers to help their students learn better*" (Bordage 1999, quoted in Bligh 2001, pp.2).

Dayan and Yu (2003) in their experiments with small rats have carried out research regarding learning and uncertainty from three perspectives: statistical theories, psychological models in which attention is paid to stimuli with an effect on the speed of learning associated with those stimuli, and neurobiological data on the influence of the neuromodulators on learning and inference. Their conclusions are - the more uncertain a stimulus, the faster the animal learns about that stimulus: "*It is obvious that learning should be occasioned by unfamiliarity*" (Dayan and Yu, 2003, pp.10). This links with the research study, - that uncertain stimuli generate learning, which is found in the current research where an uncertain and unfamiliar, or unknown context will guide the decision-maker thorough a process of dealing with that uncertainty, in order to understand it. This unfamiliar context is an uncertain context in the sense that a decision-maker (human) will have to 'familiarise' himself with it, reconstructing it with others (assuming that reality is social-constructed), in order to know it and then be able to make decisions.

In the field of Economics, Arrow states "*Learning is certainly one of the most important forms of behaviour under uncertainty*" (Arrow 1958, pp.13). Arrow argues that each individual achieves his satisfaction level at minimum cost. "*If we assume that individuals are averse to risk, individuals and firms in planning for an uncertain future may want to make sure that their demands and outputs are mutually compatible*" (Arrow, 1958, pp.268). Arrow writes about consumer behaviour and so this is a very specific form of D-M related to consumers. However, it should be highlighted that Crawford argues "*Most articles in the literature on decision making under uncertainty have the feature that the outcome of a decision is a function of the state of the environment which is usually expressed as random variables unknown at the time of the decision but governed by a subjectively known distribution function. Under this approach, no circumstances for learning arise, unless the economic agent can divine the future state of the environment* (Crawford, 1973, pp.587). Consequently, Crawford maintains the implications of introducing learning in an uncertainty model are twofold:"

1. *Learning has a stabilizing influence on price;*

2. *The net effect of learning on price may be positive or negative depending upon the specific type of information being gained.*" (Crawford, 1973, pp.596)

This means a learning process has a stabilizing effect on the emotional stress of the decision-maker in the market. This stabilization requires time, time used for things to stabilize, and provides time for the decision-maker to learn and see patterns in the environment.

The spiral of experience, emotions and facts of the living experience of learning is similar to the imagery of liquidity, expressed by Bauman (2004) quoted in Bryant (2006, pp.146). The speed of flow – learning - is somewhat related with the unknowable, unpredictable, uncontrollable in the context of uncertainty. A decision maker is not dependent in the traditional values, what they were – the relation with the 'solid world view', certainty does not have sufficient validity. This can be demonstrated in a metaphor of a glacier, which as it slowly moves, changes the landscapes and leaves a different impression – even though it moves very slowly. The values are not too relevant – they are a portrait of experience, but not a landscape of the future it could be a desired landscape, but it does not mean that it will happen. We can assume what it shall be, what others will do and think, however doing business, flying, playing, have a living experience interacting with others, and in doing this interaction, uncertainty is inserted, not by chance, but it comes to be a natural change. Others also are confronted with the reality and consequently will behave, and it is not a question of probability to know how, but how to interact and reconstruct reality.

So uncertainty introduces learning like the term 'surprisal' from Hayles (1999, quoted in Bryant, 2006, pp.49). Bryant argues that when the 'surprisal' element in the information is known, then uncertainty is reduced e.g. the first time you tell something new there may be something surprising about it.

Bernstein considers that the existence of surprise shows that uncertainty is more likely than probability, "*prevalence of surprise in the world of business is evidence that uncertainty is more likely to prevail than mathematical probability*" (Bernstein, 1996, pp. 220-1).

Shackle's ideas of "degrees of surprise" has the biggest difference from the theories based on probability – it is the one that is most unique and is a turning point - i.e. it offers a very new idea about decision making under uncertainty - instead of using "probability" we should use "surprisely".

The author considers that however it is said, or however it is measured, what is true is that learning under uncertainty is about collecting information all the time until all that information can be put into familiar and known procedures/methods to be able to make a decision.

## 4.6. Summary

This chapter provides a literature review in the sense of Grounded Theory Methodology, where the author should have entered the field with an open mind or with very little knowledge of the problem under investigation. The author chose relevant literature for his research around fields related with his background studies and also professional and personal interests. Furthermore, this research attempts to explain D-M under uncertainty and complexity, formally as a Grounded Theory, being the result of applying GTM to the research study. This chapter first made a review of the main Decision theories, namely Prescriptive Decision Theory and Descriptive Decision Theory. Then, System thinking was explained in order to establish a way of thinking that guides D-M.

The literature review was very important firstly, for the author's understanding about decision theories. Then, the multiple social constructs of meaning and knowledge on 'reality' were valued. Finally, the author investigated literature about learning theories to support the analysis of the data within decision making under uncertainty.

# Chapter 5    Research Conceptual Development – Data Analysis

## 5.1. Introduction

This chapter reports the research stages, data collection and research analysis using Grounded Theory Methodology and Actor-Network Theory. The development of the theoretical sensitivity using GTM will be shown starting with open interviews, gathering data, constructing tentative ideas about categories in the data and then examining these ideas through further empirical inquiry to write memos, develop categories and finally enhance with Actor Network Theory. The theoretical development of categories: interviews transcription, coding, memos, categories and main categories are described. An explanation of ANT analysis, developed along the research practice, is also described. Finally, two interviews were selected and a detailed explanation is presented to justify the GTM phases used throughout this research and to better understand the design of the frameworks, presented in the following chapter.

## 5.2. Research Stages

The research ran under five development stages during its duration of 2004-2008:

- The first stage consisted of modelling a way of thinking, developing hypotheses of how others should behave in order to achieve D-M, with a view to testing these in some manner. This initial research consisted in the interviewing of the first set of research participants, which led to the discarding of the hypothesis and a change of research methodology as described in the previous chapter 2.

- The second stage consisted in the development of a theoretical sensitivity to deal with qualitative data type research under GTM guidelines;

- The third stage consisted of the iterative practice of GTM analysing and enlarging further data inquiry and the development of categories;

- The fourth stage consisted of another deep exploration of data, analysing grounded categories to develop the main categories, and further literature review in order to sustain the findings;

- The fifth and final stage consisted of a consolidation of the previous stages, constructing a grounded theory of D-M under uncertainty and complexity, which was also verified.

- Finally, ANT analysis was developed throughout the research practice describing the ANT concepts and the discussion of the link with GTM categories is presented.


## 5.3. First Stage – Initial Research


The author, coming from an electrical and computer engineer background, embarked on the research programme in 2004 with the initial research idea about ways to model people's channelling of information in order to make decisions under uncertain contexts, under an assumption of traditional Information Systems and a deterministic way of thinking. This deterministic way of thinking assumes that human activities run under the assumption of an unchanging process which is maintained in order to keep the operation and functionality of the running system. The first stage of the development of the research questions consists of an initial literature review that conceived initial ideas from the literature centred in Mathematical System Modelling (Pidd, 2003), Decision Support Systems (Turban and Aronson, 2001), the development of frameworks such as Zachman's Framework (Sowa and Zachman, 1992), Information Systems Project Management and Life-cycle Control (Richardson and Ives, 2004), Software components (Herzum and Sims 2000), Business Objects (Bolloju, 2004) and Model Driven Architecture (Frankel et al., 2003). This first initial literature review was not used as the main background information for this research. It helped to understand well defined implemented processes such as Enterprise Resource Planning, since these are founded in human activities systems (HAS) and are not just on a roadmap of implementation issues and intensive people training (ERP failures in Soh *et al.*, 2000; Vogt, 2002; Martinsons, 2004). The goal of researching about the presented theories was to explain the researcher's path and to understand their main concepts, although the point of HAS is a key one to explain the ideas of complexity. Further literature review in Complexity Theory (Stacey, 2003; Arthur, 1999; Kurtz and Snowden, 2003) helped to develop the formation of initial research questions for D-M under uncertainty and complexity: '*Are decision-makers using complexity theory? Are decision-makers making some sort of risk evaluation? Are decision-makers using Decision Support Systems or other tools to help?*' The techniques were also a first initial goal: what are they, how are they used, how are they applied in the organization and how they improve the knowledge of the decision-maker. Being more specific, testing for a hypothesis from the idea that a decision-maker under uncertainty and complexity builds a model, an external and explicit representation of part of reality as seen by the informant who wishes to use that model to understand, to change, to manage and to control that part of reality.

In order to test this hypothesis, the author obtained the first data, via an open-ended form of inquiry interview, to analyse and develop further research data. The first data group corresponds to the collection of interesting responses and perspectives from which further data collection and research work could be focused. Open-ended interview questions were chosen also because they have the potential to generate rich and detailed accounts of the individual's D-M experience. Open-ended interview questions were flexible enough to allow the discussion to lead to ideas which may not have been considered prior to the research literature review but may be relevant to the research subject. In open-ended interviews, it is important to put the interviewee at ease, building up a relationship between the interviewer and the interviewee so that questioning does not cause any preconceived notions in response. Accordingly, the first two initial interviews were in Portuguese, the mother tongue of the author, and the research participants were professional acquaintances of the author.

| | Enterprise | Business Type | Date | Interview Participant |
|---|---|---|---|---|
| **Group**<br><br>**I**<br><br>2005 | DINEFER[3]<br>Portugal | Production of Connector Holders and other Equipment for the Automobile Wire Harness Industry | 11th April 2005 | CEO |
| | SONAE[4]<br>Portugal | SONAE SGPS, SA has controlling interests in different businesses: Modelo Continente (food and non-food retail), Sonae Sierra (property, development and management of shopping centres), Sonaecom (mobile and fixed telecommunications, media, internet and IT services) and Sonae Capital (tourism, construction, engineering and residential development, transports and logistics, insurance brokerage, car hire and retailing and others). The role of Sonae SGPS, SA is to manage the portfolio while it is the job of its sub-holdings to manage the businesses. | 21st April 2005 | CEO |

**Table 5. 1** – Group 1 – 2005 Interviewee's participants

The author, decided to first obtain data from the business field and thus he chose what he had to hand, asking those in business who had the availability and interest in the research topic to participate. At this point, the first interviewee accepted to be interviewed, which provided the first experience of doing open interviews under the research topic. Although it was easier to continue in this world, the author's world, where he knew the actors and businesses, the author decided to maintain a distinction from what he was used to, and to search for an unfamiliar environment. In this unfamiliar territory, the author intended to enlarge the scope, searching for new ideas that could generate hypotheses in the new data. Furthermore, the author decided to establish contact, asking for participation from the biggest private Portuguese enterprise, a business whose decisions create change, in business terms, in Portugal. This was not an easy task, and it was necessary to ask for help from the author's social acquaintances. Through this it was possible to interview the CEO and founder of the enterprise. Following this interview the participant agreed to help, referring future participants to the author, including a Professor from London Business School and a Banker from Goldman Sachs, in London. They were not an initial choice or target of the author, but came through the kind opportunity of the second interviewee and their availability and willingness to participate. The remaining participant in this first group was a choice of the author, chosen for three reasons: proximity, availability and also

---

[3] http://www.dinefer.pt/ accessed 20/Jan/07
[4] http://www.sonae.pt/ accessed 20/Jan/07

the enterprise being run by unknown business decision management rules, the Leeds Metropolitan University Vice-Chancellor. A detailed explanation of each interview follows.

The interviews started with the Dinefer CEO on 11th April 2005. The meeting was at the Dinefer headquarters, in Portugal, arranged through an acquaintance of the author with Dinefer CEO. A date was scheduled and documentation about the current work was distributed. An open interview around the topic of D-M under uncertainty and complexity was recorded and then a transcription was completed. This first interview was useful in that it also provided experience for the author in open interviews, and in dealing with the research topic questions that could appear.

Ten days later a second interview was undertaken with the Sonae CEO at their headquarters in Portugal. This was arranged through several of the author's contacts that report to the Sonae CEO. Documentation about the author's work was sent also in addition to a brief summary of the author as requested. The interview was done on 21st April 2005; it was an open interview around the topic of D-M under uncertainty and complexity. The interview was recorded and then a transcription was also written.

The research study continued involving three other informants in this first group, in order to make a comparative data analysis, thus expanding the results providing multiple perspectives on the research study. One interviewee was an expert in organizational change.

| | Enterprise | Business Type | Date | Interview Participant |
|---|---|---|---|---|
| **Group**<br><br>**I**<br><br>2005 | Leeds Metropolitan University | Leeds Metropolitan University it is one of the largest universities in UK, with over 52,000 students and 3,500 staff. | 17th May 2005 | Vice-Chancellor |
| | London Business School | Consulting and management development experience with a number of major international companies: areas of organisational change and management development. | 16th June 2005 | Professor of Organisational Behaviour |
| | GOLDMAN SACHS London | Managing Director & Vice Chairman. His responsibilities include investment banking, leadership development and strategy. | 16th June 2005 | Vice-Chairman |

**Table 5. 2** – Group 1 – 2005 Interviewee's participants (cont.)

A third interview on 17th May 2005 was recorded at Leeds Metropolitan University with the Vice-Chancellor. The Leeds Met. Vice-Chancellor generously accepted to give an interview offering his experience in D-M under uncertainty and complexity. A date was scheduled and an abstract and a brief resume of the research was previously sent to frame the research interview topic. A transcription was made.

Further help came with a fourth interview carried out at the London Business School on 16th Jun 2005. Contact with the participant came from the Sonae CEO, who referred the London Business School, and in particular the interviewee who, as an expert in organizational change, could contribute to the research. A date was arranged with the London Business School participant, and an abstract of the current research and a brief summary was sent. A transcription was made. This fourth interview has slightly different characteristics, in that although it was still an open interview around the research subject matter, it was undertaken with questions focused on the author's doubts. So, this interview differs from the others since to the other interviewees the procedures they followed or how they behaved in D-M under uncertainty was asked. With this interviewee, an expert with business experience on a number of major international companies and interested in areas of organisational change, the goal was to ask him his opinion about what is D-M under uncertainty to benefit the author's understanding, searching for guidance about D-M in an organizational context and in some way to establish the research premises, such as methodology and research adequacy, as contributions to knowledge.

A fifth and final interview in this first group of data collection was undertaken in 2005, and recorded at Goldman Sachs' London headquarters on 16th June 2005. Goldman Sachs is a leading global investment banking, securities and investment management firm. The author's contact with the firm's Vice Chairman was also provided by the Sonae CEO. Prior to the interview, a summary and research abstract was sent. This interview was in Portuguese since the participant interviewee is Portuguese.

With this first group of interviews, laborious and detailed work was carried out, working with the initial hypothesis. A decision-maker uses modelling techniques to explore which of them are used, how they are used, how are they applied in the organization and how they improve the knowledge of the decision-maker. The author was testing hypotheses such as 'Are informants using complexity theory? Are informants making some sort of risk evaluation? Are informants using Decision Support Systems or other tools to help?' but simultaneously searching for *"emergent hypotheses"* (Charmaz, 2006, pp. 101), that could be researched in this first group of interviews and lead to further empirical inquiry. From the research in this first group, these questions proved not to be visible, or not to have a foundation, consequently they were discarded in view of the fact that they did not help in explaining the outcome from the deterministic models (see table 2.1 and table 2.2 in the previous chapter 2.9). In other words, a common pattern appeared, offering a fresh and surprising view of D-M under uncertainty and complexity. Two related concepts were revealed: the decision-maker's learning account and the attention he gives to the decision-process. This can be restated as a proposition: decision-makers consider a learning process, a process from where they sense the future, acquire knowledge and a manner in which they tend to dedicate attention to the decision-process. This had a consequence of developing a new research strategy under Grounded Theory Methodology.

## 5.4. Second Stage – Theoretical sensitivity

The second stage followed, using the previous group 1 interviews. However, they were now used under an assumption of qualitative data type, under GTM guidelines. In order to proceed, the author needed to understand and develop the necessary skills to work with GTM premises, since it is a research method that operates almost in a reverse fashion to traditional research and at first may appear to be in contradiction to the scientific method (Allan, 2003). Rather than beginning by researching and developing a hypothesis, the first step is data collection. From the data collected, the key points are marked with a series of codes, which are extracted from the text. The codes are grouped into similar concepts in order to make them more workable. From these concepts, categories are formed, which are the basis for the creation of a theory, or a reverse engineered hypothesis. This contradicts the traditional model of research, where the author chooses a theoretical framework, and only then applies this model to the studied phenomenon.

The author needed to acquire the necessary skills to work with GTM, and one of the skills is developing "*theoretical sensitivity*" (Glaser and Strauss, 1967; Charmaz, 2003) which guides the development of new tentative hypotheses and concepts. In GTM, theorising means developing abstract concepts and specifying the relations between them, which signify, reflecting, pondering and rethinking about the data. To gain theoretical sensitivity, a stage within GTM, the author carried out data comparison and building on ideas. This methodological phase made part of the research data analysis, and for this reason its inclusion in this section is justified.

Research work under GTM is not a straightforward process, following Glaser (1978) it requires theoretical sensitivity from an almost open mind, free from any preconceived ideas that could distort the sensitivity necessary. At this point a reference shall be given to the author's previous professional experience as an engineer. This experience was guided by a system thinking way of doing things, looking for structure and objectivity in the practice. Another critical aspect appears in the literature review on the subject topic, which potentially biases the development of the theoretical sensitivity and the appearance of categories, in this case the bias being the author's personal interest in the initial literature, mainly strategic management and complexity theory. A curiosity in the subject guided the initial thoughts of the author. This was not passed onto to the interview topics, which were kept as open interviews around the topic of D-M under uncertainty and complexity. The outcome of the interviews was a change in the author's perspective.

By being biased by previous professional experience, naturally some habits have been transposed at the beginning such as the use of tools such as NVivo 2.0, NVivo 7[5] and Decision Explorer[6]. The tools failed, or at least they did not conform with the theoretical sensitivity necessary to analyse and let the categories appear. Theorizing about categories is a step forward and a step backward, disposing the author at a stage of abstraction, where the mind acquires the necessary creativity to sense the data. It is not just a question of method and tools, it goes deeper to a stage where the mind gets into a process of innovation and making sense of what has been absorbed. It is something that has been said by Kay, the writer trying to finalize his book in the film "Stranger than Fiction", directed by Marc Forster[7] *"Well Penny, like anything worth writing... it came inexplicably... I can't believe I didn't think of it earlier"*.

Following is a narrative and samples obtained by the tools from the author's prior experience and influenced by his curiosity in the literature.

Firstly NVivo 2.0 was used extensively, to carry out the data analysis. After a short course in April'05 NUD*IST (NVivo) the author attempted to do the analyses using NVivo 2.0 The first group of interviews were imported into NVivo and it was attempted to figure out categories there. This proved to be a difficult task, since there were no clues for data categories, except those biased in the author's mind from previous professional experience and later by research literature review.

---

5 NVivo 2.0 and NVivo 7, QSR International http://www.qsrinternational.com/products_nvivo.aspx [accessed 18/Jul/07]
6 Decision Explorer http://www.banxia.com/demain.html [accessed 18/Jul/07]
7 Stranger Than Fiction. (2006) Directed by Marc Forster. Sony Pictures [video: DVD]

For example, the first interview carried out in 01-Dinefer produced 142 total free code nodes. They should represent a theoretical sample to sense those categories, resulting from having an open mind, using only the transcription, memories from the interview meeting, and NVivo to organize and dispose the sensed codes, into categories biased from the author's previous knowledge. This was a failure. In this case, the failure was a lesson; since it has contributed to go deeper into data, finding and construct meaning. As a result, categories came from top down, i.e. categories that already existed in the mind of the author, forcing codes to emerge to fit them. In this example, categories are biased from strategic management, imposing a top down view over codes.

Another example follows when work around tools, more mechanization, and an experience with NVivo 7 was carried out. NVivo 7 has additional features, such as linkage to a database where codes could be stored and there are more utilities to produce models. This comes with a computational power cost for the machine to run the program. A completely free one month work download was available at the QSR International website[8]. The author used a free download to test it. The author's opinion is simple - NVivo 7 probably has too many utilities and is difficult to use with the initial theoretical sensitivity under GTM.

Then a return to NVivo 2 was made, working with the first three 2005 Portuguese interviews (01-Dinefer, 02-Sonae and 05-Goldman). The process still continued mechanically, trying to do all the research work with NVivo. Instead of categories appearing naturally from the data; they were biased by the strong particularities of the individuals. In this example, 612 different free code nodes were sensed in the three interviews and when it was attempted to make a theoretical sample, categories emerged from the distinctiveness of a particular participant, imposed by a view of his personality, guiding the thoughts and distorting the theoretical sampling.

Another example occurred with the London Business School interview (04-LBS) participant. Since this particular interview was undertaken in a form of inquiry, the result was grouping categories around the topics suggested; instead of letting them be made from data. Then, the sensed code's nodes were fitted under each category obtaining an advanced model of the interpretation of the data.

---

[8] http://www.qsrinternational.com/ [accessed 20/Jul/2006]

The following example shows the influence of literature. Dealing with difficulties in understanding the hidden meaning of data and difficulties in conceptualisation the author looked for additional literature. For example, Rowe and Boulgarides' (1992) work about managerial decision making and particularly their 'Four Forces Model' influenced the way the author considered what categories should be. The models from Rowe and Boulgarides (1992) were introduced into NVivo, and then the hierarchy models were constructed under NVivo. This procedure should only to be to find out how the data interviews do or do not fit with the introduced models. This is a question of data fit, and not a question of appearing and finding meaning from data. This was entirely another failure, because interviews were open, and not oriented to managerial discussion or any other topic under discussion by Rowe and Boulgarides. Another author misunderstanding was related with Rowe and Boulgaride's cognitive decision style, which ground their work.

A search for complementary tools was also undertaken, suggested by the NVivo option 'Export to Decision Explorer'. Decision Explorer is a tool for managing qualitative information that surrounds complex or uncertain situations, as in the current research. It should help to capture thoughts and ideas, to explore them, and gain new understanding and insight. The result should be a perspective of creativity and a better focus. Two data interviews were exported from NVivo to Decision Explorer. However, the problem in the current research resided within the mechanization process to deal with all the interview data, to compile them. Decision Explorer, is a modeller, it adds additional features to the modelling capacity of NVivo. But modelling is the final stage, after which a deeper understanding of the hidden meaning, the goal of the research is achieved. So, by attempting to mock up conclusions without reaching them did not make sense. Trying to input all the interviews into this scenario was unnecessary and confusing, since Decision Explorer guides the construction of models, not an understanding of their grounds.

NVivo is useful to code interviews, keep a trace of changes and localize code passages. But trying to use it to organize codes to make a theoretical sample was not adequate in the author's opinion, as explained before. Charmaz argues that relying most on in NVivo and substantive codes, "*what often results is a grounded description more than a theory... to generate categories through focused coding; you need to compare data, incidents, contexts, and categories*" (Charmaz, 2006, pp.93) and this was a personal and unique task, requiring the author to be involved in a deep stage of concentration in the research data and auxiliary documents. Furthermore, the author turned to manual techniques, finding a way to find the hidden meaning. One approach was to do it in an engineering style, to objectively pick up an interview and draw up a structure of what had been said. In other words, to draw a model that represented the accounted experience of D-M under uncertainty, by the interviewee. Why did this not succeed? It failed, because it focused on results drawing a structure to get there. The problem with this resides in the fact that the interview was not objective, receiving unstructured answers for an open topic. The interviewees recounted their experiences in decision making under uncertainty and complexity. It was not objectively asked, how they did it, what resources they used, and their feelings, values and other bounds that constrained their actions.

Having tried several techniques, the author finally decided to use a mixture of tools: NVivo 2.0, post-its and MS/Excel worksheets. NVivo was used to code and manage the associated data. Post-its were used in association with the assigned codes, enabling a close look at codes and the associated text, giving helpful support to find the hidden meaning. Through them, an A2 poster was gradually created and changed, where clusters of meaning emerged during the construction process. This proved to be a good technique in interpreting and sensing the meaning that the data interviews offered. MS/Excel worksheets were an extra tool, used to keep a trace of the analysed pieces of text, analyse ANT concepts and assign different types of meaning for the present research: passage number, code name, description, symbolic assignation and extracts from the interview. A detailed explanation is given for this procedure in next section 5.5.

## 5.5. Third Stage – GTM development of categories

A third research stage followed which entailed a second group of interviews and an enlargement of the professional background of the decision-makers. Table 5.3 contains a description of the research interviews done in this second group. The study occurred during 2006 and corresponds to a search for a generalization and saturation which is particularly valuable in theory generation as it provides multiple perspectives on the research study. This second group is related to the emerging concepts from the first set, involving a more heterogeneous selection of informants. The main tool that was used for collecting the core data for this set involved again unstructured open-end interviews. However, in this case the concepts from the earlier ones were used and the aim was to enlarge the scope of the initial findings, through searching for new ideas that could generate more hypotheses in the new data. The reason for continuing with unstructured and open-ended interviews was linked to the surprise that the results of the first set of interview caused the author. Initial expectations from the literature review were not sustained, which caused a feeling of weakness in the author. Therefore, a new process of literature review was also initiated, which is in accordance with GTM procedures.

The following four interviews, in the second round, were chosen under premises: of availability, proximity and unknown territory for the author. However, these new four participants were deliberately chosen outside the business field. The author needed to open the research context, as it was embedded in a business context only, which was not helping the formation of concepts that may generate categories. The author needed a fresh, new context away from his previous familiar world. Then the choice was a question of chance and availability of this set of researcher participants, although the researcher did not go out to the streets asking everyone if they want to participate. GTM methodology requires hard work to analyse, sense, interpret and construct meaning in others' lived experiences. The experiences in which the author was interested in were those in order to understand how they made decisions under uncertainty and complexity, and possibly represent a diverse and rich life experience.

So, with the aim of researching this new and revealing *learning process* during D-M under uncertainty and complexity, a second round of interviews was done and recorded in 2006.

The first interview in this second group began with the Director of the Yorkshire Centre for Health Informatics. She is a doctor but also a manager, with whom contact was made during the workshop[9] *Doctors, Emergency Medicine and Computers,* where she was the guest speaker. The interview meeting was on 25th April 2006 in the Leeds office of the interviewee. A summary and an abstract were also sent previously. The interview was recorded but due to technical problems, a correct recording of the information was not saved. The problem was only detected after the interview ended. Therefore a mental transcription was done on the same day and sent to the interviewee to make any amendment or correction if necessary.

---

[9] *Doctors, emergency medicine and computers,* Director Yorkshire Centre for Health Informatics, Organization: British Computer Society - West Yorkshire Branch, Venue: Met Hotel, Leeds, 14/Mar/06

| | Enterprise | Business Type | Date | Interview Participant |
|---|---|---|---|---|
| **Group**<br><br>**II**<br><br>2006 | Yorkshire Centre for Health Informatics | Director of the Yorkshire Centre for Health Informatics and Senior Lecturer in the Faculty of Medicine and Health at the University of Leeds. She has been involved in the research and teaching of Health Informatics for over 25 years and works closely with colleagues in local NHS Trusts, the Strategic Health Authorities and Connecting for Health | 25th April 2006 | Director YCHI |
| | Jet2 | Pilot Command Jet | 5th May 2006 | Pilot Command |
| | Design Group 3 Architects | DG3A is a design lead practice with a track record in the delivery of commercially projects. | 18th May 2006 | Architect Managing Director |
| | Lawnswood School | Psychologist and she is the Head of School's Sixth Form | 2nd June 2006 | Head of School's Sixth Form |

**Table 5. 3** – Group 2 – 2006 Interviewee's participants

The next interview was done with a pilot of Jet2. This interview provided a unique opportunity to explore a particular context where uncertainty is necessarily avoided well minimised, considering the extreme risk associated with the unknown consequences. The meeting with the captain pilot was established through a neighbourhood contact and an interview was arranged for 5th May 2006. The interview was recorded. This interview was of personal interest to the author. At the time, the son of the author was interested in becoming a pilot, and consequently the author searched on where and how such skills were offered. This search provided three visits to pilot schools based in the UK, from where additional information enriched the author's context for this interview. It was also deemed necessary to have an informant from where failure is not valid, everything must be planned to avoid uncertainty without doubt. In this way, the author intended to enlarge the scope of grounded categories to give them strength to enrich the data. This is thus supplied via this research into professional flying, where all the operations not only have several pre-plans, but human actions are limited by a support system.

The next interview was chosen from a context where uncertainty comes from a conceptualization of artefacts, new buildings where beauty is turned into a central concept. Through an acquaintance of the author, an architect, the Managing Director of Design Group 3 Architects based in Leeds accepted to be interviewed for the current research. The interview was done and recorded on 18th May 2006, and a transcription was produced.

The ninth interview, the last in this second group, was recorded at Lawnswood School. This environment deals with young teenagers, an awareness context, from where the Head of School's Sixth Form accepted to give an interview. One of the author's children studied at the school, and contact was established via this link, providing the interview. The interview was recorded on 2nd June 2006 and a transcription was done.

Acquiring an informant's participation was not as straightforward or as easy as it first appeared. It took time and a particular and careful attention in the way the author approached eventual participants. This was done under the ethical and privacy guidelines previously explained in chapter 3.6 and complemented with the communications described here in each interview. To complement this report a reference shall be given also to failures, interviews that did not happen. The first attempt at contact occurred in 2005 with a previous CEO of the Portuguese Telecom organization. The author was acquainted with the individual, being an old fellow student. Some e-mails and abstracts were sent to his secretary, but a provisional agenda for an interview never happened, without any particular excuse for that. A second failure derived from a British company, based in Leeds. The author was approached by a member of staff of the company after he made a presentation at INN'06[10], who was quite interested in the research subject. Consequently an e-mail with an abstract of the undergoing research was sent, but unfortunately, the interview was never realised. A third failure occurred with an artist, a British painter who was an acquaintance of a friend of the author in Leeds. In 2006 an abstract was provided, but a provisional meeting was never established. A final attempt occurred with a Portuguese pianist, Maria João Pires[11], a world-renowned pianist. She was living in the same district in Portugal as the author. It was quite easy to get in touch to her in 2006 when the author was in Portugal, but unfortunately she became sick in Spain, having to be submitted to surgery. After that she decided to leave Portugal and live in Brazil, where she currently resides.

During the first set of interviews (2005) the author was guided by a theoretical sampling, which *"requires only collecting data on categories, for the generation of properties and hypothesis"* (Glaser and Strauss, 2006, pp.69). This involved starting with data, constructing tentative ideas about the data and then examining these ideas though further empirical inquiry, this also means undertaking a comparative analysis

---

[10] Innovation North Research Conference 2006 held at Leeds Metropolitan University, 10-12July'06
http://www.leedsmet.ac.uk/inn/research2006.htm
[11] More details available at http://en.wikipedia.org/wiki/Maria_Joao_Pires [accessed 22/Mar/08]

with new interviews which were being carried out. In terms of this third research stage, this involved moving back and forth between the first set of interviews, new data collection and then again new analysis. Based on Charmaz (2006, pp. 102) the process of development of categories' properties was followed.

Before arriving at the explanation of the development of categories, it is important to explain the whole steps of data analysis.

### 5.5.1. Interview transcriptions

Each interview was transcribed and a methodical and careful analysis was made, trying to not be biased by any particular subject. This was a difficult task, since the author's life experience naturally guided his thoughts. Despite this, and knowing that no one operates from an empty state of mind, a theoretical search was carried out on the data, to discover the major themes in D-M.

| London Business School | • They focus relentlessly, passionately and endlessly on simple goals. <br>• scenic fictionalize view of the organization <br>• decisive executives don't get lost in complexity <br>• reduce objectively uncertainty is reduce the perception of uncertainty <br>• managers are action men they do experience, experiment, but they do not think very much |
|---|---|
| Leeds Metropolitan University | • Thought through what are the facts, what are the figures where else <br>• Management in universities is much more intuition based. To do that is necessary to understand how Universities work, and **feel the soul** of the university. <br>• More creative, is changing thinks to affect the values of the universities to deliver that value of a good university. |
| … | … |

Table 5. 4 – Example of key phrases from interviews

The first task in the analysis was the definition of key phrases. Those keys helped to extend the analysis, giving an initial understand and a deeper understanding of the interview. They were built after the transcription finished. Table 5.4 presents an extract of phrases from the interviews. After reading line by line the interviews' transcripts, and then paragraph by paragraph and finally the whole transcript, the author evolved his own interpretation of meaning.

## 5.5.2. Coding

The interviews were analyzed through the coding process which is defined as a vital link between data collection and developing a growing theory to give an explanation to these data (Charmaz, 2006). The author started by separating, sorting and synthesizing data through qualitative coding. Through coding the researcher attached labels to segments of data. Open coding was considered in the initial phase of analysis of the researcher's interviews. Charmaz (2006) observed that openness of initial coding should help the researcher to think and allow new ideas to come forward. This process occurs under NVivo 2.0. Charmaz (2006) recommended the data were broken into segments, which are called incidents.

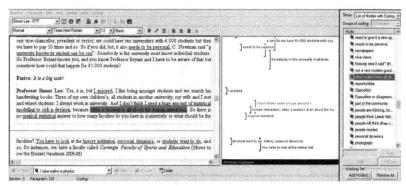

**Fig. 5. 1** – Code selection under NVivo

An incident is found in a phrase, a sentence or two but infrequently in as many words as a paragraph (Glaser, 1998). The incidents were compared with other incidents and other data, to discover or develop the code. In other words, the researcher tried to find the actions in each segment of data and coded them by using simple, short and active words which reflect these actions (Charmaz, 2006). For example, in the following sample the interviewee stated that "**I don't think I need** a huge amount of **statistical modelling to rich a decision**, because **often a decision is** all about the **human interaction**. So there is no **magical statistical** answer to how many faculties do you have in a university?" (03-Leedsmet). This incidents include actions related within D-M, need (personal), statistical (tools) and human interaction. An example of these incidents coded under NVivo 2.0 is presented in fig. 5.1:

The author used NVivo to keep a record on the codifying process and an A2 poster marked with post-its to derive the research analysis. The goal was to construct a poster from where the meaning could be extracted with the set of NVivo free code nodes which could be clustered to a new set, and in this case, a set of categories. Each time a conceptualization, an idea of clustering codes, related links or common denominators emerged, in the mind of the researcher, a memo note was also written. In the following subsection point 5.5.3 a more detailed explanation of this process is given. It follows a A2 poster of post-its, in fig. 5.2, after analysing all the codes from NVivo.

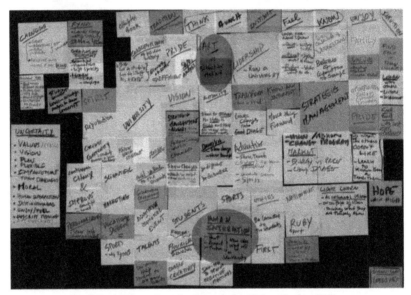

Fig. 5. 2 – A2 Poster of post-its after analyzing all the codes from NVivo.

Simultaneously, using MS/Excel each concept was characterized with more information, as shown in the following figure, in order to keep a record from the thoughts of the researcher at that moment. See fig. 5.3.

Fig. 5. 3 – Previous concepts under MS/Excel Worksheet

The author, with this example, pretends to illustrate the code process along the interview analysis, using interview transcription, coding in NVivo, the post-its development into an A2 poster and the excel worksheet, from which further explanation follows.

### 5.5.3. Memos

By making and coding numerous comparisons, the analytic grasp of the data begins to take form. The author wrote preliminary analytic notes called memos about his codes and comparisons and any other ideas about the data that occurred. In addition, a comparative process between interviews and support material helped the development of emerging ideas sustaining a process of comparison, and validation of emergent ideas. Memo writing leads directly to theoretical sampling. Memo writing has the virtue of being able to record the present ideas from a particular incident which occur at that moment the author was analysing it. They have provided the means of keeping a record of the author's reflections during the research study. But they are also a problem in terms of management, as there were so many and they all needed to be traceable and most importantly, some memos represent a consolidation of a number of memos. For each interview, the author wrote memos, but was constantly comparing with previous interviews, when an incident occurred which made it necessary to search for that cross reference. Later, a consolidated memo was used, a short list of ideas where incidents for each informant were inserted. This created mainly two types of memos: one mainly related with each interview (but still with cross-references to other informants in special incidents) and another as a consolidated memo, reflecting a summary of ideas, incidents and informant origin.

In addition, MS/Excel worksheets were maintained concurrently, which contained a summary memo description associated to each NVivo code node analysed and post-it associated.

MS/Excel was selected because of the ability to use the unstructured facilities to design tables, sort them and then agglomerate by topic. It could be substituted by any database tool, as NVivo 7 uses an external database. The problem at the beginning of this new stage was that all the variables that should be used, what they would look like, how the author will cluster and sort them, was not known. Given these constraints, MS/Excel looked as if it would be adequate to proceed with the research analysis. The result was a final excel worksheet for each interview. An example of memo is presented in fig. 5.4.

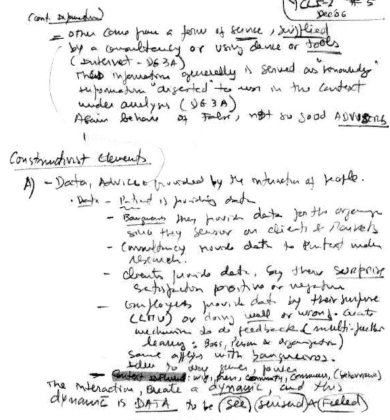

**Fig. 5. 4** – Sample of a memo

The Excel worksheet used the following columns, fig. 5.5: *Free code No represented by N*, corresponds to the number of the free code node sensed in NVivo. *1ˢᵗ passage* in NVivo represents the first analysis done. The work was never done in only one or two passages. It was a cycle of returning, reading and revising. Furthermore, the 1ˢᵗ passage (column "Jun'06") is related to a previous analysis where the focus was not clear. The designated free code name is a brief resume from the first analysis done in NVivo. 2ⁿᵈ passage (column "Dec'06") which is now the goal and describes the author's thoughts at the moment. Sometimes another name is given, which represents an eventual category to cluster the code. *Description* is an excel memo, describing what the author was thinking at the moment about that operation.

*Symbolic* is related to two premises, first the previous engineer profession of the author, decomposing things in synthetic forms. Second, related with an attempt to do a symbolic interactive approach to understand social life that focuses on how reality is constructed by the accounts of the interview participants through their interactions with their social context. It proved to be difficult, since there were too many codes, and the effort to synthesize all the symbolism written, did not give a deeper understanding. (fig.5.5)

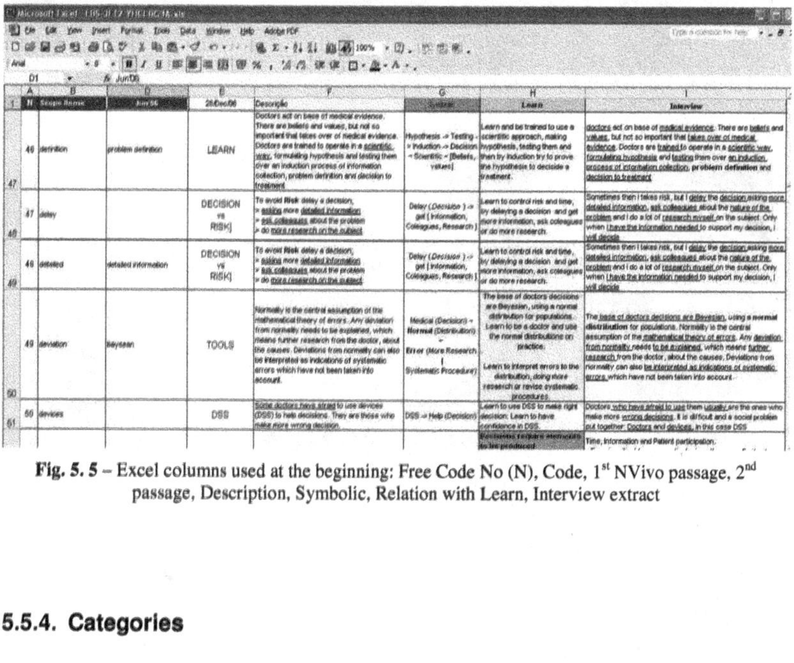

**Fig. 5. 5** – Excel columns used at the beginning: Free Code No (N), Code, 1$^{st}$ NVivo passage, 2$^{nd}$ passage, Description, Symbolic, Relation with Learn, Interview extract

### 5.5.4. Categories

The process of sensing, interpreting and creating meaning was undertaken in order to make theoretical sense of so much diversity in the data. The researcher's codes were transposed for A2 sheets where attempts to represent cluster's of codes of post-it's are drawn.

| | |
|---|---|
|  |  |
| Stage 1 - Initially to each code is assigned a post-it. The post-its were put onto an A2 sheet, and similar context post-its were put into the same area. Sometimes, a set of post-its were removed to a different area, rearranging the layout. | Stage 2 - This picture shows post-its becoming a cluster of meaning. Eventually a full cluster could be moved to a different area. |
|  |  |
| Stage 3 - This is a final representation. Now with help of associated memos, clusters of meaning shall be visible. | Stage 4 - This is a final representation of one of the participants. Now the clusters of meaning are clearly extracted from the participant's account of decision-making. |

Fig. 5. 6 – The path to draw a poster of post-it cluster representing categories

The task occurred in NVivo coding each interview, as explained previously in 5.5.2. These sets of codes were then transposed in a meticulous and lengthy procedure through the construction of a poster of post-its. To each code from NVivo a post-it was associated, where a designation for that code was re-written. Sometimes, it had the same designation, or an equivalent word, or a brief action description. Or even some codes did not have a post-it representation, since it was represented previously by another designation. These post-its were agglomerated onto an A2 paper sheet for each participant, one by one, in a form that was changing and evolving over time from the beginning. The goal was to construct a poster from where the meaning could be extracted with the set of NVivo free code nodes which could be clustered to a new set, and in this case, a set of categories. Each time a conceptualization, an idea of clustering codes, related links or common denominators, emerged, in the mind of the researcher, a memo note was also written. If there does indeed exist a method to draw such poster post-its, then diagram 5.1 shows the algorithm to do it.

These sets of categories (see fig. 5.6) are a deepened analysis of the extracted meaning, for each participant interviewee, about his account of the D-M experience. Each participant was analysed individually. Further data collection strengthened categories. This work sharpened the categories, offering a new meaning, providing a link between some, highlighting others' strengths and their structure. This process corresponded to a total of 1.680 codes from all nine interviews, as Table 5.5 shows.

| Group | Interview | Codes |
|-------|-----------|-------|
| I | 01 - Dinefer | 179 |
| | 02 - Sonae | 256 |
| | 03 - Leeds Metropolitan University | 216 |
| | 04 - London Business School | 82 |
| | 05 - Goldman Sachs | 174 |
| | *Total Free Code Nodes Group I ...* | **907** |
| II | 06 - Yorkshire Centre for Health Informatics | 193 |
| | 07 - Jet2 | 198 |
| | 08 - Design Group 3 Architects | 160 |
| | 09 - Lawnswood School | 222 |
| | *Total Free Code Nodes Group II ...* | **773** |
| | *Total Free Code Nodes Group I & II ...* | **1.680** |
| III | 10 - Chelsea FC | 212 |
| | ***Total Free Code Nodes ....*** | **1.892** |

Table 5. 5 – Total Codes used to derive categories

Theoretical sampling ensured that the author constructed categories that lead to clarify relationships between categories (Charmaz, 2006, pp.103). This was not an obvious process, it was an in-depth, thorough and, sometimes frustrating personal task, going over interview data again and again, sifting through MS/Excel worksheets, NVivo codes, A2 poster post-its and memos in order to consolidate a set of categories, with a sustained reduced process, but always resulting from the data analysed.

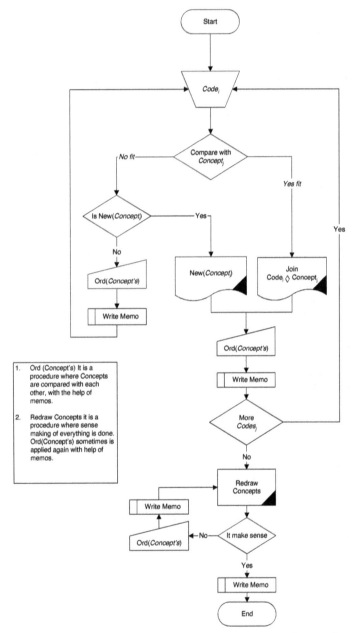

**Diagram 5. 1** – Author developed algorithm used to draw the A2 posters of post-its

As a result of the previous steps, a method of theory development sustained by the theoretical sampling, a set of categories was obtained. These categories were still a large number, they needed to be concentrated, to arrive to an abstract level, and for this purpose the comparative method was used. Charmaz (2006) states the comparative method is a combination of the *"conversion of qualitative data into crudely quantifiable form"* and the *"data inspection for new properties of his theoretical categories, and simultaneously writing memos on these properties"* (Glaser and Strauss, 1967, pp.101-2). Further steps used the comparative method to reduce previous obtained categories.

The operation was made sorting by MS/Excel into which was inputted all the grounded categories obtained from the A2 poster post-its for each interview. This task was done in two phases. Phase 1 corresponded to translating the Portuguese category name into English and then creating an MS/Excel worksheet where all the categories were in one column. This column was then simplified with a *unique* operator remaining as only one single column without any repetition of category name. Then to each category name row, in the next column an equivalent Reduced Category name was written. In phase 2, this process was repeated, copying the new Reduced Category into a new column, simplified with a *unique* operator and finally sorted. These phases reduced the original 26 different categories into 12. This was a task, based on an interpretation from each category obtained using GTM analysis, which reduced the number of categories. For example, generally the researcher obtained a category which corresponded to the interviewee's personality, profession or other interpretation: "Architect", "Doctor", "Leader", "Pilot" and "Self" were reduced to "Decision-Maker". Another example is the reduced category "Tools" which was obtained from the categories "Information Systems", "Planning", "Systems" and "Tools". In this example the author kept the designation "Tools" assigned to some of previous categories, Table 5.6 shows the fully reduced categories.

As a result of this stage of the research, the following reduced categories were obtained, taken from 26 grounded categories:

- *Culture* – response from socio-cultural values;

    o For example the interpretation evidence from 02-Sonae interview "Now there is the negative value of brands, because of the confrontation between Islamic fundamentalism and the American unique superpower" or "The Jews want to win money, they are great financiers. In this objective they are specialists, organized, very intelligent, and they discover methods, and it is very difficult to deceive the Jews".

- **Decision-Maker** – refers to the self, the interviewee referred sometimes to his profession;

  - o For example, the following sample from the interviews: "we have to be able to communicate successfully and not just say to people what you want, you have to be able to get from them, what you want." (08-DG3A) or "if it is money, and it is something that I have to be carefully I have to make a very rational decision but in my personal life I have take very stupid decisions on the basis of emotions and get carried away" (09-Lawnswood).

- **Judgment** – consequence recognition for a decision act, the resulting evaluation process;

  - o For example, the following samples from the interviews: "…when you can't go with further research, it then goes down to instinct, to judgement I suppose." (08-DG3A) or "Doctors need elements to support a medical evidence decision, but also have fear to make wrong decisions, since there could occur fatal consequences to the patient and prosecution of the doctor." (06-YCHI).

- **Leader** – refers to the ability to affect human behaviour influencing a group of people to move towards its goal achievement;

  - o "Two fundamental things: one is to have a project, a vision and another is leadership, nothing happens without leadership". (01-Dinefer) or "Leadership in universities is an art rather then science." (03-Leedsmet) or "I have a clear vision of what a good university should be." (03-Leedsmet).

- **Learning** – process to sense and acquire knowledge for unknown features of the uncertain and complex context;

- **Organization** – organizational context of the interviewee;

- **People** – network of individuals important to the organization where the interviewee also plays a part;

**Phase 1**

| Interviewee | Category | Reduced Category |
|---|---|---|
| DG3A | Architect | Decision-Maker |
| Dinefer | Clients | People |
| Jet2 | Company | Organization |
| Sonae | Culture | Culture |
| DG3A | Decision | Judgment |
| Lawnswood | Decision | Judgment |
| LBS | Decision | Judgment |
| LBS | Decision-Maker | Decision-Maker |
| YCHI | Doctors | Decision-Maker |
| Goldman | Information Systems | Tools |
| Lawnswood | Job | Organization |
| YCHI | Judgment | Judgment |
| Dinefer | Leader | Leader |
| DG3A | Learn | Learn |
| Dinefer | Learn | Learn |
| Goldman | Learn | Learn |
| Jet2 | Learn | Learn |
| Lawnswood | Learn | Learn |
| LBS | Learn | Learn |
| LeedsMet | Learn | Learn |
| Sonae | Learn | Learn |
| YCHI | Learn | Learn |
| LeedsMet | Lidership | Leader |
| DG3A | Office | Organization |
| Dinefer | Organization | Organization |
| Goldman | Organization | Organization |
| LBS | Organization | Organization |
| Sonae | Organization | Organization |
| YCHI | Patient | People |
| Dinefer | People | Society |
| LBS | People | People |
| LeedsMet | People | People |
| Jet2 | Pilot | Decision-Maker |
| Jet2 | Planning | Tools |
| Sonae | Public Opinion | Public Opinion |
| Lawnswood | Self | Decision-Maker |
| Sonae | Society | Society |
| LeedsMet | Symbols | Symbols |
| Jet2 | Systems | Tools |
| Lawnswood | Systems | Tools |
| Sonae | Tools | Tools |
| YCHI | Tools | Tools |
| Dinefer | Uncertainty | Uncertainty |
| Goldman | Uncertainty | Uncertainty |
| Jet2 | Uncertainty | Uncertainty |
| LeedsMet | Uncertainty | Uncertainty |
| Sonae | Uncertainty | Uncertainty |
| Dinefer | Values | Learn |

**Phase 2**

| Reduced Category | Category | Interview |
|---|---|---|
| Culture | Culture | Sonae |
| | Architect | DG3A |
| | Decision-Maker | LBS |
| Decision-Maker | Doctors | YCHI |
| | Pilot | Jet2 |
| | Self | Lawnswood |
| | Decision | DG3A |
| Judgment | Decision | Lawnswood |
| | Decision | LBS |
| | Judgment | YCHI |
| Leader | Leader | Dinefer |
| | Lidership | LeedsMet |
| | Learn | DG3A |
| | Learn | Dinefer |
| | Learn | Goldman |
| | Learn | Jet2 |
| Learn | Learn | Lawnswood |
| | Learn | LBS |
| | Learn | LeedsMet |
| | Learn | Sonae |
| | Learn | YCHI |
| | Values | Dinefer |
| | Company | Jet2 |
| | Job | Lawnswood |
| | Office | DG3A |
| Organization | Organization | Dinefer |
| | Organization | Goldman |
| | Organization | LBS |
| | Organization | Sonae |
| | Clients | Dinefer |
| People | Patient | YCHI |
| | People | LBS |
| | People | LeedsMet |
| Public Opinion | Public Opinion | Sonae |
| Society | People | Dinefer |
| | Society | Sonae |
| Symbols | Symbols | LeedsMet |
| | Information Systems | Goldman |
| | Planning | Jet2 |
| Tools | Systems | Jet2 |
| | Systems | Lawnswood |
| | Tools | Sonae |
| | Tools | YCHI |
| | Uncertainty | Dinefer |
| | Uncertainty | Goldman |
| Uncertainty | Uncertainty | Jet2 |
| | Uncertainty | LeedsMet |
| | Uncertainty | Sonae |

**Table 5. 6** – Comparative method used to reduce categories

- **Public Opinion** – connotation to society guided by the media. It is also termed the market;

- **Society** - the external social network of the organization;

- **Symbols** (*Inscription and translation*) – association to actor-network theory objects;

- **Tools** – referring to systems and tools used as complementary to socio-networks in sensing the unknown;

- **Uncertainty** – description for the unknown prospects.

In order to fulfil these conceptual relationships and make theoretical propositions, the author developed a new stage of reasoning, in order to achieve a synthesis for all the obtained categories and further hidden meanings.


## 5.6. Fourth Stage – Main Categories


. The fourth stage consisted of another deep exploration of data, analysing the grounded categories to develop main categories, finding other independent categories and designing new research questions which compelled the researcher to further literature review in order to sustain the findings. In this process new data was constructed and in some situations reconstructed, simultaneously with theory building. This involved a learning loop, a consult and return to data and memos, between theory and the research study. Charmaz argues for this stage of reasoning *"forming hypothesis for each possible explanation, checking them empirically by examining the data and pursuing the most plausible explanation"* (Charmaz, 2006, pp.104). Furthermore the researcher returned again to the A2 posters of post-its relating to each individual participant, and, observed them all together, in an attempt to read and interpret what was not yet shown (mainly recurring to simplified versions of the A2 poster post-its, but with associated colours). Then, the remaining hidden meaning could be found and the existing data examined to see if alternative or additional meanings could be found. Complementary work was carried out through a handwritten schema of the categories obtained; attempting to find the remaining hidden meaning that bound everything all together. Further complementary work was carried out sorting the MS/Excel worksheets, with the expectation that integrated categories would appear.

Another operation was executed over each A2 poster of post-its, observing, reading notes and transcribing an image of the categories and properties onto a separate A4 sheet of paper. Then, using coloured pens, categories were clustered, associating each one to the others with a related and sensed meaning, as figure 5.7 shows a final example. This final clustering of categories was applied in each A2 poster of post-its, providing the final four categories as table 5.7 shows: **Calculating decision knowledge, Decision-maker learning story, Impact of learning (new knowledge) on the decision-maker's professional composure (self)** and **Uncertainty**.

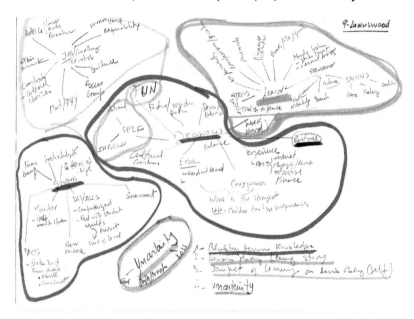

**Fig. 5. 7** – Sample of Clustering Categories

In order to validate this work, a final operation was carried out with MS/Excel clustering the obtained categories with colours and the results from phase 1 and 2, resulting in the cluster of categories is shown in table 5.7.

98

| | Calculating Decision Knowledge | Decision-Maker Learning Story | Impact of Learning on the Decision-Maker Professional Composure | Uncertainty |
|---|---|---|---|---|
| 01-Dinefer | People Organization Clients | Learning Values | Leader | Uncertainty |
| 02-Sonae | Society Public Opinion Tools | Learning Cultures | Organization | Uncertainty |
| 03-Leedsmet | People Symbols | Learning | Leadership | Uncertainty |
| 04-LBS | Decision-Maker | Learn Decision | Persons Organization | |
| 05-Goldman | Tools Information Systems | Learning | Organization | Uncertainty |
| 06-YCHI | Tools Patient | Learning | Doctor | Uncertainty (*Judgment*) |
| 07-Jet2 | Systems | Learning Planning | Pilot Company | Uncertainty |
| 08-DG3A | Decision | Learning | Architect Office | Uncertainty |
| 09-Lawnswood | Systems | Learning | Job Decisions | Uncertainty |

**Table 5. 7** – Main categories summary table

For this end, this fourth research stage and work in order to find meaning provided the major themes on D-M under uncertainty and complexity:

- **_Calculating decision knowledge_** – refers to the social network construction where a decision-maker could sense the unknown; it is associated with the decision-maker surrounded by his social web, from where he gets help to reconstruct/reframe the uncertain and complex context. Both human and non-human techniques are used to obtain information in order to support D-M.

  o For example "We have here a culture of permanent contact and communication. Not only for sharing information but especially for cooperation." (05-Goldman), "In the past I do not admit anybody without speaking with three people: the druggist, the priest and the barber." (02-Soane) or "If nothing ever went wrong, planes would not have a pilot. But we are there to make decisions, do not trust on the machine." (07-Jet2) or "in a business sense, it is to make sure you have a collection of people who have different knowledge... we have a mix, so it is like having more than a one brain" (08-DG3A).

- **_The decision-maker's learning story_** – the process from which he senses the unknown features, the story from *where*, *how* and *when* he learns to make a decision under uncertainty; it describes the learning process developed during the development of the decision. It corresponds to all the learning related categories.

- o The following phrases show the interpretation of the evidence by the researcher: "As a crew we all are going to participate in a crew decision. So we have five inputs from the crew, it is a crew decision." (07-Jet2) or "...to try change the situation and the strategy to change depends on my interpretation of the student needs, what kind of person they are. If it is a student who needs a lot of direction then he needs to be shown first and then we will develop a structure" (09-Lawnswood) or "Relationships between key players on another human level and... the thing that really determining the acquisition are in a human level." (04-LBS).

- **The impact of learning (new knowledge) on the decision-maker's professional *composure (self-control)*** – which provides the new socio-organizational context as result of the process of learning under uncertainty. It could or could not be a successful decision. The strength is on the practised experience, and on the new reality derived from the learning process; this category refers to the interpretation that the researcher makes from each interview. Each interviewee is different, as each person has a style which reveals how he makes decisions under uncertainty and complexity. Some are more rational, searching for more data to support a decision; others are more emotional, mostly deciding based on his feelings and intuitions, not waiting for information to support a decision, they prefer to decide. This experience of deciding under uncertainty, creates some behaviour which shows professional experience, acquired during a professional life. The experience of deciding under uncertainty and complexity, which is learning, is represented then under this category and the Impact of Learning on the decision-maker. Table 5.7 shows the contribution of grounded categories for this new category.

- o The following samples show the evidence: "When someone really with courage, shows up, he wins the crowd's sympathy. This is dangerous..."(02-Sonae) or "I will be able to use them as an example again to people to say: 'these individuals are climbing Everest, no problems'. We need to aim high, literally." (03-Leedsmet) or "you are accountable in the future for that decision" (08-DG3A).

- **Uncertainty** – concerns the eternally vague context of reality. There is no single answer for uncertainty. It is a common category to all interviews. It is a category that reflects the uncertain context and is treated with human interaction and understanding. The following sample shows evidence from all the interviews:

  o "Scientific advances increase uncertainty enormously. We today, for example, are extremely dependent on the invasion of computer hackers, of terrorist cuts of basic lines of communication, blackouts of energy, and explosions of a nuclear central power station... Therefore the world is the world of many commitments, where uncertainty is sometimes contained." (02-Sonae) or "The more mature society is, the more powerful and more sophisticated progress is linked to changes that are largely unpredictable and very random." (05-Goldman).

## 5.7. Fifth Stage – The Grounded Theory

The fifth research stage consisted of a consolidation of the previous stages, constructing a grounded theory of D-M under uncertainty and complexity, which was also verified. For this end, a third set of interviews was directed by the emerging concepts from the previous sets, involving a selection of informants.

This research stage was carried out to evaluate findings and confirm with previous interviewees the research findings. In addition, another goal was undertaken, in order to saturate categories and validate theory. Charmaz as well as other authors argues for categories theoretical saturation "*When gathering fresh data no longer sparks new theoretical insight, nor reveals new properties of your core theoretical categories... or nothing new happening*" (Charmaz, 2006, pp. 113). For this end, a third group of interviews were carried out, in 2007, after the grounded categories were analysed, with some questions and a validation and confirmation still remaining, which had to be done. These questions were related initially with the categories saturation, which indicate or not the necessity for more data to be collected. Secondly the role of *learning*, the central category extracted from previous interviews, needed a final validation. Finally, some open questions such as the structure of relationships grounding the knowledge acquired to make a decision, the role of family and friends in uncertain context and calculating knowledge to help D-M needed to be resolved. Posing these new research questions, a critical and rich environment where uncertainty plays a central part had to be selected. One day whilst watching a football match between Chelsea FC and Manchester United on TV, the idea that the football arena would be satisfactory occurred to the researcher. There are similarities with the business field in that it contains decision making under uncertainty, where unknown results could emerge, fast decisions are made, it deals with people's feelings and mainly with people's options, and after all it is a world wide business also, as in the first group interviews context. The most interesting fact was that the Chelsea football manager was at that time Portuguese, being one of the best football managers at the time, called by the press 'the special one'. Therefore a process in order to contact Chelsea FC was started, and after several telephone calls and e-mails, contact was established. Before a schedule was defined, an abstract of the work and a resume of the author were sent. The interview was carried out on 9th February 2007 in the Conrad Hotel, London. The interview was recorded and a transcription was produced.

A reference to validation and result confirmation should be given at this point. The reason for interviewing two previous participants for a second time is linked to the need of confirmation of ideas, to see what they had to add more. Alasuutari presents his interpretation to the participants and pushes for a dialogue about it; "*He gained confirmation of his view then pushed further later in the same conversation*" (Alasuutari, 1996 quoted in Charmaz, 2006, pp. 112). The author planned a presentation to the two previous participants, sustained by Alasuutari (1996), presenting his interpretation, aiming for a response. In addition, two other interviews were produced, to show results and receive feedback from the participants (Alasuutari, 1996). The first presentation and feedback was done at the Dinefer headquarters in 9th March 2007. The author firstly presented the initial results to the Dinefer CEO and his son, the head of another enterprise of the group. The feedback, with some surprise, presented the role of the emotional side in D-M. They were so interested in the results that they invited the author to present them in a workshop for the Dinefer staff and some outside guests. This workshop was held on 12th March 2007- 17:30 at Dinefer headquarters. Further detail is show in chapter 6.7.4.

A second interview was scheduled with the Sonae CEO, at the Sonae headquarters, Portugal for 19th April 2007. This second interview also had the purpose to give thanks for all the support and referrals of the other participants. This interview was not long, due to a time limit set by the interviewee. However the author had the opportunity to explain the findings giving the opportunity to the interviewee to reply.

Further detail is shown in chapter 6.7.4. Previous to this second interview, contact by e-mail and phone calls was established and an actual resume of the work sent.

| | Enterprise | Business Type | Date | Interview Participant |
|---|---|---|---|---|
| **Group** | CHELSEA FC | Football manager of Chelsea F.C. | 9th February 2007 | Football Manager |
| **III** | DINEFER | 2nd Interview Report Results | 9th March 2007 | Dinefer CEO |
| 2007 | SONAE | 2nd Interview Report Results | 19th April 2007 | SONAE CEO |

**Table 5. 8** – Group 3 – 2007 Interviewee participants

The remaining research work corresponded to reading memos, looking again at the data generated, writing down grounded tables, generation of the structure of relationships, reviewing each chapter's content and linking everything in order to write the book. It is important to explain the procedures that developed the structure of the relationship between categories, which follows.

The main data resides in grounded tables containing the interview analysis synthesis, and represents each interview category with all the properties. This document is central since it contains the generated data: categories and properties and an extract from the interview as table 5.9 shows. For example, the "Architect" category from the 08-DG3A interview, as shown in table 5.9, has five properties and a sub-category "Work constrains" which has four properties. It has the following representative table 5.10:

| 08-Design Group 3 Architects | Table 1 of 5 |
|---|---|
| Category **Architect** | |

An architect is someone who receives a traditional education as an artist, someone who creates something very individual or personal or novel. Creating something is working under a critical thinking process where creativity is balanced with regulations and people in order to have a product. This process develops within constrains to creativity, such as buildings regulations, health and safety, financial constrains, and aesthetic constrains and the human side constituted the planning system which have professionals, lay people and others giving aesthetic judgements. It is a constant process or continuous learning, gathering information, put into the thought process and the design process. It is very difficult for an architect to work as an individual because there is a limit to his ability to gather and handle information to be able to provide an efficient response to a client's requirements. Creating something is a participative process with the architect, community and client in a process to communicate successfully what the architect wants and also be able to get from others what the architect wants. There are also other work constrains related to efficiency that an architect has to deal with when creating something. These limitations are cost, quality, time and aesthetics. An aesthetic constrain is a judgment about the beauty of the architect's creation, an aesthetic judgment by another person who sees it by his own eyes and beauty criteria. An architect learns through experience and needs to continue learning.

| Properties | Description | Extract interview |
|---|---|---|
| **Critical Thinking** | It a process where creativity, constrains and people are balanced in order to have a product. The process develops within constrains to creativity, such as buildings regulations, health and safety, financial constrains, and aesthetic constrains and the social network, the planning system which have professionals, lay people and others giving aesthetic judgements. It is a constant process or continuous learning, gathering information, put into the thought process and the design process. We learn with our experience. | "It is all part of the thinking process. An unsuccessful architect is press hunted, is stressed every time a decision has to be made, your decision or not, logical or not. But is something that comes with learning and experience, a combination of both." <br><br> "It is a constant process, gathering information, put into the thought process and the design process." <br><br> "…you need to continue learning, like information technology, we need to continue learning about what there are up there" <br><br> "we have to be able to communicate successfully and not just say to people what you want, you have to be able to get from them what you want." |
| **Design Team** | It is a participative process with the architect, community and client. It is a process to communicate successfully what the architect wants and also be able to get from them what the architect wants. | "Very participating process it is a … we called it a design team, is very important, but it is not just being an architect it is all the other areas of expertise, but outside the design team, is the community, is the client, is the end user, at the end always… so there is a lot to take on board." |

**Table 5. 9** – Sample of a summary of categories for each interview (Grounded tables)

| Properties | Description | Extract interview |
|---|---|---|
| **Work Constraints** | Constrains relates to the efficiency that an architect has to deal when creating something. These limitations are cost, quality, time and aesthetics. | "We have to do that within constrains, severe constrains, but after all, buildings regulations, health and safety, financial constrains, and aesthetic constrains and finally we have what we call the planning system which we have professionals and other people, we have lay people, making the decisions whether your building is acceptable or not" |
| • *Cost* | Limitation on financial terms and in the ratios cost/quality and cost/time. | "...the financial constrains, we have talking about them" "...need to be efficient, cost-quality and time and they are more interested in cost right" and the price is right if the product is visually pleasant and efficient |
| • *Quality* | Limitation to quality if it is visually pleasant, good, efficient and good price. | "...cost-quality and time and they are more interested in cost right, quality right and getting on time;" "...your quality it is good, and the price is right if the product is visual pleasant and efficient so, you can't have other arguments on it" |
| • *In time* | Limitation to the delivery time | "...getting in on time; not in the next year, not in the three years time... a wonderful process we deliver on time..." |
| • *Aesthetic* | Relates to a judgment about the beauty of the architect creation, an aesthetic judgment by another person who sees it by his own eyes and beauty criteria. | "...aesthetic judgements. There is a saying 'beauty is in the eye of the beholder' so what I think is beautiful, fantastic and successful, maybe horrible, not fantastic and not successful to somebody else. And that person maybe is the person who is deciding where you can do what you wish to do." |

**Table 5. 10** – Sample of a sub-category and his properties (08-DG3A "Architect" category)

In doing this summary, the author looked again for all the generated data, grouped everything in order from excel worksheets, memos and consolidated a description summary. (See table 5.10) All was linked with an extract interview. This research task contains all the categories and properties obtained. Now another overview is taken, in order to draw a structure that links the categories with the other ones. This structure sustains the resulting theory and explains further frameworks. For example the same "Architect" category from 08-DG3A interview has the following illustration:

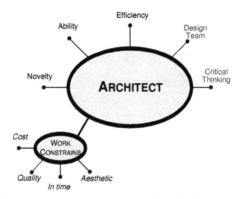

**Fig. 5. 8** – Category sample illustration (08-DG3A "Architect" category)

The yellow colour is related within the cluster of categories, used to obtain main categories, as explained previously at section 5.6.

Joining all categories from an interview the result is shown in the following figure:

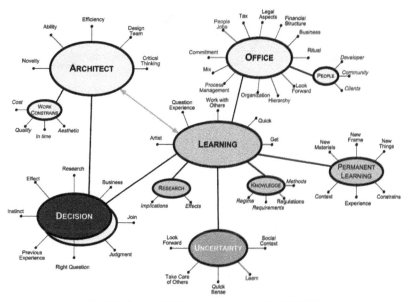

**Fig. 5. 9** – Sample of Relations between categories (08-DG3A)

The schema shown in figure 5.9 is puzzling, since it contains all the categories, sub-categories and properties obtained from one interview analysis. There are links between categories which provide a structure, however it is not yet clarified. The researcher had to work backwards to the main categories, and using the cluster categories this schema is simplified for the next one:

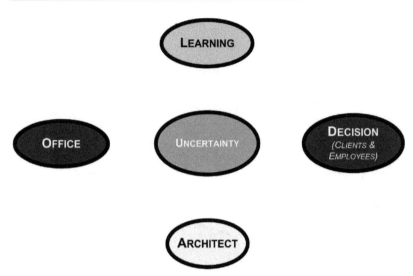

**Fig. 5. 10** – Sample illustration with cluster categories (08-DG3A)

The previous figure 5.10, showing how the cluster categories are obtained from the clustering is explained previously section 5.6. However, this simplification requires an interpretation for the links between categories, which are not yet represented.

These relationships have been obtained from summarizing all the categories, subcategories and properties generated into a single worksheet, as shown in table 5.11.

Then, the researcher made interpretative frames, which is an interpretation of his understanding of the relationships between categories. As a result, he obtained a picture which represents a specific setting in time and space from where the decision-maker develops the process of learning, how to make a decision under uncertainty.

| 01 - Dinefer | 02 - Sonae | 03 - Leedsmet | 04 - LBS | 05 - Goldman | 06 - YCHI | 07 - JET 2 | 08 - DG3A | 09 - Lawnswood |
|---|---|---|---|---|---|---|---|---|
| **Leader** | **Organization** | **Leadership** | **Persons** | **Bankers** | **Doctor** | **Pilot** | **Architect** | **Job** |
| Capacity | Public Opinion | Art | Artist | Scenario Building | Medical Evidence | Logic stand | Novelty | Work Hard |
| Delegate | Risk Behaviour | Pride | Action | Brainstorming | Start Process | Danger | Ability | Responsability |
| North | Bet | Enjoy | Leadership | Permanent Contact | Information 20% | To be the best | Efficiency | Counseling |
| Vision | Society | Know | Manager | Daily Meetings | Time | Operate | Design Team | Focus Group |
| Adviser | Pharmacy | Feel the Spirit | Organization | ICT | Problem Definition | Aircraft | Critical Thinking | Guidance |
| Present | Priest | Vision | Small | | Join Decision | Solve problem | Work Constrains | Maths/Physics |
| Experience | Professor | Hunch | Feedback | | Decide | Training | Cost | Advice |
| People | Barbershop | Instinc/Intuition | Judgment | | Doctor Type | Day work | Quality | Rules |
| Other Organizations | Vote | Tradition | Qualify | | Belief | Goal | In Time | Prosecution |
| Clients | | Family | Large | | Act | Satisfaction | Aesthetic | Constrains |
| Adepts | | | | | | Job done | | Ethical |
| Family | | | | | | | | Organization |
| | | | | | | | | Student Cultures |
| **Organization** | **Tools** | **Symbols** | **Decision-Making** | **Inf. Systems** | **Tools** | **Systems** | **Office** | **Systems** |
| Values | Agreements | History | Feelings | Confidence | Budget | Routing | People Jobs | System Software |
| Adepts | Scenario Building | Sports | Time | Collection | Software | Exact Route | Tax | Facts |
| Employees | Decision Tree | Rhinos | Consequences | Markets | Aircraft Systems | Aircraft Systems | Legal Aspects | Monitor |
| Customers | Game Theory | Reputation | Leadership | HR Management | Statistic | Technical Systems | Financial Structure | Focus Group |
| Capacity | Chance | Chapter Book | | Trading | Afraid to use | Weather Systems | Business | Individualize |
| | | | | Clients | Ask Others | Air Traffic Systems | Ritual | Patterns of Life |
| | | | | | | | People | Government |
| | | | | | | | Developer | Show Evidence |
| | | | | | | | Community | |
| | | | | | | | Clients | |
| | | | | | | | Look Forward | |
| | | | | | | | Hierachy | |
| | | | | | | | Organization | |
| | | | | | | | Proc. Management | |
| | | | | | | | Mix | |
| | | | | | | | Commitment | |
| **Learning** | **Learning** | **Learning** | **Learning** | **Learning** | **Learning** | **Learning** | **Learning** | **Learning** |
| Create new Leaders | Speculation | Sports | Business | Use Tecnology | Dialogue | Plan ahead | Artist | Students |
| Others | Politics | History | Math's | Innovate | Collection | Crew Decision | Quest. Experience | Data |
| Experience | Power | Hope | Action | Not Waste Time | Read | Common sense | Work with Others | Culture |
| Clients | Pleasure | Lift Spirts | Kolb's | Control Uncertainty | Divide & Conquer | Avoid Uncertainty | Quick | Feelings |
| Values | Fears | Positive Feelings | | Client Needs | Analysing | Pick Solution | Get | Structure |
| Liberty | Courage | Disagreements | | Decide Fast | Scientif Way | Alternatives | Perm. Learning | Family |
| Responsability | Time | Students | | Make Business | Delay | Systems | New Materials | Balance |
| Respect | Decision Impact | Human Interaction | | | Experience | Make Plan | New Frame | Capture Knowledge |
| Transparency | Cultures | Other People | | | | Weather | New Things | Stress |
| Loyalty | USA | | | | | Route | Const | Research |
| Availability | Islamic | | | | | Fuel | Experience | Expertise |
| Flexibility | Jews | | | | | Precise Solution | Knowledge | Financial |
| Reactivity | Europe | | | | | React to Situation | Methods | Monitor System |
| | Switzerland | | | | | In the Air | Regulations | Student Targets |
| | Russians | | | | | Crew | Requirements | Personal Needs |
| | | | | | | Telephone | Regime | |
| | | | | | | Manual | Implications | |
| | | | | | | Research | Effects | |
| **Clients** | **Public Opinion** | **People** | **Decision** | **Organization** | **Patient** | **Planning** | **Decision** | **Decisions** |
| People | Apathy | Constant Change | Political | Culture | Cause of Disease | Plan | Instinct | Cult. Constrains |
| Capacity | Bureaucracy | Families | Leaders | Bankers | Treatment | Alternatives | Effect | Work Hard |
| Caprice | History | Be connected | Information | Human Capital | Consequences | Deviate | Research | Experience |
| | Brand | Distinctiveness | Timing | | Futures Diseases | Passengers needs | Business | Balance |
| | Media | Sports | Soft Data | | Commitment | Airports | Join | Fun |
| | | Be the first | | | | Conditions | Judgment | Self |
| | | Nationwide | | | | First Plan | Right Question | Rational |
| | | | | | | | Prev. Experience | Impulsive |
| | | | | | | | | Information |
| | | | | | | | | Factual |
| | | | | | | | | Emotional |
| | | | | | | | | Partner |
| | | | | | | | | Advice |
| **Capacity** | **Nature** | **Ethics** | **Uncertainty** | **Uncertainty** | **Uncertainty** | **Uncertainty** | **Uncertainty** | **Uncertainty** |
| Capacity | Nature | Ethics | | Innovation | Wrong Decision | To be avoid | Look Forward | Goal |
| North | Unpredictability | Vision | | Progress | Court | Not impinging | Take Care of Others | Path |
| Believe | Limits | Plan | | Cultures | Tie | Ask someone | Quick Sense | Loss |
| Vision | Science | Flexible | | Aggregate | Afraid | Danger | Learn | Feel |
| | Risk | Human Interaction | | Risk | Collateral Effects | Plan ahead | Social Context | It never Stops |

**Table 5. 11** – All interviews categories, subcategories and properties

Following the example from the 08-DG3A interview, "Decision" is the goal for the Clients or Employees needs, from where the Learning process is needed, and that need is what moves the decision-maker, presently the "Architect". Does he have previous experience or not? May he use some tools or other mechanic developed with previous experience? If not, he is presented to the unknown and other ways to satisfy the need must be developed, reconstructing and reframing the reality. From this interpretation we have, for previous figure 5.10:

- "Learning" <u>link</u> with "Decision" – **Need** – the decision goal

- "Learning" <u>link</u> with "Office" – **Unknown** – the developing process which is unknown, facing uncertainty and complexity at the beginning of the process

- "Architect" <u>link</u> with "Decision" – **Why** – The motivation for the learning process

- "Architect" <u>link</u> with "Office" – **Mechanicistic** – The structure of previous experience in uncertainty and complexity contexts.


Now the "Uncertainty" also provides interpretation links with all the categories. Following the same example from the 08-DG3A interview, the "Uncertainty" context will guide the "Architect" to turn operational "Office" in order to define a tacit approach to "Decision". This operational tacit will depend on the experience of the "Architect" dealing with "Uncertain" context of the "Decision". So the "Architect" will develop the cognitive means to the "Learning" process. Consequently, this "Learning" process under "Uncertainty" will have an impact on the "Architect", e.g. in his experience. From this interpretation we have, for previous figure 5.10:

- "Uncertainty" link <u>with</u> "Decision" – **Tacit** – The approach to deal with the decision context

- "Uncertainty" <u>link</u> with "Office" – **Operational** – The means to develop knowledge and support for the "Decision"

- "Uncertainty" <u>link</u> with "Learning" – **Cognitive** – The way that the "Architect" enlarges his cognition capacity in order to make an informed "Decision"

- "Uncertainty" <u>link</u> with "Architect" – **Impact** – The resulting experience of "Decision" under "Uncertainty" will be reflected on the "Architect" experience and the way he is seen by others.

Following the interpretation, as a result from comparing common properties between categories, forming a causal explanation for the decision accounted experience, the author developed the following structure (Fig.5.11). This structure reflects the links between properties in all interviews.

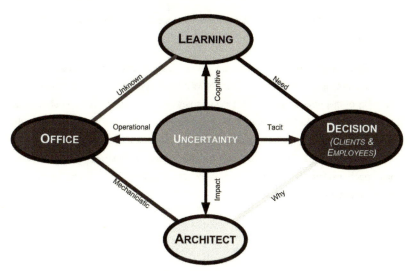

**Fig. 5. 11** – Conceptual Schema – GTM main categories relationships (08-DG3A interview)

## 5.8. ANT Analysis

The constructs developed from using Grounded Theory Method, were then enhanced and elaborated through the use of Actor-Network Theory. Using Actor-Network Theory terminology it was investigated - how *inscription* and *translation* explains the D-M process, and how the ANT concept of *punctualisation* was applied to the D-M process:

- *Inscription* refers to the way practical artefacts symbolize patterns of use. In research terms, what the meaning and the function of the objects are used in the decision-process;

- *Translation*, the strength and collective order that are repeatedly negotiated as a social process of aligning interests (Callon, 1999). In D-M research terms, translation is the practice the decision-maker works out to configure a strategy to capture knowledge for over what he will make the decision;

- *Punctualisations* or black boxes (using ANT terms) shall be used to deal with bounded rationality. In research terms, does a decision-maker simplify the context to help thinking? If so, what simplifications are used to help the D-M process? What is used to make inferences about the context that helps the D-M process?

This analysis work was achieved using written memos for A2 posters, NVivo containing interviews with codes and finally MS/Excel worksheets. The problem at the beginning of this new stage was all the variables and type that would be used. Given these constraints, MS/Excel looked as if it would be adequate to proceed with the research analysis. The result is a final excel worksheet for each interview, the same used in section 5.5.2 Coding, but now the ANT concepts interpretation are added. Again each worksheet is complemented by more written memos that guided the thought flow of the author.

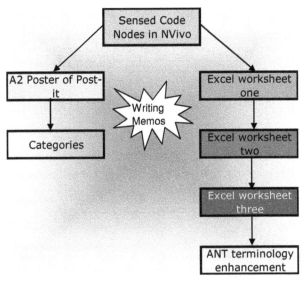

**Fig. 5. 12** – Paths that sensed free nodes codes from NVivo for analysis.

From this Excel worksheet, through the enhanced codification a second one appeared. Laborious and patient work within MS/Excel was undertaken in order to merge cells. The merging provided clusters around each new enhanced codification. Figure 5.13 shows a sample

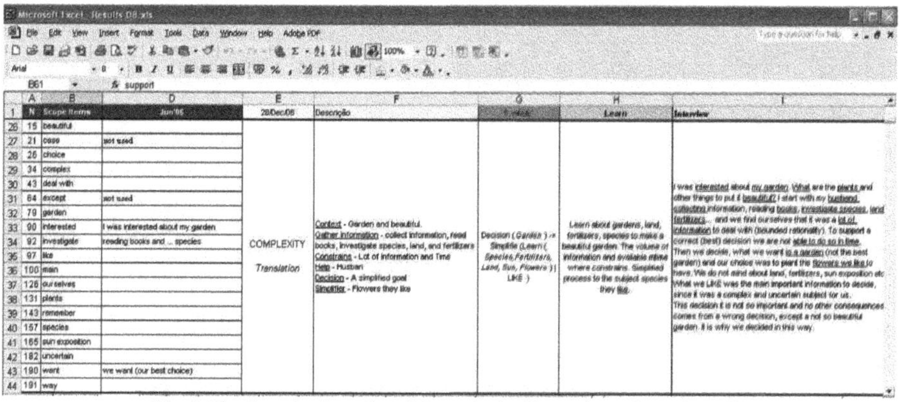

**Fig. 5. 13** – Second enhanced worksheet, obtained by sorting and merging cells

The reading from the sample shown at figure 5.13 is: from the left side there are the sensed free node codes and in the right column the extract from the interview. The middle four columns contain the joined enhanced code, a brief description, a symbolic interpretation and an explanation to the research focus i.e. a worksheet for each data interview was produced as well as a set of memos (figure 5.4 shows a memo sample) that accompany each interview.

Finally, all the individual interview worksheets were grouped onto one worksheet. The extra columns were removed so that only five columns remained. This final worksheet was then sorted by the renamed column *concept*. A sample is shown in figure 5.14.

This final worksheet, together with memos and the categories obtained from the A2 poster post-its, represents the working method used to analyse the research data, for ANT analysis. All the ANT concepts were extracted and a further reading and revising, guided the construction of ANT summary tables. Each ANT concept had a researcher interpretation from the previous steps. The following sample shows this process:

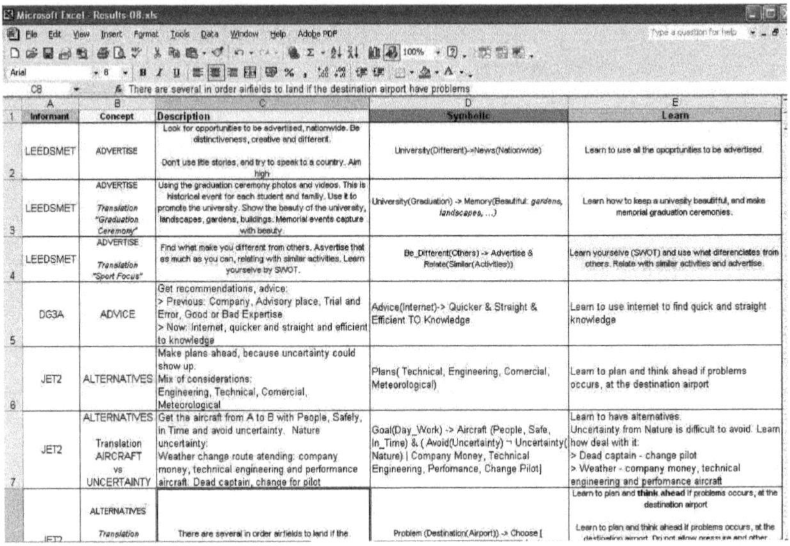



| | A | B | C | D | E |
|---|---|---|---|---|---|
| 1 | Informant | Concept | Description | Symbolic | Learn |
| 2 | LEEDSMET | ADVERTISE | Look for opportunities to be advertised, nationwide. Be distinctiveness, creative and different. Don't use litle stories, and try to speak to a country. Aim high | University(Different)->News(Nationwide) | Learn to use all the opoprtunities to be advertised |
| 3 | LEEDSMET | ADVERTISE *Translation "Graduation Ceremony"* | Using the graduation ceremony photos and videos. This is historical event for each student and family. Use it to promote the university. Show the beauty of the university, landscapes, gardens, buildings. Memorial events capture with beauty | University(Graduation) -> Memory(Beautiful: *gardens, landscapes, ...)* | Learn how to keep a univesity beautifful, and make memorial graduation ceremonies. |
| 4 | LEEDSMET | ADVERTISE *Translation "Sport Focus"* | Find what make you different from others. Asvertise that as much as you can, relating with similar activities. Learn yourselve by SWOT. | Be_Different(Others) -> Advertise & Relate(Similar(Activities)) | Learn yourselve (SWOT) and use what diferenciates from others. Relate with similar activties and advertise. |
| 5 | DG3A | ADVICE | Get recommendations, advice: > Previous: Company, Advisory place, Trial and Error, Good or Bad Expertise > Now: Internet, quicker and straight and efficient to knowledge | Advice(Internet)-> Quicker & Straight & Efficient TO Knowledge | Learn to use internet to find quick and straight knowledge |
| 6 | JET2 | ALTERNATIVES | Make plans ahead, because uncertainty could show up. Mix of considerations: Engineering, Technical, Comercial, Meteorological | Plans( Technical, Engineering, Comercial, Meteorological) | Learn to plan and think ahead if problems occurs, at the destination airport |
| 7 | JET2 | ALTERNATIVES Translation AIRCRAFT vs UNCERTAINTY | Get the aircraft from A to B with People, Safely, in Time and avoid uncertainty. Nature uncertainty: Weather change route atending: company money, technical engineering and performance aircraft. Dead captain, change for pilot | Goal(Day_Work) -> Aircraft (People, Safe, In_Time) & ( Avoid(Uncertainty) ¬ Uncertainty( Nature) \| Company Money, Technical Engineering, Perfomance, Change Pilot] | Learn to have alternatives. Uncertainty from Nature is difficult to avoid. Learn how deal with it: > Dead captain - change pilot > Weather - company money, technical engineering and perfomance aircraft |
| | JET2 | ALTERNATIVES *Translation* | There are several in order airfields to land if the | Problem (Destination(Airport)) -> Choose [ | Learn to plan and **think ahead** if problems occurs, at the destination airport Learn to plan and think ahead if problems occurs, at the destination airport. Do not allow pressure and other |

**Fig. 5. 14 –** Third and final enhanced worksheet, obtained by merging all the worksheets from each interview. Some columns are removed and the worksheet is sorted by the column *concept* which represents the key work column from 1st and 2nd worksheets.

### ANT inscriptions

- "White" has an inscription for "Cleanness and discipline", from 01-Dinefer interview: "Have painted white walls in the factory plant, creates a mechanism of careful cleanliness and discipline"

- "Rynos" has an inscription for "Low charge (low fees) and high impact (good values)" from 03-Leedsmet interview: "The animal rhinoceros is low charging, meaning that £2.000 is a low price but it is like rhinoceros, low charge, and high impact"

### ANT translations

- "Agreements" represents a translation for "Social network within politics, agreements and speculation of the surrounding social relations of the organization (constructed reality), to achieve with pleasure and courage what he wants with his decisions." (02-Sonae)

- "Critical thinking" represents a translation for "Critical thinking stands in a social web of people, a process where creativity develops under

constrains which are balanced with people in order to have a product"
(08-DG3A)

**ANT punctualisations**

- Divide and Conquer, Medical Procedures 20% of Information, Join Decisions and Commitment are used by 06-YHCI: "An experimental doctor avoids unimportant information, selecting the best to analyse. It is a process of divide and conquest and going step by step in a roadmap of medical procedures" or "Joining decisions and commitment with the patient and on-call colleagues into the participation of the understanding of the nature of the problem" or "20% of information at least is necessary" (06-YCHI)

- Systems (aircraft, weather, traffic control, company) hide the detailed technological and political complexity, and deal only with the surface, important on flights, and are used by 07-Jet2: "The Company is obviously deciding where we are going to go and they will put the route into the system, exactly the route where to go. They decide the countries where we fly to, they clear that with, if there is any political considerations, permissions, the routing has to be accepted by the main traffic control centre. So that, to a degree, it is decided for us...we decide how to run the aircraft." (07Jet2)

After this stage a link to the main categories, obtained from GTM come into view, after all, the GTM main categories are constructed from the same data interviews, but constructed under a different guideline. However, the author cannot separate them since the main categories also give rise to similar meaning as ANT concepts.

For this evidence we have the following table 5.12:

| GTM main category | Interpretation | ANT conceptualization |
|---|---|---|
| Calculating decision knowledge | The decision-maker surrounding social web, from where he gets help to reconstruct/reframe the uncertain and complex context | This relates to the human and non-human techniques used, which will provide the **information** needed to achieve decision making, which is also related with ANT *translations* |
| Decision-maker learning story | The process from which the decision-maker senses the unknown features, e.g. the story from *where*, *how* and *when* he learns to make a decision under uncertainty | The process of **reframe/reconstruct** the uncertain context. How simplifications are made with others, which relates with ANT *punctualisations* |
| Impact of learning (new knowledge) on the decision-maker professional composure (self) | Some decision-makers are more rational, searching for more data to support a decision; others are more emotional, deciding more based on his feelings and intuitions, not waiting for information to support a decision, they prefer to decide. This experience of deciding under uncertainty, creates some behaviour which are from the professional experience, acquired during his professional life | This relates to the **experience** of the decision-making through his professional life, which also relates with his experience using ANT *inscriptions*, and how he may succeed or not |
| Uncertainty | Vague context reality, which is better treated with human interaction and understanding | How a decision-maker deals with and interprets uncertain and complex contexts. The justification is found in the ANT concepts analysis. |

**Table 5. 12** – Linking GTM main categories with ANT concepts

The previous table 5.12, linking ANT analysis with GTM main categories, provides an enhancement of the GTM categories. This interpretation centres the **Decision-maker's learning story** as being a human, someone who has feelings, behaviours and actions which evolve through his life experience. This evidence derives from links between main categories (as figure 5.11 shows on page 110), however enriched with ANT concepts:

- *Calculating decision knowledge* links *Impact of learning (new knowledge) on the decision-maker's professional composure (self)* with common meaning between categories, under ANT concepts, deriving in **experience** (see fig. 5.15):

    o The evidence is shown in the following sample in 08-DG3A interview; this **experience** link is provided between categories "Decision" with "Architect" and "Office", as the following figure shows:

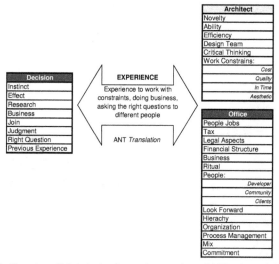

**Fig. 5. 15 – Experience** link derivation from main categories and ANT enhanced (08-DG3A)

- *Calculating decision knowledge* links *Uncertainty* with common meaning between categories, under ANT concepts, deriving in **facts:**

  o Using the same sampled interview 08-DG3A: this **facts** link is provided between categories "Decision" with "Uncertainty", as the following figure shows:

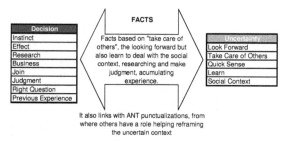

**Fig. 5. 16 – Facts** link derivation from main categories and ANT enhanced (08-DG3A)

- *Impact of learning (new knowledge) on the decision-maker professional composure (self)* links *Uncertainty* with a common meaning between categories, under ANT concepts, deriving in **emotions:**

o The same sample from interview 08-DG3A: this **emotions** link is provided between categories "Architect" and "Office" with "Uncertainty", as the following figure shows:

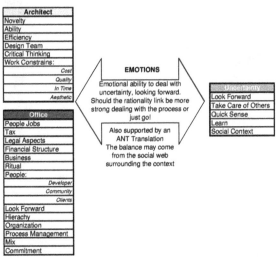

**Fig. 5. 17 – Emotions** link derivation from main categories and ANT enhanced (08-DG3A)

Fig. 5.18 synthesises the research conceptual development paths followed by the author to analyse the data gathered for this research.

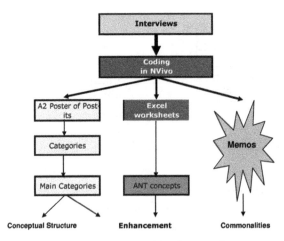

**Fig. 5. 18** – Research Conceptual Development paths

## 5.9. Examples of the Interviews' analysis using the proposed methodologies

The research method was explained in detail in the previous sections. The author decided to choose only two interview's analysis (06-Yorkshire and 07-Jet2) to present, in detail, the way they were explored.

### 5.9.1. Interview 06 – Yorkshire Centre for Health Informatics

The interviewee was the Director of the Yorkshire Centre for Health Informatics and Senior Lecturer in the Faculty of Medicine and Health at the University of Leeds. She has been involved in the research and teaching of Health Informatics for over 25 years and works closely with colleagues in local NHS Trusts, the Strategic Health Authorities and Connecting for Health. Her major interest is in providing relevant, evidence-based information to improve decision making by clinicians and patients. The researcher developed 193 codes from the interview. Research work was applied with GTM resulting in the construction of the A2 poster. The result shows five categories, as illustrated in figure 5.19.

A brief analysis from this interview shows a social network made of Doctors, Patient and Tools to support decision making.

The researcher's interpretation of the **Doctors** category, explains how Doctors are trained to operate formulating hypotheses and testing them over an induction process of information collection, problem definition and decision to treatment. New doctors with little experience occasionally have difficulties with the amount of information to process, however experienced doctors, with more skills, know how to avoid unimportant information. Until medical evidence is attained, a doctor searches for the necessary information. During problem definition, colleagues are consulted, and new hypotheses are formulated. Values, beliefs and other constraints although important, are always secondary to medical evidence. A decision act is taken within a learning process of collecting information until medical evidence is sufficient to decide on a treatment. This medical act is personal and free, although subject to the organizational strategy and rules which the doctor has to confront. Finally, accepting the risk, the doctor makes a joint decision, involving the patient's participation, which is founded on data and commitment. In this category ten properties were interpreted: *Start Process*, *20% Information*, *Time*, *Problem Definition*, *Join Decision*, *Doctor Type*, *Medical Evidence*, *Belief*, *Act* and *Decide*.

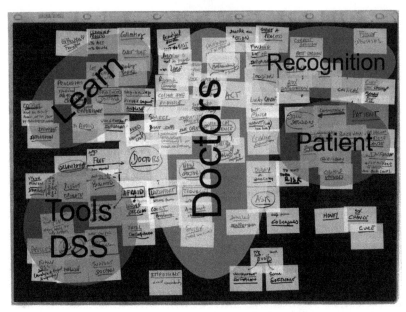

**Fig. 5. 19 – Grounded** Categories from 06-Yorkshire Centre for Health Informatics interview

The **Tools** category corresponds to the techniques used to deal with the contextual nature of the problem. Doctors are trained to operate in a scientific way, using normal distribution and other statistic tools. The doctor's commitment to the hospital's mission and the patient's financial capacity to support the treatment are far beyond these mathematical tools. There is specific software to help doctors to find information, although there is a socio-technical problem, in the interviewee's words, in putting doctors and devices together. Doctors are embedded in a social network constituted by themselves, patients, patients' family and other colleagues who contribute in some way to the decision making process. In this category six properties were interpreted: *Budget*, *Software*, *Afraid to use*, *Statistic*, *DSS* and *Ask Others*. The balance between doctor intervention in the decision process and the mathematical and statistical techniques constitute risk assumption, because doctors can decide using their beliefs or experience when taking a decision or they can follow the mathematical techniques.

The **Patient** category considers the interactive element between the doctor and the doctor's decision. The doctor collects and analyses information, in the interviewee's words, using a 'Bayesian distribution' and the deviations from the 'normal' for further research, to detect the cause of disease. When medical evidence is reached, a medical decision follows, relating to the treatment. Despite careful procedures constructing a reality from which a treatment follows, unintended consequences may happen. Uncertainty is not definitively excluded, no matter how precisely and carefully the roadmap of medical procedures has been followed. In this category five properties were interpreted: *Cause of disease, Treatment, Commitment, Future diseases* and *Consequences.*

The **Learning** category is interpreted as a learning story. A decision act, as defined before, is the learning process of collecting information constantly until medical evidence is sufficient to transform information into knowable procedures that guide a medical decision. This practice starts with communicating with the patient to collect information, and eventually with colleagues about the nature of a problem. The process is guided by a scientific approach formulating hypotheses and then testing them over an induction process of information collection, problem definition and decision to treatment. In some situations the information requires techniques of analysis such as step-by-step analysis and checking with the roadmap of medical procedures, and even discussion with more experienced doctors. Delay is a technique to gain more time to get a better understanding of the nature of the problem, during which time is used to ask colleagues, get more information and do more personal research. Despite all the attention and care given to the medical procedures, uncertainty and risk are always present. In this category eight properties were derived: *Dialogue, Collection, Read, Divide & Conquer, Analysing, Scientific Way, Delay* and *Experience.*

The category **Recognition** relates to the *uncertainty* and the unknown unintended consequence that can result from a medical decision. Uncertain events could occur as subsidiary effects and result in prosecution of the doctor. The actual risk reduction is made by the doctor who undertakes a joint decision with the patient, but this does not avoid the feeling of fear and discomfort in the doctor. Other techniques are used such as: a statistical approach (Bayesian Normal distribution) and a risk assessment for each treatment, or a surgical decision, or delaying in time to learn more about the nature of the problem which in itself can also be a risk. In this category five properties were interpreted: *Collateral Effects, Court, Afraid, Wrong Decision* and *Time.*

Regarding these categories and properties, uncertainty was interpreted as Recognition, a process of relationships between known and unknown information, an unintended consequence from a medical decision. The social construct is provided through a joint decision between doctor and the patient. Despite this, some extended consultations are undertaken with the doctor's colleagues in order to have a better understanding of the nature of the problem. The learning story is rooted in medical procedures, guided by a scientific approach, where experience counts, formulating hypotheses and testing them over an induction process of collecting information until the medical evidence is sufficient to transform information into knowable procedures to guide and make a medical decision.

**Relations between categories**

The relations between categories are shown in figure 5.20, which contains visual information showing what has been explained. The decision-maker, a doctor, learns from medical procedures and experience guided by a scientific approach and dealing with bounded rationality. Despite this scientific approach there is a social interaction between doctor and patient through communication and understanding of symptoms and the collected information until medical evidence is reached. Tools such as Statistical approach and Risk assessment for each treatment and DSS are used to deal with information, and in this case a network constituted by non-human techniques and human colleagues was included which provided an extension to the comprehension of the problem. However, as referred in section 5.7, in this schema (fig. 5.20) it is difficult to capture all the richness, because all the categories, subcategories and properties are shown. After all, this schema is, a visual representation from the data generated from GTM analysis. But GTM also has provided main categories, and through recurring to them another conceptualization is more perceptible. Here follows an explanation of the conceptual schema obtained for this interview.

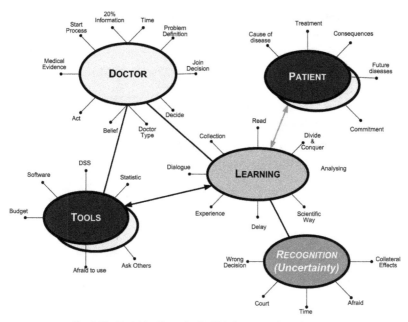

**Fig. 5. 20** – Yorkshire Centre for Health Informatics – GTM Categories

## Yorkshire Centre for Health Informatics – Conceptual Schema

GTM is a "bottom up" coding method. The researcher raised those categories that rendered the data most effectively to theoretical concepts, i.e. the categories that contained important properties that made data meaningful. As a result, after subjecting the categories to an analytic refinement they became main categories. However, concepts are considered as interpretive frames offering understanding of relationships between main categories.

- **Doctor** – Is the decision-maker who needs to investigate the cause of disease for a particular "Patient":
  - o Instance of *Impact of Learning on Decision-Maker* which is the Doctor category;
- **Patient** – The subject under the decision context:
  - o Instance of *Calculating Decision Knowledge* which is "Tools" and "Patient" categories (patient is used also in the process to obtain the information needed to a decision);

- **Tools** – Tools or other mechanism developed from previous experience:
  - o Instance of *Calculating Decision Knowledge* which is "Tools" and "Patient" categories;
- **Learning** - the cognitive process which results in the learning process in order to be informed for D-M;
  - o Instance of *Decision-Maker Learning Story* which is the Learning category;
- **Uncertainty** - is the Recognition category:
  - o Instance of the *Uncertainty* main category

Following the example, "Patient" is the goal that "Doctor" solves, from where the Learning process is needed. Does "Doctor" have previous experience or not? May he use some tools or other mechanic developed from previous experience? If not, he is presented with the unknown, and other ways to satisfy the need must be developed, reconstructing and reframing the reality. From this interpretation we have:

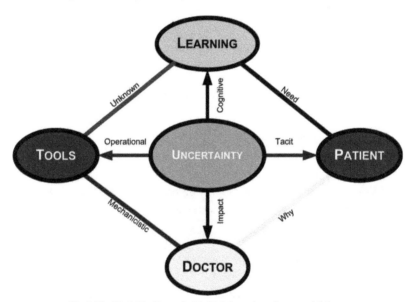

**Fig. 5. 21** – Yorkshire Centre for Health Informatics – Conceptual Schema

As observed in figure 5.21 above, the central category is Uncertainty, which has relationships with other categories namely Tools, Learning, Patient and Doctor. The interaction between Uncertainty and Tools is established through operational steps;

Uncertainty is linked with Learning in the sense that decisions are made facing or not facing a known or unknown situation and Learning is the cognitive process that results from the whole established learning; Uncertainty is related with Patient through dialogue and consensus; Uncertainty has impact during the decisional medical processes. This impact is a failure or success in consequence of the learning to solve the *need*.

Tools are a mechanical medium of interaction with Doctors; the type of Learning that comes from the use of tools is unknown until tools are experienced and the doctor's decision is made. Learning is always evident in relation to Patient in the sense that patients need to learn what the doctor told them, they need to learn the way to deal and behave with the sickness they suffer, they need to learn the way to take prescriptions and they need to learn the contexts of health care systems. Patient is the role element between the Doctor and the doctor's medical decision. They are a very important actor within the decision process.

A sample reading from the conceptual schema: *Why* a "Doctor" (decision-maker) *needs* to investigate the cause of disease for a particular "Patient" – this is the *tacit* position. Through these questions he will search information from *"mechanicistic"* means (medical patient analysis, medical newspapers, talking with the patient, books, asking other doctors etc.) and he will research the remaining *"unknown"* in order to get better informed – this is an *operational* position. During this process the decision-maker is "learning", capturing knowledgeable information – he is reinforcing his *cognitive* capacities facing the "uncertainty". At some stage, the doctor may or may not make a decision which will have consequences and will have an impact on him and on the patient – decision *impact* as result.

## ANT Analysis

As explained in Chapter 5, section 5.8, ANT analysis, three important concepts within ANT were verified: *inscriptions*, *translations* and *punctualisations*.

This analysis of the interview offers some interesting incidents that can be understood as ANT *inscriptions*. Inscriptions are here understood as all the types of communication media used by actors (human and non human). It is a process of creating text and communication verbalizations that enhance and maintain the interests of the actors.

The Tools category has a double interpretation, both being non-human objects, tools in a sense to help doctors operate in a scientific way and being human and social.

In the former, tools support doctors' decisions in Bayesian normal distribution or mathematical theory of errors. In the latter, there is a human interchange and dialogue between Doctor and Patient in an attempt to fill the lack of information.

Another association is the use of Decision Support Systems, where special software is designed to help doctors to deal with information, although there is a socio-technical problem, in the interviewee's words "It is a difficult and a social problem put together – Doctors and devices".

In terms of ANT *translation* in the analysis given, it becomes clear that the interviewee is a Doctor, the medical act relates to the decision, which stands in a learning process following medical procedures, formulating hypotheses and testing them over an induction process of information collection, problem definition and decision to treatment. Despite this scientific approach a doctor also establishes an auxiliary support through a social network with patient and colleagues in attempts to fill the lack of information and commitment from the patient through the treatment or surgery.

From the interview, ANT *punctualisations* are used to deal with bounded rationality through the new doctor's inexperience dealing with the amount of information. This bounded rationality is solved with time or with a divide and conquer strategy - a process of divide and conquest and going step by step through a roadmap of medical procedures. Auxiliary help is found through joint D-M and commitment with the patient and bringing colleagues into participation for the understanding of the nature of the problem.

### 5.9.2. Interview 07 – Jet

The interviewee is a Type Rated Captain Pilot of the Jet Company. The researcher developed 198 codes from the interview. Research work was applied with

GTM, resulting in the construction of the A2 poster. The result shows six categories, as illustrated in figure 5.22.

A brief analysis from this interview shows the importance of the social network to support D-M. There is the reconstruction of uncertain context through the crew, the cabin crew, the passengers, technical personnel support, air traffic control and eventually the company.

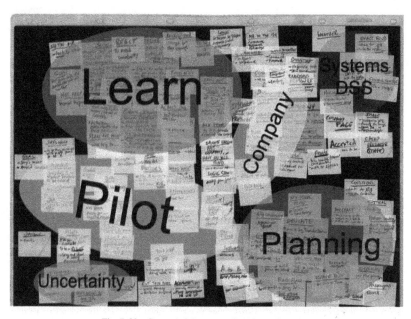

**Fig. 5. 22 – Grounded** Categories from 07-Jet interview

The **Pilot** category emerged from the Pilot's job information, which is limited considering that she performs the best possible work trying to save the company money. It is a dangerous profession, with identical liability of that of doctors as stated by the interviewee: "In my job, safety is critical the most, I guess. We, like doctors, can kill people". The operation of an aircraft is the responsibility of the Pilot and is the essential achievement in a day's work i.e. getting the aircraft and its passengers to its destination safely and on time. The Pilot's role is, according to her own words: "The whole point of my job is to avoid uncertainty where we can, to prevent anything that leads us to that situation". To become a pilot involves learning throughout several years of experience and training in real situations under a close regimentation. In the interviewee's words "It is a long and slow way and it is very regimented too". In this category eight properties were interpreted: *Danger*, *To be the best*, *Operate*, *Aircraft*, *Solve Problem*, *Logic Stand*, *Training*, *Day's Work* which has sub-properties *Goal*, *Job Done* and *Satisfaction*.

The **Company** category concerns the pilot's work environment and established relationships. Pilot and company have different but complementary roles. The company's responsibility is to put the route into function, to decide where to go, which countries to fly to, if there are any political considerations, arrange the necessary permissions and establish the route with the main traffic control centre. A Pilot is responsible for her decisions when operating the aircraft, for creating a good company image and saving the company money. A Pilot can ask the company for options during the flight, but she has the final decision. Different pressures come from the company culture when a decision under uncertainty has to be made. Commercial pressure over the pilots can arise, for example, when facing problems, they must do what the company wants instead of what the pilot thinks should be done. In the interviewee's words "commercial pressures are enormous and faced with minor technical problems their pilots are being pressured into making a decision as to what the company wants". In this category eight properties were interpreted: *Delay*, *Ask*, *Culture*, *Image*, *Values*, *Saving*, *People*, *Pressure* and *Make Money*.

The **System** category relates to the implemented systems from where a Pilot obtains information in order to reach D-M. These systems are: aircraft systems, technical engineering systems, weather systems, air traffic control system and company systems. A Pilot makes a decision avoiding uncertainty which can be caused by, for example, bad weather conditions, a passenger that becomes sick or from a technical aircraft problem. The pilot's decisions sometimes deviate from the main plan and a change in the route or of the destination airfield occurs. In the interviewee's words "We have to check the procedures from network traffic, safety procedure". He reacts to situations deciding the best, under the global airway systems and the company's indications i.e. the exact destination, dealing with political considerations and the route allowed by the traffic control centre. The overall air traffic operations are run under a system that manages procedures from network traffic and safety. The weather system provides weather consideration for the route and the destination, and the pilot makes decisions based on it. Technical engineering systems provide help assimilated through quick courses or just a technical manual on board. In this category six properties were interpreted: *Aircraft*, *Exact route*, *Routing*, *Air Traffic*, *Weather* and *Technical engineering systems*.

The **Learning** category arises from a learning story, the Pilot gathered information and their interpretation in order to arrive to D-M. A Pilot is always learning, avoiding the uncertain events that oblige a change to the flight plan. In the interviewee's words "everything is planned and we react as the situation continues to avoid uncertainty". The context change and new realities lead to making subsequent decisions whilst maintaining the previous goals, i.e. getting the aircraft and passengers from A to B, safely and on time. On the ground, there is constant planning, to provide a plan of alternatives for uncertain events that may occur during the flight such as fuel, route and weather conditions. In the interviewee's words "But when one's on the ground then we are back to plan, planning, planning and more planning". Pilots also learn how to deal with uncertain events like reading systems such as aircraft, weather, traffic control and sensing what the crew has to say. This is a collaborative environment where all the crew participates in the final decisions. In the interviewee's words "As a crew we all are going to participate in a crew decision. So we have five inputs from the crew". Those inputs are reaction, sensing, search for new alternatives, decisions, adjustments and new realities. Pilots learn by telephone if necessary, when they need advice from the company to reach a decision. A Pilot learns how to produce the best guessing with the available information in order to make a decision solving a problem. In this category twelve properties were interpreted: *Plan ahead*, *Crew Decision*, *Avoid uncertainty*, *Alternatives*, *Systems*, *Make plan* (which has four sub-properties *Fuel*, *Route*, *Weather* and *Plan*), *In the Air* (which has three sub-properties *Manual*, *Telephone* and *Crew*), *React to situation*, *Impinging*, *Common sense*, *Pick solution* and *Precise solution*.

The **Planning** category is complementary to the Learn category and concerns the planning activities. Planning is creating alternative scenarios, from which a choice is picked if an uncertain event occurs during the flight. Planning is the pilot's job on the ground, which will continue during the flight although it can be recalled and adjusted according to contextual information. The process of learning happens once the pilot faces, for example; some technical aspects of the machine, or a system for rerouting the flight, or even a system to deal with passenger's problems. Pilots learn how to produce the best guessing with the available information in order to make a decision to avoid uncertainty and adjust the flight plan. In this category eight properties were interpreted: *First plan*, *Plan*, *Alternatives*, *Deviate*, *Aircraft*, *Passengers needs*, *Airports* and *Conditions*.

The **Uncertainty** category corresponds to the role of uncertainty and how it affects the interviewee's job. Uncertainty is always present, but limited under control from which the flight plan evolves. It occurs when the context information changes and a new decision must be taken. The ideal situation is to avoid uncertainty. In the interviewee's words "The whole point of my job is to avoid uncertainty where we can to prevent anything that leads us to that situation". Suggestions from the Company or from the Crew help to find meaning for the uncertain reality and therefore help D-M. The pressure caused by the organizational culture makes D-M difficult under uncertainty. The Pilot's job and role is to avoid uncertainty despite unexpected constraints, through prevention, planning and reacting. In the interviewee's words "If nothing went wrong, planes would not have a pilot. But we are there to make decisions". Uncertainty avoidance through prevention is concerned with any anticipated situation which allows decision in a precise moment; planning ahead and defining alternatives; reacting to a situation to avoid uncertainty, keeping control of the situation. In this category five properties were interpreted: *Plan ahead, Danger, Ask someone, Not impinging* and *To be avoided.*

Throughout all categories and properties, uncertainty was interpreted as something natural and central to the pilot's job. Her main concern is to avoid uncertainty and constraints that lead to those situations. A Pilot learns how to produce the best guess with the available information in order to make a decision to avoid uncertainty and adjust the flight plan. The learning story is rooted in how information is obtained from the systems, from the crew and in the event of uncertain incidents how the pilot reacts, deciding to avoid the uncertain context. A Pilot reacts to situations deciding the optimum, under the global airway systems to fulfil the day's task of working safely and on time. Decisions stand in a socio-technical network, where the human contribution arrives from the crew, colleagues from the company giving auxiliary options, engineering technical personnel giving quick courses and the personnel at air traffic control systems. The non-human aspects are the aircraft itself and weather systems. Uncertain contexts have a pre-construction within flight plans, and in flight they are adjusted to the new situations.

**Relations between categories**

The relations between categories are shown in the figure 5.23 in a visual form. The decision-maker, a pilot, learns from systems readings and tries to avoid uncertainty. Despite this machinery-based approach, D-M is made through reacting to situations in collaboration with personnel from air traffic control systems, from the company and also from cabin crew. They relate to each other through communication and options understanding in order to reach D-M, which reconstructs context, and adjusts the flight plan accordingly. D-M does stand for the best possible decision, because it is an in-flight reaction, and in the interviewee's words "we only do the best guess with the information we have". Learning happens in a variety of situations, through events reactions and sometimes through technical short courses. As referred in the previous interview, the schema is complex, since it contains all the categories, subcategories and properties. This schema is a visual representation from the data generated from GTM analysis. However, GTM has also provided main categories, and through re-referring to them, another conceptualization is more perceptible. There now follows an explanation of the conceptual schema obtained for this interview.

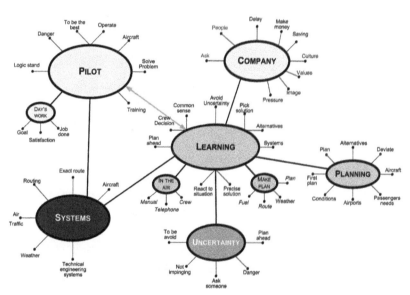

**Fig. 5. 23** – Jet – GTM Categories

## Jet2 Conceptual Schema

From section 5.6, the main categories obtained for this interview are:

- **Pilot** – Is the decision-maker who needs to investigate the uncertainty caused to the flight "Plan":

- o Instance of *Impact of Learning on Decision-Maker* which is the "Pilot" and "Company" categories;
- **Plan** – The subject under the decision uncertain context:
  - o Instance of *Decision-Maker Learning Story* which is "Learning" and "Planning" categories (Planning is re-used in order reconstruct/ reframe new plan under the uncertainties);
- **Systems** – Tools or other mechanic systems available from which "Pilot" knows how to use from previous experience:
  - o Instance of *Calculating Decision Knowledge* which is "Systems" category;
- **Learning** - the cognitive process from which the result is the learning process in order to be informed for D-M;
  - o Instance of *Decision-Maker Learning Story* which is Learning category;
- **Uncertainty** - is the "Uncertainty" category:
  - o Instance of the *Uncertainty* main category
- **Company** - Supplementary category which is associated with "Pilot", since the Pilot's D-M may be supported by the company and the decision *impact* affect both as well.

(The main categories referred are explained section 5.6)

As figure 5.24 shows, below '"the central category is Uncertainty which has relationships with other categories such as Systems, Plan, Pilot and Company. The interaction between Uncertainty and Systems is established through operational steps; Uncertainty is linked with Learning through situations where known or unknown decisions are made. Learning is the cognitive process that results from the whole established relationships between concepts. Uncertainty is related with Plan through tacit knowledge; uncertainty has impact during the decisional piloting processes. The Pilot has collaborative support from the Company.

Systems are a mechanical medium of interaction with Pilots; the types of Learning that comes from the use of Systems are unknown until Systems are experienced and the Pilot's decision is made. Learning is always evident in relation to Plan in the sense that they need to learn what are the changes, pilots need to learn the way to deal and behave with uncertain events, they need to learn the way to avoid uncertainty and they need to learn the contexts of failure systems. Plan is the interactional element between the Pilot and the pilot's decision. It is a very important actor within the decision process since questions are made bidirectional. The Pilot can also contribute to the recognition of uncertainty, which has an impact in his behaviour. In this Conceptual schema, Pilot collaborates with the Company, having support from it and also supports the Company through his "day's work".

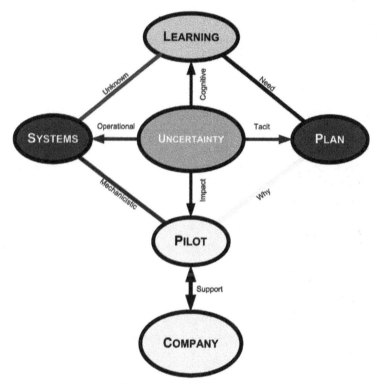

Fig. 5. 24 – Jet – Conceptual Schema

For example, facing a context of uncertainty, from where great changes will occur, the "Pilot" will question "why" and what he "needs" to be better informed – this is a *tacit* position. Through these questions he will search for information from "mechanicistic" forms (aircraft systems, weather systems, air-traffic systems, asking the company, asking crew, board manuals, etc.) and "Pilot" will research the remaining "unknown" in order to be better informed – this is an operational position. During this process the "Pilot" is learning, capturing knowledgeable information – "Pilot" is reinforcing his *cognitive* capacities facing the uncertainty. "Pilot" has *support* from the

"Company". At some stage, the "Pilot" may or may not make a decision which will have consequences and will have an impact – decision impact on "Pilot" as result: good or bad pilot, whatever happens.

## ANT Analysis

This analysis interview offers some incidents that are understood as ANT objects. The first one is *inscriptions* which refer to the way technical artefacts embody patterns of use. *Telephone* is interpreted as the medium that provides the conversation with technical engineering personnel. The *flight plan* is an important pattern of use, and represents the route and the alternatives to do the job safety and in time. This *flight plan* represents the intensive planning done on the ground and it works like scenario building, contexts options, used in conditions of uncertainty. Another inscription is the *machine,* a complex engineering technology, the aircraft, which carries passengers, safely and on time, it is the central part according the interviewee.

In terms of ANT *translation* and from the previous analysis it can be said that the interviewee is a Captain Pilot, who makes decisions in the flight as a free act. Sometimes the Company intervenes within the decisions as do other collaborators such as the crew, technical personnel, air control systems, weather systems and other sort of ICT communication media. Decisions are reactions to avoid uncertainty and are made within the occurrence of constraints, e.g. technical or weather problem observed out of the flight plan. The context within which a decision is made is very complex once time and consequences are critical. The entire actors that take part in the pilot's decisions have a relevant role.

The evidence from the interview of ANT *punctualisations* or black boxes, used to deal with bounded rationality is found in intensive planning on the ground. This planning provides a set of alternatives to deal with the complexity of possible context and amount or lack (in this case) of information during the flight. So a flight plan could be interpreted as a form of dealing with bounded rationality. However, other uncertain events could occur, and the pilot sets a social network from where he reconstructs the context in order to react and make a decision even if it is outside the flight plan. Other *punctualisations* are related to support systems of global prevision conditions, air traffic control situations and the aircraft systems dealing with the complex technology. The company also has an associated *punctualisation* dealing with political considerations and permissions for the flight route.

## 5.10. Summary

The current chapter introduced the research stages, data collection and research analysis using Grounded Theory Methodology and Actor-Network Theory. This was done exposing the interview participants as well their organization, the established contact and the distributed documentation. The development of the theoretical sensitivity using GTM was explained starting with open interviews, gathering data, constructing tentative ideas about categories in the data and then examining these ideas through further empirical inquiry. The theoretical development of categories: interviews transcription, coding, memos categories and main categories are described and all these steps are analysed in order to support the results presented in the following chapter. A final explanation of ANT analysis, developed from the research practice, is also described. Finally, two interviews are explored in more detail as an example of the work the author did during this research. In chapter 6, the research results are explained.

# Chapter 6 Decision Making under Uncertainty - Frameworks

## 6.1. Introduction

This chapter explains the development and validation of the Grounded Theory of Decision Making (GTDM). Firstly, an explanation of the set of definitions that are at the basis of the current research, such as Knowledge, Information, Experience and Facts is given. Secondly, a discussion of the independent categories found in all the interviews is made.

Subsequently, the resulting developed main categories of D-M under uncertainty are presented, explaining a conceptual framework, an ANT network and the enhancement provided by ANT over the conceptual framework. Then the GTDM under uncertainty is explained. A comparative analysis with theories analysed in Chapter 4 - Literature Review is then included, and finally the verification of the theory, with reference to a supplementary interview showing the categories' saturation and the validity of independent categories is explained. The supplementary interview is discussed and it is revealed how this corroborates the theory. A final confirmation and presentation of the theory to two interviewees and a small group is then discussed. A brief critique of the used methodology is presented.

## 6.2. Pattern Interpreted Definitions

In the GTM analysis, the author undertook the analysis as a process of interpretation and meaning-making using material from interviews and other sources to construct a GTM of D-M, using Charmaz's idea of constructive GTM as a guide.

- *Decision-Making context* encompasses the ways in which the decision-makers base themselves in their experience, factual personal data and social network;

- *Knowledge* is an interpretation for "what is best" within a learning process by a network composed by people and organizations. The researcher's interpretation of knowledge changed afterwards, because knowledge is not a static fact;

- *Recognition* stands in this research as the cognitive operation by which someone establishes relationships between elements, known and unknown. It is the transformation process from the unknown to known realities to establish the entire elements which lead to the decision making process;

- *Learning* – is within the process of collecting information constantly until evidence is sufficient to transform information into knowable procedures that guide a decision act;

- *Information* – evidence which the interviewees obtain from the internet, magazines, computer systems, navigation systems, balance sheets and events from experts in some subjects;

- *Fact* is data used within information. This data is obtained from a data collection process in order to balance the decision-maker's experience and emotional feelings contained on a decision;

- *Experience* is a set of occurrences that forms and guides an individual through his life experience. It stands for observing and interpreting the surrounding social context; for structuring a strategy to capture information from the social context and learn; and establishing a verbal interchange with the social context, through dialogue and conversation and from being a member of the social context, who understands this context, its premises, structure, language and actors;

- *Irrational* and *non-rational* is a judgment interpretation of a decision made in an uncertain context. *Irrational* is interpreted when a decision is made against a perspective interpretation in context; *non-rational* is used when a decision is made; however not all the context premises are understood in context.

These terms are the result of coding using GTM of the data gathered from the interviews. Some of them were used by the interviewees and others are the result of the interpretation made by the author.

## 6.3. Independent Categories

Independent categories reflects a summarised interpretation from common categories obtained from all the interviews. The author's interpretation characterizes them as independent categories since they appeared from the work of interpretation when taking notes, summarizing what has been common to all interviewees. They correspond to expressed data that have been interpreted as having a similar meaning which cross the interviews. Furthermore, this point offers commonalities (see figure 5.18 - Research Conceptual Development paths in chapter 5.8) that have been interpreted in the previous interviews. Learning; Uncertainty modelling refutation; Creating a Social Network that involves the decision-maker searching for information; Situated Reality; Reframing-context; Using support systems: non-human and human; Having pleasure; Family dependency; Working hard; Confidence and Recognition.

### 6.3.1. Learning

Learning was the focus, the central concept in this research work. It is common to all interviewees and this interpretation is expanded from initially five interviews in Table 2.2 in chapter 2.9 to all nine interviews. The author looked for how decision-makers make meaning to produce decisions, i.e. how they acquire the knowledge that guides a decision, how they structure a network of people that can help to understand what is the best under the uncertain context. This process of learning is interpreted according to the interviewees' words as being a process of learning through experience, and sensing others' needs, and being capable to answer them. The process of learning includes learning the organization's history and values, learning through disagreements and opposition, learning to observe and be prompted to decide, not delaying the reduction of uncertainty, recognising it is a continuous practice and learning. It allows constructing a new frame, a new context, to work with constraints, to speak to others, always learning, avoiding the uncertain events. All of this process is made through the use of a human approach, dialogue and interaction with social-actors in the uncertain context.

## 6.3.2. Uncertainty Modelling Refutation

From all the interviews there is no evidence about a modelling way to think about uncertainty, and the way to deal with it. No interviewee as a decision-maker under uncertain and complex context referred to using any modelling technique. Searching for a model, as an external and explicit representation of part of reality, was seen by the people who wish to use that model as a way to understand, to change, to manage and to control that part of reality. This is not intended to be an unequivocal claim: all decision-makers do not use models under uncertainty. This affirmation must be understood as the interpretation from the current research's nine interviews, using GTM methodology. This is not a conclusion from quantitative research asking a representative population if they use a model or not when deciding under uncertain contexts. As explained previously, using GTM methodology, interviews were open, giving freedom to interviewees to speak about a topic, and not their position about a direct question. The answers were then meticulously analysed under GTM guidelines, offering a deep interpretation to the author.

## 6.3.3. Creating a social network

The interviewees initially received information which was used to construct a reality. However, it was understood that they shared commonalties and repeated patterns which stand in a social network. The primary context becomes real in their mind. The social network is a consequence of the lack of information, a search in other humans for the answers to fulfil the knowledge needed for the D-M. This process of searching from others' support for D-M is a translation in ANT terms, a translation of digested information from the members in the social network, which is transformed into knowledge in this translation process. Therefore D-M under uncertainty and complexity does not only depend on the decision-maker's risk behaviour, it depends also on feeling of being supported by others, creating a social-network of information, standing all together for knowledge, building on the lack of information which results in the construction of a new reality. This new reality is not something that becomes real in a common sense. It continues to be a vague sense of consequences from the decision made, from the interpretation that resides in the mind, "*in the eye of the beholder*" (DG3A interview). The closed social-actors related with the decision are a common conception for the network.

### 6.3.4. Situated Reality

Situated reality is the denomination the author found to explain the understanding that reality changes. Following Suchman (1987) the purposeful human action is not primarily rational, planned, and controlled, but is described as situated, social, and in direct response to the physical and social environment. The reality changing process found in this research was due to the variety of social-actors and to the strategies adopted by decision-makers in order to fulfil a lack of information that occurred within the decision process.

It was understood that human interaction using dialogue permits a direct meaningful conversation where meaning can only be understood with reference to the 'actual' situation, which establishes the action to D-M under uncertainty and contributes to reduce uncertainty. The uncertain context is characterized as lack of information, being an uncompleted reality that is reconstructed with the dialogue interaction between social-actors in the context. Dialogue is the basic interactional construct, which stands for a set of other interactional constructs depending on the context in the sense of the learning and sharing process that occurs between social actors: Understanding, Agreements, Disagreements, Opposition, Order and Power, Permanent Dialogue, Commitments, Guidance and Focus Group. All of these constructs are shown in table 6.1 – Situated Reality Summary Table.

This table represents from left to right the interviewees' identification, utterances from interviewees, the identification of the social actors involved in the interaction and the actions that resulted from the author's interpretation as situations within the context of each utterance. The interactional constructs are those presented in the 'actions' column. They are important concepts related to D-M under uncertainty and contribute to reduce uncertainty.

| Interview | Utterances from Interviewees | Social actors | Actions |
|---|---|---|---|
| 01-Dinefer | "Playing caprices with customers, learning under this interaction, creating a new understandable reality, a link for the business future".<br><br>"Creating new leaders, cause employees in order to create new leaders, to push for us." | Customer's, Employees | Dialogue, Understand others |
| 02-Sonae | "It can be the woman, for example, to put order, to put the things in the trail."<br><br>"Commitments between the economy of taken risk or risk not taken, and the politics."<br><br>"Using symbols of power over a crowd "with fear of the cannon and therefore in an uncertainty environment, it appeared there" | Wife, Political agreements<br><br>Using power | Dialogue, Agreements, Order, Power |
| 03-Leedsmet | "With disagreement and opposition contesting decisions, a new reality is constructed: "Opposition or disagreement is not a bad thing. It is good; it is learning too for your organization." | Board Directors, Personnel | Dialogue, Disagreement and debate |
| 04-LBS | "Negotiated political acts under complex and uncertain events, the politics reconstruct, redefine the reality and in doing that they explained, influence others justifying their decisions." | Public opinion | Dialogue, Reconstruct context, Justify Decisions |
| 05-Goldman | "Interacting, brainstorming, search for the lack of information and then make a decision, provide changes in the uncertain context, which are observable, sensed in the market. These changes are then analysed and used as feedback mechanism, and adjust previous decisions. In this case the public market, this gives the market actors the possibility to learn, and to change also." | Market actors | Permanent Dialogue, Surprise decisions |
| 06-YCHI | "A joint decision, doctor and patient, guiding a treatment or surgery. This decision occurs under risk and commitment from the patient, but it changes the uncertain context, constructing a new one or a failure occurs, which is also a change. It is not because a treatment, the symptoms were detected but because a joint decision follows guiding the future treatment." | Doctor and Patient | Dialogue, Joint decision and commitment |
| 07-Jet2 | "React to uncertain events and make a decision to avoid them, change the context. The actions taken guide to a new reality."<br><br>"Crew decisions, the act of deciding changes the context, the sense of uncertainty is modified or reduced to a new reality, a new context." | System actors (Flight Crew, Weather, Air Traffic) | Dialogue and Crew Decision |
| 08-DG3A | "Very participating process it is a ... we called it a design team, is very important, but it is not just be architect it is all the other areas of expertise, but outside the design team, is the community, is the client, is the end user, at ends always... so there is a lot to take on board." | Design Team, Client, Community, Developer | Dialogue and Discussion (Participative Process) |
| 09-Lawnswood | "You know, my culture throught the way I live my life has an impact on the decisions"<br><br>"You looking where they need to be severe aspiration and that also affect the decisions you make about them and what opportunities you give to them for guidance"<br><br>"When you make a decision... You have more decisions, you have afterwards, it never stops." | Students and Students Family | Dialogue, Guidance, Focus Group |

**Table 6. 1** – Situated Reality summary table

### 6.3.5. Re-Frame the Context

The interviewees as decision-makers reframe the context, justifying their decisions, and redefining their meaning, from the hidden meaning contained in the spoken words. In an attempt to understand social-actors in the decision context, the interviewees simplify things, in order to fill their lack of information. Knowing is not having a full head of available information, it requires time to construct a place for one's knowledge. Sometimes only after a decision has been made and confirmed the decision has effects. This requires constructing a reality where information makes sense, a reframed reality in the eyes of the decision-maker. Interviewees justify their decisions, re-framing uncertain context. In doing this reframing they try to reconstruct what in their view is the best option for their decisions at the time. For example, in a design process (08-DG3A), a creative meeting where social-actors discuss their ideas, they try to generate a common understanding.  Or in attending customers (01-Dinefer) and giving responsibility to employees, the interviewee reconstructs reality in his own eyes, from what he thinks others are (capable of). Or a doctor by deciding on some treatment (06-YCHI), or on some action they wait and see what happens. What is common is that doubts are present, there is a lack of information, but a need for a decision to be made, however the decision-maker needs to justify, or to believe himself that what he is doing is good. For example a leader decision-maker do not reduce uncertainty, objectively, what he does is reduce the perception of uncertainty – he reconstructs the context. For example, "*...in the Iraqi context; when Blair and Bush to legitimize decisions they reconstructed the context*" (04-LBS).

### 6.3.6. Using supporting systems: non-human and human

Facts are interpreted as being data that is measurable under mechanisms that provide a reading for the interviewee which can be analysed and interpreted in accordance with the uncertain context. The author's interpretation is that interviewees do not intend to represent the lack of information; they just intend to present another complementary view and another situational analysis which serves as a balance. For example, market, deviations, weather, money, finance situation etc. To measure these facts, there are no common systems, as table 6.2 shows. An exception may be considered, if taking into consideration that running a business requires the knowledge of the financial situation, although this was not referred to by the Architect interviewee, being also a business man.

| Interview | Researcher Interpretation from Interview | System | Data used for... |
|---|---|---|---|
| 01-Dinefer | Information System | Accounting, Clients | Financial Situation Customer position |
| 02-Sonae | Information System | Finances | Availability to invest |
| 03-Leedsmet | Information System | Accounting, Finances, Students | Financial Situation Student numbers |
| 04-LBS | N/A | " | " |
| 05-Goldman | Information System & ICT | Markets, Cases, Mail, Videoconference | Markets numbers, Memory cases, Permanent Contact |
| 06-YCHI | Decision Support Tools | Information analysed to the doctors | Help Diagnose |
| 07-Jet2 | Aircraft Systems, Weather Systems, Traffic Control System, Organization Information Systems | Navigation, Weather, Air Traffic, Run Business | Situational navigation, Avoid uncertainty |
| 08-DG3A | Technology Design Systems and Internet | CAD and Internet Search | Design and Search Information |
| 09-Lawnswood | Monitor Systems/Pastoral Systems | Monitor Students | Deviations to normality |

Table 6. 2 – Non-human Systems Information summary table

Although the use of non-human devices or systems is common to all interviewees, the use of human techniques or human systems that provide auxiliary information for the lack of information is also common. These human interaction techniques are founded in a dialogue between social-actors in the uncertain context, in order to understand the context. These techniques vary from: Playing with Customers, Meetings, Making Agreements, Brainstorming, Defining Scenarios, Communicating with the patient, Asking Colleagues, Dialoguing with human-actors in control systems, Meetings with Crew, Critical Thinking, Focus Groups, etc. For example "A company acquisition is a judgment about soft data and often acquisitions work when there is very good fast relationships between key players on another human level" (04-LBS) or "There are very frequent brainstorming meetings, in which we have a problem to solve, we do not know how to deal with the issue and then we organize a meeting to do a little bit of brainstorming and try to see a little, make a little light of a situation that is very dark." (05-Goldman) or "...get the clients, the developer or the community, maybe all three different people, who are not usually the same, and we have to get them to understand and what are we doing in this process ritual go on" (08-DG3A) (more detail is shown in table 6.3 - Human interaction techniques summary table).

| Interview | Researcher Interpretation Technique from Interview | Information used for/to... |
|---|---|---|
| 01-Dinefer | Clients Caprices, Create new Leaders, Give Responsibility | Gain Confidence and construct context |
| 02-Sonae | Barbershop, School, Priest, Pharmacy, Decision Tree, Agreements and Scenario Building | Better understanding and constructing context |
| 03-Leedsmet | Meeting Senior Executive Team, Connected to students, Graduation Ceremony | Learn and construct context |
| 04-LBS | Relationships between key players on human level | Learn and Feel in order to reconstruct the context; justify decisions, make business fusions |
| 05-Goldman | Permanent Contacts, Daily Meetings, Brainstorming, Scenario Building | Being informed and constructing context |
| 06-YCHI | Communicate with Patient, Ask Colleagues | Help Diagnose, construct context causes for the disease |
| 07-Jet2 | Dialogue with human-actors in aircraft systems, Dialogue with human-actors in weather systems, Dialogue with aircrafts technicians, Dialogue with personnel in the organization, Meetings with Crew | Learn situational navigation context, construct new context to avoid uncertainty |
| 08-DG3A | Critical Thinking, Communicate in the Design Team (Clients, Community, Developer, Architect), | Learn the common understanding to construct a common understanding context |
| 09-Lawnswood | Focus Group, Guidance, Counselling, Individualize and Dialogue with Students and Parents | Strategy to capture student information to understand the student context problems |

**Table 6. 3** – Human interaction techniques summary table

## 6.3.7. Having pleasure

In all the interviews it was interpreted that the interviewee shows some pleasure, some happiness in working under uncertainty, developing the means to do their tasks. This 'pleasure' was interpreted as being related to the D-M success. What matters is doing it with pleasure. Pleasure is a consequence and a precondition to work with others, the social-actor network. If this interaction is done unpleasantly, it will be sensed by others. For example *"In the Sonae I am a risk taker and eventually an exaggerated risk taker. How it gives joy to me, the world of business! I am not a bureaucrat, I am an anti-bureaucratic..."* (02-Sonae) or *"a decision is produced, not only when a doctor is satisfied but also when there is medical evidence to support it"* (06-YCHI) or *"Achieve the goal, working with pleasure, getting the aircraft with the people from A to B, safely and on time and not under pressure"* (07-Jet2) or *"that it not only a wonderful process we deliver on time"* (08-DG3A).

### 6.3.8. Family dependency

Family, wife, friend, husband and partner are terms used by the interviewees referring to the closest person who they go to when asking for support. Some interviewees make a direct reference, others an indirect reference to their family, which is interpreted by the author as being also important in an uncertain context. These support people were mentioned by the interviewees without any reference given by the author. The interest in this dependency is based on the importance that some interviewees give to the role of family. For example "...*it can be fans, it can be whatsoever organization, can be the proper family*" (01-Dinefer) or "*The uncertainty in a moment for others becomes certainty, because somebody compels it. It can be the woman, for example, to put order, to put the things in the trail.*" (02-Sonae) or "*whatever be their familiarity, they deal with them to find business opportunities and bring them to the firm*" (05-Goldman).

### 6.3.9. Work Hard

All interviewees refer to their work to get the best results as being hard. This hard work becomes another common characteristic of D-M under uncertainty. This interpretation suggests that D-M under uncertainty is not a question of chance, it requires hard work, to structure the social network, sense from others, study information and facts, research and give time to understanding how the things are going. Furthermore, hard-work is an interpretation of the process of D-M under uncertainty, from where decision-makers spend their time concentrating, structuring and finding the lack of information. It was not interpreted as the opposite, i.e. D-M without work, impulsive decisions. Indeed, if an option based on chance has to be taken, it still follows from a previous hard labour of dismantling complexity, arranging things, discussing the situation etc, and only if even then the answer remains obscure, then eventually the decision-maker will toss a coin or pray. In an interviewee's words "*I can disassemble the uncertainty and go arranging the situations until I arrive at a zone that is exactly dark. Toss a coin, pray...*" (02-Sonae).

### 6.3.10. Confidence

Confidence is related to the capacity and belief in dealing with the uncertainty, the context to be solved in order to make a decision. The author interpreted it as being common to all interviewees: each interviewee believes in his capacities and he is confident in the consequences. Otherwise, they can not risk a decision. So, confidence, like pleasure and hard work, is a characteristic that a decision-maker feel in order to achieve D-M under uncertainty.

### 6.3.11. Recognition

Recognition refers to the consequences of the decision i.e. the process where unknown and known information is analysed before a decision is made. The author's interpretation and meaning's finding, from all interviewees, is founded on the responsibility that the interviewees expressed they feel. From that feeling, they create two sides, interpreted as a duality, with one side having a more risky tendency and the other a more rational tendency, where decisions require less emotional participation. However, in these nine interviewees it was not possible to make an interpretation of risk behaviour. For example in the words of two interviewees: "*if it is money, and it is something that I have to be careful with, I have to make a very rational decision, but in my personal life I have been taken by very stupid decisions on the basis of emotions and got carried away*" (09-Lawnswood) and "*Personally I take minimum risk. I do not take any compromise, I will not give any guarantee to anyone on property, about my family, and I do not mortgage anything of what is the family core business. In the firm I am completely a risk taker and possibly a prohibitively risk taker. What gives me joy, in the business world is that*" (02-Sonae).

## 6.4. Conceptual Framework

The defined concepts refer precisely to what is common to a class of objects. They are important features of the social interaction presented and they provide guidelines for this research. Sensitizing concepts as stated by Charmaz are "*those background ideas that inform the overall research problem*" Charmaz (2003, pp. 259). At some stage they provided starting points for building analysis.

From the GTM analyses of interviews, and the conceptual schemas for each interview, a common concept to all interviews is shown in figure 6.1. This Conceptual Framework is a consequence of all the interviews' conceptual schemas.

The main goal of this framework is to give us a vision through time and place of the decision process. It can be used in the D-M cases within uncertainty environments. This conceptual framework permits us to describe the uncertainty environment and inform what a person does and will do. For example, facing a context of uncertainty, from where great chances will occur, the decision-maker will question *"why"* and what he *"needs"* to be better informed – this is a *tacit* position. Through these questions he will search for information from *"mechanicistic"* forms (newspapers, books, the internet, asking others, brainstorming with others, doing medical analysis, market analysis, etc.). He will also search for the remaining *"unknown"* in order to get better informed – this is an *operational* position. During this process the decision-maker is learning, capturing knowledgeable information – he is reinforcing his *cognitive* capacities facing the uncertainty. Eventually, the decision-maker has *support* help from someone (family or company). At some stage, the decision-maker may or may not make a decision which will have consequences and will have an impact on the decision-maker – decision *impact* on decision-maker as result.

The presented framework is the result of the analysis carried out on chapter 5.

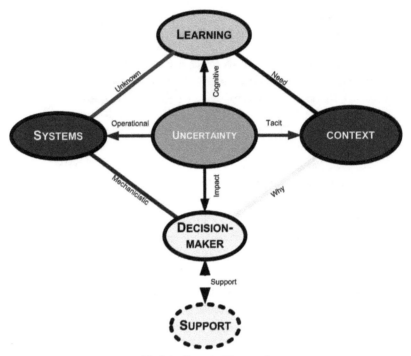

**Fig. 6. 1** – Conceptual Framework

The **Concepts** shown represent:

**Uncertainty**    The central concept that represents the unknown context, driving two axes: The horizontal represents the operational and the tacit to deal with uncertain context. The vertical is linked with the decision-maker's cognitive, communicative and social capacities, which have an impact on him as human being.

**Context**    The concept for the undefined reality, where uncertainty evolves and is reframed, resulting in a redefined context in order to achieve D-M. It represents the D-M goal.

**Learning**    The concept that drives the decision-maker to understand the context, constructing a social-web in order to understand and reframe the context.

**Systems**             The concept that represents the set of human techniques to build on the lack of information: scenarios, brainstorming, group meetings etc.; however it also stands for computer systems and other system devices built in order to provide factual, measured information from the defined reality.

**Decision-maker**      The concept that represents the role of decision-maker actor from which comes "why", the lack of information in order to reach D-M.

**Support**             A volatile concept, depending on the decision-maker's contextual uncertain world. It could be Company (Organization) or Society (People) or Family.

**Internal Links referring to the decision-maker:**

Cognitive               It is related with the process of knowledge construction within the social-web, created by the decision-maker; it stands for understanding the uncertain context;

Impact                  It is related with the decision-maker, the consequences of the decision;

Operational             It relates to information channel from pre-defined computer systems and/or systems devices. Operational also refers to human techniques in order to get information from brainstorming, scenario building, group meetings, etc.

Tacit                   Refers to how the strategy to reframe the uncertain context is developed, how tacitly the uncertain context is re-constructed.

External **Alignments** show how uncertainty is sensed:

Mechanistic             Previous experiences and tools to deal with facts

Why                     The personal desire to know, to understand the context

Unknown                 Uncertain territory, no tools or anything whatsoever to measure or obtain facts

Need                    Call for reconstruction or re-definition of the uncertain context

**Usefulness**

This Conceptual Framework presents the results to consider D-M under uncertainty. It is the GTM methodology's outcome applied in the current research study, within nine participant interviewees. This Conceptual Framework is a constructed interpretation from the interviews analysis.

A generic reading for this Conceptual Framework follows:

The Uncertainty centres on the concepts Systems, Learning, Decision-Maker and Context, which represent a frame for an uncertain context. The interaction between Uncertainty and Systems is established through operational steps; Uncertainty is linked with Learning in the sense that decisions are made facing or not a known or unknown situation and Learning is the cognitive process that results from the whole established relationships; Uncertainty is related with Context through tacit knowledge; uncertainty has impact during the decisional processes and with the decision results on the Decision-maker.

Systems are a mechanical medium of interaction with the Decision-maker; the type of Learning resulting from the use of Systems is unknown until tools are experienced and the decision is made. Learning is a need in relation to the decision Context in the sense that they need to learn what the Decision-maker has to do and later has done in order to reframe and reconstruct the reality in order to achieve D-M. The decision-maker collaborates with or has support from the concept Support. This concept can be considered as unpredictable since it is not always present.

## 6.5. ANT Enhancement

As referred to previously in chapter 5.8, the use of Actor-Network Theory terminology was investigated in how *inscription* and *translation* explains the D-M non-human associations, and how the ANT concept of *punctualisation* is applied to the D-M process, reframing the context because of the bounded rationality of the decision-maker. This section reflects firstly a summarised interpretation from the ANT summary in all interviews. Secondly, how ANT relates with relation between categories schemas will be shown, followed by a process over each of these schemas taken in order to have an ANT Network or Process framework for D-M. Finally this ANT Network will enhance the Conceptual framework, resulting in the Behavioural framework which derives the Grounded Theory for Decision Making.

### 6.5.1. ANT summary objects

- *Inscription* refers to the way technical artefacts embody patterns and the meaning and role of the objects at hand within the decision-process. From the analysis and interpretation from all interviews, no common patterns of use appear, as table 6.4 shows. These patterns of use are dependent on each interview and context. Some interviewees labelled symbols as having strong connotation of a particular use and others so. A remark about all the interviewees is that in some way they assign symbols to patterns of use, which varies from Module, Tank, Supermarket, Sports, ICT, Machine and Internet but without a particular common use or function. In terms of GTM, there are patterns of use, which are represented by GTM grounded categories, however in terms of ANT inscriptions, patterns of use, are not inscribed in any artefact;

- *Translation* refers to the social order that is continually negotiated as a social process of aligning interests in the decision context. In D-M terms, *translation* is the process the decision-maker works out to make the decision over. This particular ANT concept offers a common interpretation for all interviews. The author sensed, interpreted and found meaning for all interviewees – and the point to make is that the interviewees are all involved in a process of translation given the observations about dialogue, networks and so on, meaning that they construct a social network in the decision context from where they try to learn, to capture the lack of information and feel supported in order to make a decision. This structural process of constructing the social-network in the decision context contributes to the learning process and the reconstruction of the uncertain context to D-M;

- *Punctualisations* or black boxes', using ANT terms, is used to deal with bounded rationality. *Punctualisations* are used to analyze how decision-makers simplify the context to help thinking, how simplifications are used to help the D-M process and what is used to make inferences about the context that helps the D-M process. However, all the interviewees present the simplification using other human-actors in the social network of decision-context. For example, Delegation, Responsibility,

Construct Scenarios, Organization History, Interchange between key players, Joint Decisions and Commitment, actors in Systems (aircraft, weather, traffic control, company) and Mix of different people. Examples are presented in chapter 5.8.

| Interview | Researcher Sensed *Inscription* | Researcher Sensed, Interpreted and Constructed Meaning |
|---|---|---|
| 01-Dinefer | Module | Know clients better |
| | Colour White | Cleanness and discipline |
| | Mobile telephone | Being present |
| 02-Sonae | Tank | Symbol of Power to reframe uncertainty |
| | Wife | Finish uncertainty |
| | Ferrari | Autonomous decision-maker |
| | Train | Non Autonomous decision-maker |
| | Old Rag | Digital (new) versus Analogue (old) devices |
| | Supermarket | Job for someone who does not like to learn |
| | Barbershop, Pharmacy and Church | Emotional Picture |
| | Professor | Transmitter of culture, be useful to society |
| 03-Leedsmet | History | Room (non-human object) and reputation (human) representing strong history incidents |
| | Sports | Effort, hard work and success |
| | Rhinos | Low charge (low fees) and high impact (good values) |
| | Reputation | Strong historical connotations |
| | Chapter Book | Best interpretation for the past and takes it forward |
| 04-LBS | N/A | --- |
| 05-Goldman | ICT | Non-human artefact interpreted as giving confidence, allowing rapid adjustments to decisions that need to be adjusted |
| 06-YCHI | Scientific way | Support their decisions in Bayesian normal distribution or mathematical theory of errors |
| | Decision Support Systems | Special software is designed to help doctors to deal with information |
| 07-Jet2 | Telephone | Conversation with technical engineering personnel, having a quick training course |
| | Flight plan | Works like scenario building, contexts options used in conditions of uncertainty |
| | Machine | Aircraft being a complex engineering technological entity ; carries passengers, safely and on time |
| 08-DG3A | Internet | Substituting the "finger on knowledge", the search for expertise knowledge |
| | ICT Technology | Put what have been learn into the design process and the management |
| 09-Lawnswood | Books, Magazines and Internet | Use and Non use - "I will draw on instinct of my experience". A clear distinction between what she knows, uses experience, and what she does not know, uses others resources. |

Table 6. 4 – ANT *inscriptions* summary table

## 6.5.2. Process Framework – ANT Network

From each interview analysis is considered the conceptual schema from which was derived the conceptual framework. As explained in chapter 5.8 (table 5.12) linking ANT analysis with GTM main categories, provides an enhancement of the GTM main categories. This understanding centres the Decision-maker's learning story as being a human, with feelings, behaviours and actions which change through his life experience. This evidence derives from links between GTM main categories, enriched with ANT concepts: *information*, *reframe/reconstruct* and *experience* as following figure 6.2 shows.

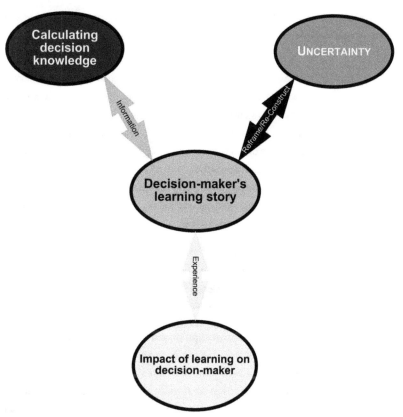

**Fig. 6. 2** – Process Framework or ANT Network

This is an ANT Network, however not a common ANT Network, from where concepts are drawn from a structure. As explained in chapter 3.4.2 - Actor Network Theory, this ANT network results from the categories obtained from GTM. These GTM categories now are enhanced through an ANT network. The network is revealed from these ramifications, through the use of GTM categories, created as a sustained bottom up ANT network. This provides a D-M social network structure from where a decision-maker bases his decision process.

This ANT network is a process framework resulting from the ANT analysis. The concepts used were the same as those used within GTM. A decision is not an act that happens it is an act that takes time to happen. This dynamic framework describes the decision process itself which varies from person to person. The framework's categories are the global categories resulted from GTM, under an ANT conceptualization.

- **Calculating decision knowledge** - a mix of tools and systems, non-human *inscriptions* such as computer programs or wider, global systems such as weather systems, navigation systems, market systems were used. Human correspondence is based in brainstorming, counselling, advising, meetings, dialoguing, joint decisions, crew decisions, whatever characterizes the found meaning in order to have knowledge, the best probable reality in the context of the decision. This is a *translation*, from those involved directly in the process of D-M, such as bi-directional learning, constructing knowledge, constructed reality from the direct participant in the process.

- **Decision-maker's learning story** - the definition of a social-web from where to gather information, the construction of the human elements that provide the ways to calculate decision knowledge. It also relates to the involvement of non-human objects, into the social-web which uses it.

- **Impact of learning (new knowledge) on the decision-maker's professional composure (self)** - What is the risk feeling, controlled risk behaviour in order to achieve D-M. It relates to the amount of knowledge which satisfies the decision-maker in order to make the decision. It also affects the surrounding social-web, who are sometimes surprised, only understanding the full impact after the decision has been made and effects are visible, permitting judgment. In some interviewees words "*Show others how I am right*" (03-Leedsmet), and "*creating new leaders*" (01-Dinefer). This category also explains the social strength between the decision-maker and the social-actors.

- **Uncertainty** – Uncertainty is a common category to all interviews, and stands for the eternally vague context reality with no single solution and is treated with human interaction and understanding.

The ANT links represent (see table 5.12):

**Information**
The result of Calculating Knowledge from the social-network. Each participant contributes with his own knowledge and interpretation in order to reframe and reconstruct the uncertain context.

**Experience**  Each actor obtains Experience in each decision context. This experience will enrich the social-network links and will define the images of collaborative work.

**Reframe/Re-construct**  Common understanding for the uncertain context. It will be further reconstructed during time and space. It is developing a process of re-framing and changing the context for D-M, accommodating not a solution but a change, which is in accordance with SSM.

In the process framework or ANT network a reading can be done:

The decision-makers, their dimensions, and what they are and do, all depend on the relations in which they are involved. For example, interests, projects, expectations and preferences and, the most important, a social network, who they may ask for more information or for help to sense the unknown. The evidence is the flow of information from "Calculating Decision Knowledge", the circulation, the connections provided in the ANT resulting network. However, this flow and correspondent meaning depends on the Decision-maker's first interpretation of the uncertain context. Furthermore, he will initiate a process of *translation*, defining a social-web for calculating decision-knowledge used to reframe/reconstruct uncertainty, developing a process of changing the context for D-M, accommodating not a solution but a change. This process will have impact in his self-professional composure, the image he offers in collaborating with others.

### 6.5.3. Behavioural Framework

The behavioural framework (see fig. 6.4) is obtained by adding together the conceptual framework and the process framework (fig. 6.2). The GTM conceptual framework (fig. 6.1) works as a contextual frame of actors, accounted for the uncertain context. Through it, it is possible to explain *tacit, need, unknown* and the *mechanicistic* involved. Inside, looking at the decision-maker's actions it shows the flux of cognition (new knowledge) and its impact on the decision-maker. Horizontally it will provide an operational way to define a tacit in order to reach D-M.

The process framework or ANT Network (fig. 6.2) works differently, not showing any detail, however concentrating all the detail in ANT concepts. The importance now is in the links between ANT concepts, guiding a process reading for the constructed/redefined reality. These are related to knowledge (existing in the social-network) and knowing (the need to reconstruct an uncertain context). These are commitments and agreements with respect to the social-network context, built for the decision-maker to share knowledge with and among actors, finding meaning, and a social rationality in order to make decisions.

Furthermore, a connection between both frameworks provide an extra enhanced explanation and results in a behavioural explanation, as derived in chapter 5, section 5.8. The basic concepts found within this derivation are: *emotions*, *facts* and *experiences* which were enriched with the concepts of *novelty*, *leadership* and *rationality*. The outcome of this combination allows the characterisation of decision-makers through the way they decide. This is a behavioural framework which has impact on the decider, because D-M under uncertainty provides experience, the cognitive result from the learning process. This experience has an impact in the decision-maker's behaviour for further situations, as a result of the success of previous ones. For example: "...*it is experience which is telling us when to speak strong or soft, when we must be present or absent, and let the people eventually commit errors...*"(01-Dinefer) or "*When someone really with courage, shows up, he wins the crowd's sympathy. This is dangerous...*" (02-Sonae) or "*An unsuccessful architect is press hunted, is stressed every time a decision has to be made, your decision or not, logical or not. But is something that comes with learning and experience*" (08-DG3A).

A new framework is then presented with the conceptual framework and process framework (ANT network) which is the result of the joint of the conceptual framework as the context, and the ANT network, as the process. The outcome of this combination (fig. 6.3) allows the characterisation of people through the way they decide. This is a behavioural framework which has impact on the decision-maker (see section 5.8).

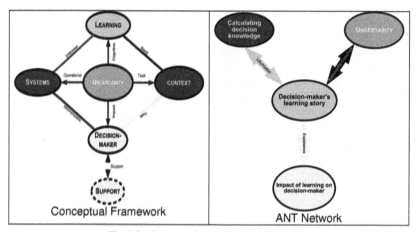

**Fig. 6. 3** – Conceptual Framework and ANT Network

| Meaning | Link | Contextual | ANT Concept | Enhancement |
|---|---|---|---|---|
| Cognitive (Knowledge) | Cognitive/Impact | Social-web | Learning Story | **EMOTIONS** |
| Resource | Operational & Tacit | Systems Techniques | Calculate Decision Knowledge | **FACTS** |
| Process (Experience) | Behavioural External alignments: why, unknown, need, mechanicist | Experience | Impact on the Self | **EXPERIENCE** |

**Table 6. 5** – Behavioural Table

- **Emotions** – are feelings, expressed in a social context constructed under a Decision Learning Story, from where knowledge, the cognitive aspects, is obtained.

  o For example: *"Some of the aspects of decision-making will be artistic rather then scientific. It is a matter of feeling rather then a matter of knowledge"*(04-LBS) or *"in my personal life I made very stupid decisions on the basis of emotions and got carried away"* (09-Lanswood)

- **Facts** – are data facts, representing information from systems and other techniques under the concept of Calculating Decision Knowledge. They represent the operational and tacit resources.

o For example: *"people make decisions on a basis of information, and they use them differently"* (04-LBS) or *"It is all a balance to try to solve it all and not to create more problems."* (07-Jet2)

- **Experience** – represents the behavioural characteristics of the actors, which have been subject to an impact from previous D-M on their image. It represents the process (experienced actors) in dealing with the external conceptual alignments such as: *why, unknown, need* and *mechanistic.*

  o For example *"New doctors with little experience, sometimes are in trouble with the amount of information to process"* (06-YCHI) or *"we work on the context of what we have learnt"* (08-DG3A)


Table 6.5, which joins the conceptual framework and process framework (ANT network), improving and enhancing conceptual finding, offers the final enhancement conceptual framework or behavioural framework, shown in fig. 6.4.

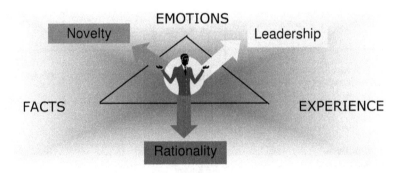

**Fig. 6. 4** – Behavioural framework

- **Novelty** - where a decision is based on facts and emotions. A decision in these terms is a balance between factual information and the decision-maker's emotional behaviour, where experience does not play a part – it is related to novelty, new business opportunity and surprise.

- **Leadership** comes with previous experience, the history of organizations, where emotions play a role in guiding a vision, feeling the experience of D-M. D-M under these circumstances is a balance between the decision-maker's experience and emotional behaviour, where actual information does not have great importance in the eyes of the decision-maker. It is common to leaderships and decision-makers with experience, where uncertain and complex context have modelled their behaviour. Reality is as it stands in front of them, as facts they know, which do not require more social interaction to be better known, since they feel what to do, and feel supported to do it.

- **Rationality** is based on facts and experience. It takes time to produce a decision. Tools, systems and human interchange techniques are used to help in the decision-process by reconstructing the uncertain context. This rationality stands also for social order, the rational reality, systematic creation of rules and systematic control systems to measure, to observe deviations and react to abnormal events. A decision in these circumstances is a balance between factual information and the decision-maker's experience, which avoids the emotional feelings that constraint or may bound a decision.

Further readings, explanations and examples are shown, but under the Grounded Theory of Decision Making under Uncertainty, which follows.


## 6.6. Decision Making under Uncertainty - The Integrated Theory


D-M in uncertain and complex situations is a balance between facts and the decision-maker's previous experiences. In uncertainty the obtaining of facts is difficult, and the experience in uncertain and complex context is difficult to define in terms of its usefulness, because of the particularities and vagueness of the reality context under analysis. Even with this particularly adverse set of circumstances, decision-makers still make decisions. What drives a decision-maker are the emotional forces, which guide a D-M process or the decision-maker's learning story, constructing a social web from where he tries to obtain information to fill the lack of it and support the emotional feeling for what is the best, by reconstructing the vagueness of the context to make the decision. During this learning story process, decision-makers calculate the best from the available facts, using non-human devices and systems balancing the obtained factual measurements with human interactional tools, reconstructing the uncertain context. This process is based on hard work done with pleasure and confidence, a continuous learning practice: making a new frame, new context, working with constraints, speaking to others, avoiding the uncertain events, whilst using a human approach, dialoguing, interacting with social-actors in the uncertain reality context.

Facing uncertainty, as figure 6.5 shows, a decision-maker calculates decision-knowledge within a decision-maker's learning story, constructing a social-web decision context from where he tries to obtain the lack of information and the feeling of emotional support in order to reach D-M. The decision consequences reflect a new context which also affects the social-web decision context, strengthening the links, the organizational culture and the decision-maker's characteristics.

EMOTIONS

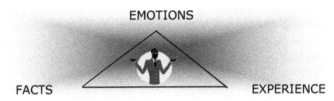

FACTS                                    EXPERIENCE

Fig. 6. 5 – Decision-Maker options under Uncertain Context

The experience of D-M under uncertainty shapes the individual decision-maker's characteristics, determining his future behaviour. This is an assumption that has been sensed, interpreted and its meaning found from the research, following an ANT Enhancement of Conceptual framework, which figure 6.5 shows.

A decision-maker facing an uncertain and complex context, from where he has to make a decision, has four optional ways, as the author understood, to calculate decision knowledge in order to do the best:

Case 1) In the first case, we may assume there is no experience in the context. A decision in these circumstances is a balance between information and the decision-maker's emotions. If a decision has to be produced, then the lack of experience will be based on the available information obtained through the hard work of calculating decision knowledge. In these conditions the result will be a novelty, a surprise decision, as figure 6.6 shows. It may be considered an instinctive decision, a surprise decision. For example "*The question of investing is not a point; the point is whether or not we are willing to accept the risks, to accept the uncertainty.*" (05-Goldman) or "*So I have to do a quick engineering course on the telephone as well to check the aircraft for a heavier landing before I could continue"* (07-Jet2).

**Fig. 6. 6** – Decision with lack of Experience

Case 2)   In the second case, as figure 6.7 shows, there is no factual information in this context. A decision in these circumstances stands mainly with the decision-maker, who balances the decision between his previous experiences and his emotional feelings under the circumstances, with courage and risk behaviour, avoiding the factual information, even if detectable. However the decision-maker may have experience, the emotional behaviour experience from being under pressure, experience of the unknown and having to deal with it which gives him the behavioural characteristics to work without knowing the facts. The calculated decision knowledge now is based upon human interactional techniques, such as scenario building, meetings, and permanent contacts, between the social-web decision context which helps the decision-maker to reframe and construct the uncertain reality in order to achieve D-M. This requires qualities of dialoguing, communication and participation in the decision-maker in order to reconstruct reality with other actors. A decision in this circumstance may have impacts on the decision-maker's professional composure (self), if the decision succeeds, giving to the decision-maker leadership and/or communicative characteristics. For example, *"Action man. You know experience, experiment, experience, experiment, but they do not think very much"* (04-LBS) or *"good leaders know a lot about the timing of things and the requirement to the situation"* (04-LBS) or *"Then all the decisions I make are based on emotion and experience that is really more important when I actually I am working with the students, because a lot of the time I have factual, objective data to work from, that shows if there is a problem."* (09-Lanswood).

**Fig. 6. 7** – Decision with lack of Factual Information

Case 3) In the third case, as figure 6.8 shows, there is no Emotional data in the context, the lack of emotions within the decision-maker and the surrounding social-web. This may be understood as being a decision without a proper social interactional dialogue or interchange guiding a well formed reality, where facts are more or less visible depending on the effort and time spent to obtain them. He who makes a decision alone after a long time spent investigating all the options may be extremely meticulous. A decision in this context stands for pushing rationality, removing the decision-maker's feelings from the context of the decision-maker. A decision in these circumstances is a balance between factual information and the decision-maker's previous experiences, which avoid the emotional behaviour in the learning story used to calculate decision knowledge. For example: *"ask colleagues about the nature of the problem and I do a lot of research myself on the subject"* (06-YCHI) or *"if it is money, and it is something that I have to be carefully I have to make a very rational decision"* (08-Lanswood).

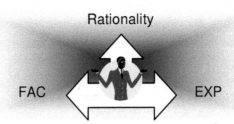

**Fig. 6. 8** – Decision with lack of Emotional Information

Case 4) A fourth and final case may be considered, a decision which is taken instinctively without a learning story and the consequent calculated knowledge. This case may result in D-M without a proper dedicated effort calculation of the factual and emotional data, without creating a supportive social web, the decision-maker being lost in the context, making decisions alone, conducting to an unknown future: having luck or not. However, in a reality where social actors do not matter, reality is offered as-is to the decision-maker, with which he does what he wants. For example: *"in my private life, my emotional life I am not like that, I am very impulsive... like following my heart or feelings of anybody and make silly things."* (09-Lanswood) or *"I start with my husband collecting information, reading books, investigating species, land, fertilizers... and we find ourselves that it was a lot of information to deal with, then we decide, to plant the flowers we like to have. We do not mind about land, fertilizers, sun exposition etc. What we like was the main important information to decide, since it was a complex and uncertain subject for us"* (06-YCHI).

## 6.6.1. Dynamic Experience

The Grounded Theory of Decision Making under Uncertainty stands in a dynamic process of evolution. This evolution dynamic is caused by the construction of reality, the transformations that uncertain contexts have caused by the decision learning story and the effects of calculating decision-knowledge, reframing the vague context in order to clarify it to be able to make decisions. D-M consequences also affect the context, having an impact of learning (new knowledge) on the decision-maker's professional composure (self) and consequently in the social-network decision context. As explained previously (see section 6.3.4 Situated Reality) the uncertain context is characterized by a lack of information, being an uncompleted reality which is reconstructed through the dialogue interaction of social-actors in the context. Dialogue is the basic interactional construct, which is composed of a set of other interactional constructs depending on the context: Understanding, Agreements, Disagreements, Opposition, Order and Power, Permanent Dialogue, Commitments, Guidance and Focus Group. All of these constructs result in a modification of the reality, at least, as seen by the social-network under decision-context. Whether it succeeds, as expected by all actors, is another question[12], but it will be different in the eyes of the social-actors in the decision-context. Knowing is not a full head of available information, it requires

---

[12] Not object of the current research being a future research direction – decision-making expectations and judgement

time to construct a place for own knowledge. Sometimes only after the decision has been made, is the effect seen. This requires constructing a reality where things as information make sense, a reframed reality in the eyes of the decision-maker and social-actors in the decision context. For example: "*...we were gradually, and slowly constructing our image*" (01-Dinefer) or "*...what you are able to do and what you aren't to. Complete a new learning curve, starting with nil and then you start and now you have a chance to learn gradually, go from there to there very quickly*" (08-DG3A).

## 6.6.2. Comparative Analysis

A first question (see 4.2 – Prescriptive Decision Theory) relates to why a decision-maker does apparently act non-rationally:

- Newell and Simon's (1972) theory of Bounded Rationality. There is a cost of obtaining and processing all the information;

- Biswas (1997) states "*calculating the expected utility function and the expected utility for each lottery is a lengthy procedure and people are likely to use their intuitions*" (Biswas, 1997, pp.6);

- Tversky and Koehler (1994) believe that "*probability judgements are attached not to events but to descriptions of events... the judged probability of an event depends upon the explicitness of its description*" (Tversky and Koehler, 1994, pp. 548 quoted in Bernstein, 1996, pp.279);

- Chase *et al.* (1998) argue that the classical definition of rationality also has problems: universality of conception of probability which makes content and context unnecessary.

The GTDM answer places the discussion of non-rationality in the social-network of D-M. The decision-maker's learning story and the calculated decision knowledge are based on a dialogue, feelings and interchange between social-actors, which will define a common understanding for what is irrational to do, in the constructed and negotiated context. Other understanding from outside actors is possible, eventually producing what is seen to be an irrational behaviour or non-rationality. Only after the D-M consequences are in place are the outside actors able to understand. Consequently,

GTDM places irrationality enclosed under the social-network decision-context, where its validity is understood.

A second question is associated with the rational behaviour of the decision-maker on the termed *Allais paradox* (see chapter 4.3), where either the rational decision-maker could make irrational decisions, or the expected value theory is wrong.

- Kahneman and Tversky (1979) propose the Prospect Theory of which the main distinctive features are: Individuals evaluate uncertain prospects in terms of gains and losses. For a small fair bet, the individuals are risk averse and the probability weighting function assumes to place more importance on low probability events;

- Biswas (1997) argues violations to prospect theory are frequently observed in real life and *"A positive theory of choice under uncertainty which seeks to explain the behaviour of individuals dealing with uncertain prospects is expected"* (Biswas, 1997, pp. 56);

- White (2006) complements this discussion with knowledge: *"whether we use objective measures or subjective measures, subjectivity must enter into their derivation. Such measures must depend on the knowledge content, of the individual"* (White, 2006, pp. 64);

- Einhorm (1982) argues *"Knowledge is difficult to achieve because of the inductive way in which we learn from experience"* (Einhorm, 1982, pp. 282).

The GTDM position places the decision-maker as having knowledge from being human. In another way, his psychological state is changed as a consequence of the learning story's 'effort' to calculate decision knowledge in order to make a decision, so the knowledge, the social-network structure, is different in this new stage, and it is in this enclosed social world where irrationality or non-rationality is defined and the expected values calculated. Then we either have a decision-maker acquiring knowledge (contradicting Einhorm) or he does not change his state and Biswas is wrong. The exception is that both are right, that the decision is unconscious, without any 'effort', and taken instinctively without a learning story and the consequent calculating knowledge. For example *"I am very impulsive... like following my heart or feelings of anybody and make silly things."* (09-Lanswood).

A third question is based in the D-M learning process.

- We have Simon with the *"satisficing"* ( a strategy to consider alternatives, one by one, until a satisfactory one is found) and other bounds that influence the way a decision-maker behaves;

- From Kahneman and Tversky (1979, 1982) we have emotions and risk behaviour;

- Rowe and Boulgarides (1992) offer a framework where values play a central part on the decision style;

- Gigerenzer and Goldstein (1996) state a probabilistic mental model trying to justify a 'guessing' theory of probability cues;

- Thaler (2000) and Bazerman (2006) add more bounds to our rationality;

- Bernstein argues *"The heart of our difficulty is sampling. We use shortcuts that lead us to erroneous perceptions, or we interpret small samples as representative of what larger samples would show"* (Bernstein, 1996, pp. 271).

The GTDM position stands in the Learning and Knowledge definition referred to previously (see 6.2). Learning is a process of structuring a strategy to capture information, to structure a social-network of actors in the uncertain decision context and knowledge is interpreted as a network of people and organizations that can make a judgement as to what is the best. This has nothing to do with bounds, behaviour or rationality. The GTDM approach is with a constructivist learning view, in which the learner, in this case, decision-maker, constructs new ideas based upon current and past knowledge supported by a community of actors in the decision context. However pleasure, working hard, family/partner and confidence count in bounding decision-makers under uncertainty.

A fourth question relates to the GTDM position with system thinking and organizational studies.

- In system thinking a boundary around the system is drawn, framing a reality. It is then essentially a choice to include or exclude other incidents that may participate in the construction of reality under analysis. System thinking needs a problem, something real, visible and understandable that works as a focus, and then in a systematic manner, using specific methodologies which manages the problem, trying to find solutions to resolve it;

- Second order systems thinking, fundamentally from Checkland proposes with SSM that systems are the mental constructs of observers, integrating multiple viewpoints of participants in order to assist them to predict and control the changes to their systems in vague situations. SSM output is learning which leads to a decision to take certain actions, knowing that this will lead not to the problem being solved but to a changed situation and new learning.

The GTDM position aligns with the system view, enclosing a social-context and then with Checkland SSM, integrating multiple views in this social-context. As referred to previously in 6.3.4 this leads to a situated reality, not a solution but a changed context, after which follows new learning. For example "*They reconstruct the context; they simplify and reconstruct the context. For example, in the Iraqi context; for Blair and Bush to legitimize decisions they reconstructed the context.*" (04-LBS) or "*Decide quickly and see what happens to perceive and act.*" (05-Goldman) or "*Anticipate, reacting avoiding uncertainty... Deviate, not creating more problems*" (07-Jet2) and finally "*It is between the idea and the delivery. So it's a whole process that has to be put in place and that's where we work on the context what we have learned*" (08-DG3A).

The main difference from other theories is based in the social-network of decision context, which influences the decision-maker's behaviour when facing uncertainty. This influence is measured in terms of calculating decision knowledge which is based on factual data but also for human interactional techniques, helping in the construction of the reality. In this context, risk behaviour becomes different from that of an individually isolated analysis, here there exists cooperation and not a defined goal, but one constructed under negotiated premises for what is the best.

## 6.7. Theory Verification

In the Chelsea interview, the author continued with open interviews, the difference from the previous interviews, being in the premise that deciding under uncertainty is learning which gave the central theme for the interview. At this stage, the author had established a GTDM, and the validation for the Learning process, in what the interviewee participant had to say about it, speaking about his experience. The remaining verification was done, again under GTM methodology work, i.e. the interview analysis was like the previous, but now whenever incidents were interpreted as linked with the theory, a note was taken. This process lead to the construction of a large amount of memo notes – much greater than the previous interviews. Later, the reference memo notes from the Grounded Theory are used to consolidate the explanation of the theory.

Furthermore, the analysis structure of the Chelsea FC interview follows the previous interviews: Transcription, A2 poster post-its, Memo notes and MS/Excel worksheets, Conceptual schema and ANT analysis.

### 6.7.1. Theoretical Saturation

To concentrate all the grounded categories, in a general integrated meaning, this research practice work was explained in chapter 5, resulting in the final clustering of grounded categories. This work also provides the ANT Network (explained in section 6.5.2). Now, table 6.6 shows all categories, including this last interview. In the author's interpretation, this table shows that the main categories are theoretically saturated (it is an expansion to the table shown in chapter 5.6, table 5.7). The obtained grounded categories are all enclosed in the previous main categories.

An explanation for the main categories obtained in this Chelsea interview, follows:

- **Calculating decision knowledge** – Non-human systems and inscriptions such as computer programs allow the player data to be inputted which is then treated scientifically by software and viewed in a palm consecutively in real-time, reading the miles, intensity of run and levels of fatigue from each player during the game. The human correspondence is based in the assessment of the social network of each player in order to sense the psychological and other problems each player has previous to each game, by talking with wives, close family and managers;

| | Calculating Decision Knowledge | Decision-Maker Learning Story | Impact of Learning on the Decision-Maker Professional Composure | Uncertainty |
|---|---|---|---|---|
| 01-Dimele | People Organization Clients | Learning Values | Leader | Uncertainty |
| 02-Bonas | Society Public Opinion Tools | Learning Cultures | Organization | Uncertainty |
| 03-Leedsmet | People Symbols | Learning | Leadership | Uncertainty |
| 04-L88 | Decision-Maker | Learning Decision | Persons Organization | |
| 05-Goldman | Tools Information Systems | Learning | Organization | Uncertainty |
| 06-YCHI | Tools Patient | Learning | Doctor | Uncertainty (Judgment) |
| 07-Jet2 | Systems | Learning Planning | Pilot Company | Uncertainty |
| 08-DG3A | Decision | Learning | Architect Office | Uncertainty |
| 09-Lawrisbrook | Systems | Learning | Job Decisions | Uncertainty |
| 10-Chelsea | Systems | Learning | Self Family Futebol | Uncertainty |

Table 6. 6 – Main categories summary table

- **Decision-maker learning story** - the definition of a social-web from where to gather information, the construction of the human elements that provide the ways to calculate decision knowledge. In this interview, the actors were players and family too, as well as associated staff, club board directors and all knowledge which may help when facing future uncertain events. It also relates to the involvedness of non-human objects, by the social-web which uses it, in this case final scientific game statistics and real time data from players; for example "...*in the background, is a bit of preparation, we must be prepared - I know my entire opponent tomorrow. The decisions that I have taken in relation to the game of tomorrow, I have a process of study and analysis*".

- **Impact of learning (new knowledge) on the decision-maker professional composure (self)** - What is the risk feeling, controlled risk behaviour in order to achieve D-M? It relates to the amount of knowledge, satisfying the decision-maker to make the decision. It also affects the direct surrounding social-web, which sometimes is surprising, only understanding the full impact after the decision has been made and the effects are visible, permitting judgment. Being a football game, the impact is visible. For example: "*I am losing 0-1 in 1 second, I have to be able to react immediately. Basically this is how you learn how to prepare your decisions*" (10-Chelsea).

- **Uncertainty** – Uncertainty is the world of football and it never finishes. What the interviewee does is work hard, preparing each game, trying to reduce the uncertainty.

## 6.7.2. Independent Categories and Conceptual Framework

If the GTDM is placed in the findings of the previous interviews, then the independent categories (common patterns) sensed, interpreted and created meaning shall be also valid in Chelsea interview. For that verification, a table summary containing all the independent categories constructed at section 6.3.1 to 6.3.11 is shown in table 6.7. An author's note shall be referred to again, that the interview was conducted openly, and none of the independent categories were asked directly or indirectly to the interviewee.

For example, the use of supporting systems: non-human and human, is an interesting and challenge case. Does the interviewee use non-human devices to help decision making during the calculations, the uncertain context? The answer is yes, as the interviewee explains he uses software to help read player data in real time during the match: body temperature, running miles, physical effort spent. In the interviewee's words "*What we do currently, in the games we have in our home... a system, a wireless system that we have now which gives us in real-time the technological analyses of the game.*" This is used to complement the physical information from players. In terms of human interchange, before the interview the author was thinking that the interviewee commands players what to do. In fact, this is not what happens, the interviewee tries to understand the social circle of players in order to understand them. During the game he does the same, as he explains "*If during the game I realize that my team is unable to win, then a tie is good. So I will change my decisions, according to the feedback they give me... I use the break to lead my players for decisions that they have to take themselves on the pitch*".

Pleasure, Work hard and Confidence are other common factors, which again are verified. The interviewee works hard preparing for the game (uncertainty) but the most important thing is that he has pleasure working under pressure, as he states: "*I always prepare myself very well for my work, to have the capacity to respond under pressure... People have an idea that we suffered greatly, that our life is a life of much tension and stress of having to decide, and the stress of not know what about. It is exactly the opposite.... the ability to feel comfortable in that environment."*

| | Extract from Interview | Researcher Sensed, Interpreted and Constructed Meaning | |
|---|---|---|---|
| Uncertainty | "Basically my world, is a world of great uncertainty, a great unpredictability and what I try to do in my business is ... the game is the most important moment in my activity, the game, are 90 minutes. What I try to do is reduce the maximum the unpredictability of the game." | Deal with | Uncertainty is |
| | | Vision, Flexibility and Human Interaction | Permanent, never solved |
| Reality Change | "If during the game I realize that my team is unable to win, then the tie is good. So I will change my decisions, according to the feedback they give me...the approach that I will make facing the game, sometimes not according to what I think, or not on the basis of what is my feeling for the situation but according to what I look to them" | Social actors | Actions |
| | | Players, Family Players, Entrepreneurs, Club Management | Dialogue, Reconstruct Context, Disruptions, Surprise Decision, Join Decision and Commitment |
| Reframing Context | "Ultimately the decisions that I take during a match, are teaching them, to decide according to the situations that could put us ahead. I help them to find solutions and responses that they have to put in practice"  "Decision-making for me also has much to do with the analysis that I do to their personal life..." | Interpretation | Reframe for... |
| | | Make a decision, and look what happens, if it goes as expected or not | Justify a decision to see what happen |
| Non-Human Information Systems | "During the game I know now the body temperature of my players because they have a sweater with a microchip that allows me to read the temperature of the body." | System | Data used for... |
| | | Wireless Network to sense in real time data players | During a match, analysis player's data |
| Human interaction techniques | "I have 20 women players... I have 20 entrepreneurs of players... I have 20 parents of players... players from other coaches"  "...at management level I origin disruptions at a steering level." | Interpretation | Information |
| | | Dialogue Emotional disruption | Learn from others to construct contex |
| Pleasure | "...that our life is a life of much tension and stress of having to decide, and the stress of not know what about. It is exactly the opposite.... ability to feel comfortable in that environment." | Interpretation | Why? |
| | | Being adapted with pressure, having pleasure working there. | |
| Family Dependency | "A decision by example, which is about a radical change in my life and that drags the family at all levels also - I like to see things from a global perspective."  "My life is all full of risks that in my family has to be zero risk" | Duality | Interpretation |
| | | Football - Risk Taker Family - Risk aversion | Wife, the leader, the rational side where things are in order. |
| Hard Work | "Always prepared myself very well for my work, continue to prepare myself for my work, to have the capacity to respond on pressure... The decisions I have taken in relation to the game tomorrow, have a process of great study and analysis" | Interpretation | |
| | | Keep working, improving and perfecting | |
| Learn | "I basically learned the decisions that I can take tomorrow and I prepare the best possible for the unpredictability of those 90 minutes. Now if during the 90 minutes, I can control all aspects of this unpredictability, I have to be able to respond and that you will learn, then it is a life experience, in this case a bank experience, an ability to learn to take the decisions" | Interpretation | |
| | | Learn to observe and be prompted to decide, not delaying reducing uncertainty, improve, research notes, use emotional ruptures, ask others | |
| Confidence | "...in terms of leadership is important because they feel that we are to lead and or have great confidence in us or not have" | Interpretation | |
| | | Believe, be capable and confident | |
| Recognition | "It is a great pressure, the decisions that are taken and often have direct influence on the success or failure of group work." | Interpretation | |
| | | Decisions responsibility and consequences - different risk position from family and firm business. | |

**Table 6. 7** – Validation Independent Categories in Chelsea FC Interview

Another difficult and particular GTDM characteristic is related to the role of family dependence. Without any question related to the interviewee's family, he spoke often of their importance, in terms of uncertain decisions. His words guided a construction of a category related with this family dependence. In the interviewee's words "*A decision by example, which is about a radical change in my life and that drags the family at all levels also - I like to see things from a global perspective.*" or "*The importance is us, our family. We as family, we are family in London, Madrid, in China or Japan*".

A final note is for Recognition, referring to the process where unknown and known information is analysed before a decision is made. The author's interpretation and meaning, from all interviewees is based in the responsibility that the interviewees feel. From that feeling, they separate the business field from the private, which again, interpreted in the words of the interviewee, is interpreted as a duality. One part has a more risky tendency and the other more rational, where decisions require a less emotional participation, in this case, the Family part. In the interviewee's words "*My life is all full of risks that in my family have to be zero risk*".

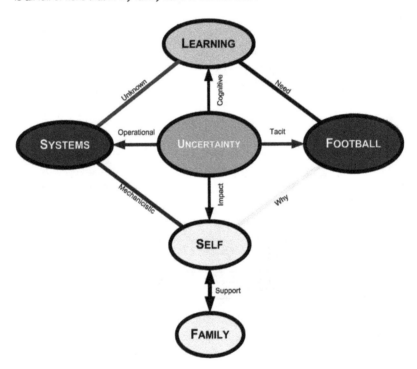

**Fig. 6. 9** – Chelsea – Conceptual Schema

In terms of the conceptual schema fitting, the Chelsea interview corresponds to the general conceptual framework discussed at section 6.4. For this interview follows the correspondent conceptual schema as fig. 6.9 shows. The main concept is Uncertainty which has relationships with other concepts such as Systems, Learning, Football and Self. The interaction between Uncertainty and Systems is established through operational steps; Uncertainty is linked with Learning in the sense that decisions are made facing or not a known or unknown situation and Learning is the cognitive process that results from the whole established relationships; Uncertainty is related with Football through tacit knowledge; uncertainty has impact during the decisional processes, since uncertain events may change during the match. For example *"Not losing is good? It depends! During the game if I see that my team is unable to win the tie is good."*

Systems are a mechanical medium of interaction with Self; the type of Learning that comes from the use of Systems is unknown until systems are experienced and the Self's decision is made. Learning is always evident in relation to Football in the sense that deciders need to learn what the Self told them, they need to learn the way to deal and behave with the tactic, they need to learn the way to follow instructions and they need to learn the contexts of the game. Football is the interaction element between the Self and the Self's decision. In this Conceptual schema, Self collaborates with the Family, having support from it and also supports the Family through his "most important thing".

For example, facing a context of uncertainty (e.g. a change of team) from where great chances will occur, the "Self" will question *"why"* and what he *"needs"* to be better informed – this is a *tacit* position. Through these questions he will search for information from *"mechanicistic"* forms (newspapers, books, internet, asking others, brainstorming with others, asking family, etc.) and he will research the remaining *"unknown"* in order to get better informed – this is an *operational* position. During this process the "Self" is learning, capturing knowledgeable information – he is reinforcing his *cognitive* capacities facing the uncertainty. The "Self" has *support* from his "Family" whatever he decides. At some stage, the "Self" may or may not make a decision which will have consequences and will have an impact on him – decision *impact* as result.

In relation to the ANT translation to common objects, it is possible to understand uncertainty, in this case football, as a social network, which progresses through a permanent learning from players and opponents' behaviours and with hard work, analysing previous games and routines in order to reduce the uncertainty.

### 6.7.3. Chelsea fitting with Theory

One aspect from D-M under uncertainty is the intuition that looks to guide some of our decisions. As explained in the fourth case of the application of GTDM (see section 6.6, case 4), this is a decision which is taken instinctively without a learning story and the consequent calculating knowledge. In the Chelsea case, the interviewee spoke about making instinctive decisions, because of the pressure to react to the circumstances of the game. However, the interviewee explains "*I did that because I had that instinct but now I will try to reason, to think about why I had acted like that: what happened in the game that made me to react that way, I have to find reasons... Writing my experience, it helps to think, I do so much. I call that, theorize my practice I did this, now I have to find reasons, why I decided well and basically try to theorize my decision*" and for that reason he takes notes for later research on them finding causes for his behaviour. So, the interviewee's interpretation offers that instinct is something that could be improved, researching the reasons that guide it. However, instinctive decisions happen, and when instinctive decisions are made, a high risk behaviour is assumed, no matter the consequences, the decision is made without a learning story and the consequent calculating of knowledge.

Another interesting application is given in the interviewee's words: "*Decision-making for me also has a great deal to do with the analysis that I do within my players. I, for example, I take decisions on how my team go to play the game, or the approach that I will take to the game, and not very much according to what I think*". This is GTDM in application. The risk behaviour and calculated knowledge do not stand in the individual decision-maker, because GTDM calculates decision knowledge in the social-network. Consequently a decision does not depend only in the self-reality but on how the decision-maker understands the jointly constructed reality. In the interviewee's words: "*So I will decide according to what happens, so I sometimes see the game that can be in view of 'I will play to win' and during the game so I say 'Hey, I play not to lose'. So, my decisions depend on me, but I also depend on the players*".

Another example refers to the interviewee's evolution of technique, with experience and whenever he needs real-time data there are technicians to help the research, expanding the social-network decision context. It is a continuous and increasing learning system, improving each game with research analysis and complementary notes from each game. This is Learning from experience under uncertainty, balancing the lack of factual data to decide between experience and emotional behaviour. This experience under uncertainty increases the taking of notes, making schemas and later analysing and discovering the reasons why instinctive actions have been taken, *"theorizing the practice"*. In addition, it is improving also the emotional side, learning to have pleasure under the pressure of the game and preparing the game, in order to use the emotional intelligence, the capacity to respond quickly under the great pressure of the game.

### 6.7.4. Theory Confirmation

A first presentation of the GTDM occurred at an interviewee's firm. The interviewee was accompanied by another staff member. They listened to the explanation, which was followed a presentation. Whilst they listened the author felt that they have understood but they were also surprised. The younger participant, who was not interviewed, argued, he supposed D-M in uncertain and complex contexts is a process of searching for data and facts where experience could be applied to help D-M. He never thought about the emotional side, which is the reason why he was surprised. The other participant, who had been interviewed, showed also some surprise, however he agreed with what had been explained. The next step was an invitation to the author to make a presentation to employees of the firm and outside guests. A date was scheduled and the author explained his research work and how he finally obtained GTDM.

From this second presentation, the author felt again some admiration from the audience about the theory, something new, never before heard which has captured interest. Most of the participants were surprised, since the organization is composed of engineering personnel, and the author expected that they were expecting to use some sort of computer programme to help D-M. This was not the case, and people started to think how important is to maintain dialogue and a permanent interaction inside the organization. It is not common inside departments under uncertain contexts, to have a proper human dialogue and communication. Usually, in their words, they think they are more communicative with each other, and with other departments in the organization, but really they close themselves in, and, for example, with low customer orders or other problems, they are not so participative and communicative, and instead of trying to solve problems or create a commonly understood reality, they prefer to use their own one. Another discussed topic came from the *experience* side, people thought it is only a question of thinking, but in this context, experience is also having courage, being participative in constructing solutions for the unknown and uncertain future. It requires experience, doing things, but also participating, feeling and communicating with each other, learning all together and being closed, not wanting the tension to confront the uncertain future. Those tasks, in their minds, are others' problems, solving that reality and letting them work. The *emotional* side and the balance with *facts* also captivated their attention, offering some discussion about where is the turning point, from were a decision must be made. This discussion follows a positivist way of seeing things, where things can and must be measured in order to be known. For example, one participant asked if it is possible to know the *emotional* tendency from someone, from what the author responded, with the expected theory, using risk behaviour facing some investments. Then reframing for the organization reality, people thought having the courage to communicate, being more participative and avoiding problems is also an emotional, behavioural tendency, which they can permanently improve, regardless of how to measure this *emotional* personal side, or what are someone's measured characteristics. The balance, the action point is somewhere in a common understanding of reality when facing uncertainty.

A third presentation, to another interviewee was also made in the same terms as the first presentation. The intent was to confront the participant with the theory and listen to what he has to say about it. Unfortunately, this interview was not very long, thus not having the opportunity to explain everything in detail, as in the previous. However, aspects of *Facts*, *Emotions* and *Experience* were explained, giving the opportunity for the interviewee to reply. Comments about the emotional side, which characterizes us as human beings, from the interviewee participant, show an agreement with the results obtained.

As a summary, the theory was not rejected or dismissed. The author's interpretation was accepted as possible and understood by the participant interviewees and guests. It offers a fresh and creative way to see decisions under uncertainty, and the interviewees saw their experience under the theory, as well a valid description for the interaction importance under uncertain context, the construction of a social-network in order to acquire more information and reframe uncertain context. Critics may point to the fact of it being a more qualitative, descriptive form which gives difficulty in its application in practical terms. It needs to have some measurement inputs in order to measure decision-makers characteristics or successful decisions.

## 6.8. Research Evaluation

The aim of this research is to examine D-M in the context of uncertainty and complexity. This is a descriptive theory about D-M, and grounded in the living experience of the research interviewees. According to Fawcett and Downs this type of theory "*describes or classifies specific dimensions or characteristics of individuals, groups, situations, or events by summarizing the commonalities found in discrete observations*" (Fawcett and Downs 1986, pp. 4 quoted in Gregor, 2006, pp.623-4).

The author undertook the procedures using GTM principles and processes as much as it is possible, therefore coding conceptualization, theoretical sensitivity and a deep reasoning were followed in order to accomplish the resulting theory. Literature review was used interchangeably with each stage of the analysis process in order to evaluate the similarities and differences that guided further steps of the research. Using ANT, conciliations and enhancements were made to categories, giving an understanding of inanimate objects and material systems as actors or co-agents of human intentional actors.

Glaser and Strauss (1967) provide some guidance for evaluating the empirical grounds of GT. These can be summarized as follows: fit, understanding ability, generalized ability and control. For this end, the author argues that with the current data, theoretical sensitivity and deep reasoning lead to the result theory. An evaluation was provided following Alasuutari's (1996) position, confirming with two of the interviewees in a later stage, with the resulting theory. Consequently a workshop was given as an extension to this exposition, as requested by one of the informants, in order show the theory to a community, in this case, extended to middle management staff of the organization and some outside guests. Generality was demanded, and this was supported with the heterogeneity of research participants, from Portuguese to English informants, from small to large organizations, from a professional management CEO to a diversity of professional expertises away from management, for example by including an architect, pilot, doctor and football coach. GTM was used, providing the way to control the development of the theory with regard to action, the social network construction that supports the phenomenon of D-M under uncertainty and complexity.

Charmaz exposes four criteria for Grounded Theory Studies (Charmaz, 2006, 182-3): Credibility, Originality, Resonance and Usefulness. Regarding these four criterion the author's answer is:

- Credibility – GTM principles were followed, the researcher having achieved close familiarity with the research topic and GTM methodology. The data used were the data needed to acquire the theoretical saturation of categories. He made systematic comparisons between observations and between categories and supported this by literature reviews;

- Originality – A learning process in D-M under uncertainty and complexity proved to be a new insight of D-M, not common in literature. It was only possible through GTM analysis which provides this new concept from the data. Social and theoretical significance can be sustained by the participative embracing of informants: as an example, the later workshop provided by one organization for their staff members and some outside guests;

- Resonance – The grounded categories portray D-M under uncertainty and complexity, describing the fully studied experience. Data from large to small organizations, from individuals within heterogeneous professional experience was gathered with ethical and privacy issues, building a good relationship with them. The resulting grounded theory made sense to the participants when presented to them;

- Usefulness – The analysis results offer interpretations that people can use in their every day worlds, it is an actual social representation from a real discrete set of experiences. Further research is exposed in the conclusion chapter, as a result of the analysis. The research contribution to knowledge is the theoretical frameworks from which the experience of learning in D-M under uncertainty and complexity can be explained as a social network from where decision-makers try to sense the unknown future. Another contribution is related to the research methodology, conciliating grounded categories with ANT objects, providing extension and enhancement description for the theory.

## 6.9. Critique of the Methodology

This research is sustained by a Grounded Theory Methodology and Actor-Network Theory, which are criticized for their qualitative nature. According to Hammersley (1992) a constant criticism of qualitative methods is their inability to relate to characteristics of the real world, although it is generally established that they have their own internal logic and strength.

Citing Bryant *"A constructivist approach means more than looking at how individuals view their situations. The resulting theory is an interpretation and depends on the researcher's view, it does not and cannot stand outside of it"* (Bryant, 2002, quoted in Charmaz, 2006, pp. 130). Besides, the research goal is to understand social relationships, in certain time and located in specific social contexts, accounted for the participants in the research. In a changing world, these relationships change equally ensuring that any new experience into such processes is likely to be new and even temporary. Uncertainty and complexity context creates *per se* a changing world, which means, when resolved, a new reality emerges again and a new uncertainty and complexity will show up, creating again new contexts to solve.

Theories can be classified by their level of generalization: Substantive theory, Formal theory and Mid-range theory. Moreover Gregor proposes that *"Substantive theory is developed for a specific area of inquiry... based on analysis of observations and is contrasted with formal theory, which is developed for a broad conceptual area"* (Gregor, 2006, pp. 616). About Mid-range theory Gregor refers *"to theory that is moderately abstract, has limited scope, and can easily lead to testable hypotheses"* (Gregor 2006, pp.616). However Hood (1983) proposes a different interpretation for Substantive Theory. Paraphrasing Charmaz (2006, pp. 140), Hood presents an identification of variables, specification of events and actions conditions to occur and an examination of consequences. She also considers what people do and the sources for actions are identified.

This substantive theory of Hood (1993) is not the Grounded Theory, which the researcher constructed because it does not find testable hypothesis that could guide further action, namely as a normative guide for D-M under uncertainty and complexity. We are all different, and the resulting Grounded Theory of D-M is an explanation grounded on the experiences of a set of discrete informants. This theory explains the commonalities observed and constructed under GTM, not standing as an argument for "Person X will make a decision Y under this Grounded Theory". The resulting Grounded Theory of D-M under uncertainty and complexity is a Substantive Theory in Gregor's terms (2006).

The use of ANT provides a sustaining and "*sensitizing device*" for a Theory of Explanation, as Gregor argues "*Explanations of how, when, where, and why events occurred may be presented, giving rise to process-type theory*" (Gregor, 2006, pp. 624) when using "*actor-network theory, an understanding of inanimate objects and material systems as actors or co-agents of human intentional actors*" (Latour 1991 quoted in Gregor, 2006, pp. 624) which provide a "*sensitizing device at a high level to view the world in a certain way*" (Klein and Myers 1999, pp. 75 quoted in Gregor, 2006, pp.624). This has been carried out in this research, using the conciliation between GTM categories and ANT objects, providing as a result an enhancement and enrichment of the grounded categories. So, it will also stand for a Theory of Explanation.

Grounded theory is also criticized as being empiricist; because it is grounded too closely on the experimental data and in the personal researcher's interpretation (Parker and Roffey, 1997). It considers the working data as the foundation of its hypothesis and lays itself down against the use of preceding theories. Bryant stated that "*There are some profound problems with this approach; in particular the unproblematic conceptualization of data, and a level of methodological flexibility that can degenerate into methodological indifference and result in superficial and ambiguous conclusions*" (Bryant, 2002, pp.25). Fendt and Sachs prefer to use the term *malaises* to criticize Grounded Theory Method: "*These malaises may well have a multitude of causes, such as:*

- *actual inconsistencies in the* method *itself;*

- *semantic inconsistencies in the method, for example, because of époque vocabulary;*

- *inconsistencies because of the fact that, ever since the ontological bifurcation of the GTM founding fathers, several versions of GTM exist, some similar and some conflicting;*

- *misconceptions because of 'misreadings of seminal texts' and probably subsequent 'miswritings" and 'misteachings';*

- *a lack of methodological training by the researchers regarding qualitative research in general and GTM in particular;*

- *insufficient attention to process, especially coaching of the researchers;*

- *an inapt fit between research question, researcher, and GTM; and/or*

- *a combination of the above*" (Fendt and Sachs, 2007, pp.3).

These Fendt and Sachs' *malaises* generally characterize GTM. Concerning the *époque* vocabulary, Grounded theory was developed in a period when other qualitative methods were often considered not scientific and thus became the main qualitative method accepted as academic. The split of the founders Glaser and Strauss contributed to the misunderstandings about GTM, which caused misconceptions and inconsistencies in the literature. As Walker and Myrick argue *"Perhaps, it is simply more a science with Strauss and more an art with Glaser. Again, it is not the differences that matter so much as the understanding of these differences and the making of informed and knowledgeable choices about what one will do in their research. Perhaps it is more about the researcher and less about the method. The value of this discussion might not reside in picking sides but exist in the discourse itself'* (Walker and Myrick, 2006, pp. 558). The lack of methodological practice and attention to the process it is not a sufficient excuse for GTM itself, but for the research where it applies. This is why Glaser and Strauss (1967) required that field researchers think about the scientific theories that might be developed out of apparently isolated studies. Silverman argues *"We no longer need to regard qualitative research as provisional or never based on initial hypotheses. This is because qualitative studies have already assembled a usable, cumulative body of knowledge"* (Silverman, 2005, pp.63).

The author's experience of using GTM synthesizes it with three malefactors in using GTM: mechanization, focus in individuals and biased top down categories. Mechanization refers to an auxiliary and complementary use of information systems doing the research work of coding and management of the data research under analysis. This helps in reality, but the researcher's mind becomes in some way lazy by the facilities provided, which can lead to influence the researcher into attempts to organize codes into categories, releasing the mind from the hard work of looking for the hidden detail, providing the interpretation and construction of meaning. Focus in Individuals is being captive by the personalities and consequently drawing up categories around informant distinctiveness and particularities that captivate the researcher's mind; and finally top down categories are those that emerge biased from previous experiences and literature that capture the researcher's sensitivity.

However, GTM has been criticized by qualitative researchers in that it fails to give appropriate attention to both data collection techniques and to the quality of the gathered material (Charmaz, 1983). In the current research, the author kept the open interviews giving the interviewees the opportunity to express their views freely. Simultaneously, the researcher attempted to avoid preconceived conceptions by keeping himself distant from their opinions, paying close attention to exactly what they said, recording the interviewees and later listening carefully several times, being immersed in each scenario according to what was being said by the experience in D-M under uncertainty and complexity.

Actor-Network Theory criticisms reside in claims that it is characteristic of non-humans, making no distinction between humans and non-humans, or things. ANT adopters defend this by answering that they do not make attributes properties similar to humans and non-humans, at least intentionally. Associations between humans and non-humans are sustained by heterogeneous associations between subjects (humans) and objects (non-humans) (Callon, 1999). In the researcher's view the connotations reside in the ambiguities that humans use to attribute properties values to non-humans things. For example in the present research 'white' was associated with 'professionalism', the rhinoceros is associated with 'low charge and high impact'. For this end, network associations are not intentional; they come from the experience of D-M under uncertainty and complexity, accounted by the research participants and then later, those heterogeneous associations were interpreted, which could be different in each research participant's experience.

Other criticisms argue that ANT is amoral. Bijker (1995) has responded to this criticism by stating that the amorality of ANT is not a requirement. Moral and political positions are possible, but one must first describe the network before taking up such positions. In the author's opinion, the amorality resides in the lack of knowledge, a wide interpretation of the phenomenon under study. For example 'demolitions' could be interpreted as immoral, since buildings cost money. We need to see more associations, the network ramifications, to make a better understanding what is in it. In the current research 'demolitions' are associated with a dynamic of change, building beauty for others, understanding appreciation. Thus, ANT requires a careful interpretation of the objects that come out in the research subject.

## 6.10. Summary

This chapter has shown the Grounded Theory of Decision Making development and validation. A set of recurring definitions used in the present research was presented. Common independent categories observed in all interviews were presented and discussed. Then it explained three frameworks: the Conceptual framework, the Process framework and the Behavioural framework. .

The Grounded Theory of Decision Making under Uncertainty was explained and discussed as well a comparative analysis given, with previous theories analysed in Chapter 4-Literature Review. The theory's verification was discussed, using an extra interview, demonstrating the categories saturation, independent categories and conceptual framework validity. Also, how the theory fits with this extra complementary interview was demonstrated and then the theory verification and confirmation with participant interviewees and a small group was presented and discussed. Finally, a research evaluation and a critique of the used methodologies were presented.

# Chapter 7  Conclusion

## 7.1. Introduction

This chapter provides an overview of the research, summarising the main contributions the research makes to the ongoing task of elucidating how decision-makers under uncertainty and complexity learn, developing a social-web context to calculate how decision knowledge and learning have an impact on the decision-maker's professional composure. It also discusses the significant issues and recommendations emerging from this research. A heuristic use of the Grounded Theory of Decision Making under uncertainty is exposed. A critical analysis of the research is also included. Finally, limitations and directions for future research are presented.

This research was conducted through a set of discrete interviews under GTM guidelines. It aims to explore the D-M under uncertainty specifically concerned with a Learning process. The following research objectives were achieved:

1. Investigation of the current extent of D-M under uncertainty in general and to find out about the actual extent and the nature of learning process under uncertainty;

2. Discovery and analysis of the conditions and factors which influence D-M under uncertainty;

3. Assessment of the extent to which issues of D-M apply in the context of uncertainty and complexity and determine the conditions under which D-M under uncertainty has been or might be explained;

4. Examination of the relationship of D-M to uncertainty and complexity, growing out of the role of knowledge and information acquisition within a

general social context;

5. Explanation of the ways in which D-M under uncertainty and complexity is a social interaction and allows calculating knowledge through a learning story activity; to present recommendations and suggestions that may contribute to explain and enhance D-M under uncertainty and complexity.

To answer and meet these research objectives, a variety of methods have been used, including face-to-face interviews (both open ended questions and structured interviewing), a first empirical case-study and literature review.


## 7.2. Overview of the Theory


The impact of D-M under uncertainty and complexity theory has one core category which is for Learning under uncertainty. This Learning central category has sub-categories which are Decision-maker's Learning story, Calculating Decision Knowledge, Impact of learning (new knowledge) on the decision-maker's professional composure (self) and Uncertainty. All these four theory elements have been enhanced with ANT providing three concepts from where D-M under uncertainty is explained:

- **Emotions** derive from the Decision-maker's learning story's cognitive capacities, through working out uncertain elements over a social-web in order to obtain knowledge;

- **Facts** derive from Calculating Decision Knowledge's operational and tacit capacities in order to obtain through whatever system techniques (human or non-human) information in order to enrich decision knowledge

- **Experience** derives from Impact on the Self, the previous experiences working with external sensitive alignments elements of uncertainty contexts: *need, why, mechanicistic* and *unknown*.

Within each of the theory elements there is a set of theoretical concepts that connect the theory's element with each other. These theoretical concepts serve to explain the vital elements of the proposed theory in more detail.

- **Context**    The concept of context for the undefined reality, where uncertainty evolves and is reframed, resulting in a redefined context in order to achieve D-M. It represents the D-M goal.

- **Learning**    The concept that drives the decision-maker to understand the context, constructing a social-web in order to understand and reframe the context.

- **Systems**    The concept that represents the set of human techniques to build on the lack of information: scenarios, brainstorming, group meetings etc.; however it also stands for computer systems and other system devices built in order to provide factual, measured information from the defined reality.

- **Decision-maker** The concept that represents the role of the decision-maker actor from which comes "why", the lack of information in order to reach D-M.

- **Support**    A volatile concept, depending on the decision-maker's contextual uncertain world. It could be Company (Organization) or Society (People) or Family.

**Sensing Uncertainty:**

- **Mechanistic**    Previous experiences and tools to deal with facts

- **Why**    The personal desire to know, to understand the context

- **Unknown**    Uncertain territory, no tools or no experience or anything whatsoever to measure or obtain facts

- **Need**    Call for reconstruction or re-definition of the uncertain context

**Decision-maker Features:**

- **Cognitive**    It is related to the process of knowledge construction within the social-web, created by the decision-maker; it stands for understanding the uncertain context;

- **Impact**    It is related to the decision-maker, the consequences of the decision;

- **Operational**       Relates to channel's information from pre-defined systems and/or systems devices. Operational also refers to human techniques in order to get information from brainstorming, scenario building, group meetings, etc.

- **Tacit**       Refers to how the strategy to reframe the uncertain context is developed, how tacitly the uncertain context is re-constructed and reframed.

## 7.3. Summary of the findings

Based on the analysis of the qualitative data offered and discussed in previous chapters, a summary of the most important findings and conclusion follows:

1. Learning process under uncertainty explains how rationality, and a constructed reality, is formed in order to facilitate D-M;

2. Verbalizations and dialogue stand for interactional constructs in a social-context under which an uncertain reality is re-framed to define rationality for D-M. However, measuring and other verbal-probabilistic propositions were not considered important, being substituted by the grounded proposition "Calculating Decision Knowledge" for D-M under uncertainty. The individual risk behaviour was seen conjointly with the directly surrounding social-web;

3. Pleasure, working hard, family/partner and confidence counted in bounding decision-makers under uncertainty. It was also shown how bounded rationality was resolved within the directly surrounding social-web under the decision context;

4. Learning was mainly related with a formation of reality, i.e. how the uncertain and complex context was made understandable; how meaning was formed through social interaction to frame a system where a system approach could be applied, finding not only a solution but providing also a change, from the point of view of the current research question, where D-M occurred;

5. This research study explained how decision-makers had a common understanding about uncertainty, an eternally vague contextual reality that is reconstructed under negotiated premises for what is the best, and is better

treated with human interaction and understanding. As the world moved more uncertainty became visible, requiring more decisions, where emotional behaviour has a part in this process.

As a findings summary the author states that:

- Learning is a process of collecting information constantly until the evidence is sufficient to transform information into knowable procedures that guide a decision;

- D-M under uncertainty and complexity is an ongoing dialogue and interactional process between the decision-maker and the social-context involved to reframe and re-construct the context in order to facilitate D-M.

## 7.4. Research Contribution

First of all the value of the research outcomes in this book indicates primarily that the Learning concept was proposed as an explanation for D-M under uncertainty and complexity. This theory was grounded on the empirical data that was collected from a set of discrete informants that agreed to participate on the research study. Through this obtained empirical data from interviews, new data was generated that is related to D-M application in relation to uncertainty and complexity.

The second contribution was related to the set of independent categories obtained from the research methodology used. These independent categories explained how: Pleasure, working hard, family/partner and confidence count in bounding decision-makers under uncertainty. It was also shown how bounded rationality was resolved within the directly surrounding social-web under the decision context.

The third contribution was the D-M under uncertainty explanation which has been supported by the frameworks. These frameworks were the result of the current research methodology, namely GT with the help enhancement support from ANT, providing a visual explanation of the interaction elements between categories.

Three frameworks were designed from the gathered and analysed data: a conceptual framework, an ANT network framework and a link between both frameworks provided an extra enhanced explanation, resulting in a behavioural framework.

- The **Conceptual framework** has five main concepts derived from GTM analysis: systems, learn, context, uncertainty and decision-maker and a sixth one that depends on the decision makers' contextual uncertain world. It also has internal links referring to the decision-maker: cognitive, impact, operational and tacit; and external alignments showing the way uncertainty is sensed: mechanistic, why, unknown, need. This framework can be used in the D-M cases within uncertainty environments. Its main goal is to give us a static vision through time and place of the decision process.

- The **Process framework** is an ANT network which is the result from the ANT analysis. The concepts used were the same as those used within GTM: calculating decision knowledge, decision-maker's learning story, impact of learning on decision-maker and uncertainty. However, the concepts were enriched with ANT during the construction process and later enhanced through an ANT network. The links between concepts are: information, experience and reframe/re-construct. This is a dynamic framework where it is understood that a decision is not an act that happens but it is an act that takes time to happen, and is sustained under a reframed/reconstructed context which corresponds to a change. The framework describes the decision process itself, which varies from person to person.

- The **Behavioural framework** resulted from joining the conceptual framework as the context, and the ANT network, as the process. The basic concepts found within this framework are: emotions, facts and experiences which were enriched with the concepts of novelty, leadership and rationality. The outcome of this combination allows characterising people through the way they decide. This is a behavioural framework which has impact on the decider.


Moreover, there is a contribution that was related to the mixture of research methodologies: the GTM process that was used to generate the theory. Firstly, the researcher undertook more than one field-work and he used all the GTM steps.

Further, the author has done literature reviews more than once to understand the data gathered and to sustain his initial expectations.

This research study may be considered as the starting point for other researches in D-M, in general and under uncertainty and complexity in particular. In other words, this research provides to other researchers the opportunity to present a more complete picture of the D-M under uncertainty process.

### 7.4.1. Research GTM Questions

The research questions were a result of the research conceptual development (Chapter 5) analysis that were 'tested' to an extent by the last interview and the later stages of the research:

Research question 1: **How is a process of learning in D-M under uncertain and complex contexts mobilized?**

- From the interpretation of the data from the interviews, the process is mobilised based on a *need*, something necessary in order to understand the uncertain context, for example, from where the business is run, to understand the employees and business adversaries, or to understand the symptoms of a disease. A representation is given within the conceptual framework (see chapter 6, section 6.4).

Research question 2: **What are the organizational/managerial mechanisms which facilitate the process of learning in decision making under uncertain and complex contexts?**

- The interpretation from interviews supports the concept of a 2nd order system thinking social interaction. People decide through being supported in a social web and, following 2nd order system authors, people observe, redesign frontiers, in order to form a common understanding. Dialogue is used to promote a change, reality is reconstructed and solutions to decision-making are accommodated, along with having brainstorming, and group meetings participation which is in accordance with Soft Systems Methodology

(Checkland, 1981). A process description is given within the ANT Network (see chapter 6, section 6.5.2).

Research question 3: **What is the contribution of learning to decision making in uncertain and complex contexts?**

- The interpretation from interviewees is that the learning phase is not decisive; a new reality follows uncertainty, or a less vague one, but uncertainty is still present, there is no single solution for uncertainty. In the words of the interviewees, "the only stable thing is uncertainty" (02-Sonae) or "the world has moved on and we need to be much more flexible" (03-Leedsmet) or "if we are willing to accept the risks, to accept the uncertainty" or "If nothing went wrong, planes would not have a pilot. But we are there to make decisions" (07-Jet2) or "you're left with more decisions you have to make afterwards, it never stops" (09-Lawnswood). The main contributions from the interviewees' inputs are better understanding between people and context knowledge acquisition. A description is given within the behavioural framework (see chapter 6, section 6.5.3).

Insightful questions, which appear during the researcher's GTM methodological analysis, were:

- **Why do decision-makers want to learn?** – From the researcher's interpretation, all the interviewees want to succeed in re-constructing the uncertain context, learning how to make change;

- **Do decision-makers think that they are better off if they learn than if they do not?** - It was common to all interviewees that they agreed that information is important on which to base a decision, and with that information they can learn to make better informed decisions and alleviate the emotional charge in D-M under uncertainty, an uncompleted reality;

- **How do they learn?** – The interpretation from the interviews was the creation of a social network, where the interviewee is also a participating member, and from this network generates the knowledge that strengthens the facts and lightens the emotional feelings, in order to make a decision;

- **Do they search for knowledge or just information?** – All of the interviewees agreed that information is important on which to base a decision, but information per se is not a sufficient condition. With information they can learn to make better-informed decisions and alleviate the emotional tension in decision-making under uncertainty. So information is obtained from the internet, magazines, computer systems, and navigation systems, balance sheets, dialogues with patients and eventually from experts in some subjects. However, making decisions under uncertainty is not just about information, it is a matter of interpreting that information and transforming it into knowledge, feeling the situational context, understanding the timing all together as requirements for decision-making. A decision-maker also senses a knowledgeable support from the social-actors, a participative process that in some way gives the feeling of sharing the risk-taking accompanying the decision;

- **Is the learning process always desirable?** – Learning is the process of collecting information constantly until evidence is sufficient to transform information into knowable procedures that guide a decision. According to the interviewees learning is desirable because if there is no learning, then there is no other way to evaluate a direction, a guide in the dark, and then one may just as well "toss a coin" or just "pray" for better luck. Learning contributes to finding solutions and to succeeding. However surprise happens, even without a knowledgeable context, assuming the risk of decision-making is not unquestioned. Innovation is also assuming the risk, assuming the unknown. Typically the professional or business world characterizes the interpretation directed on winning, a business success depends on the risk in accepting uncertainty and how surprise decisions succeed;

- **Is it possible to measure the value of learning?** – From the interviews the researcher's interpretation is based on a resulting solution and change caused by the decision-making action. As explained in chapter 6.3.4 Situated Reality, decision-making under uncertainty changes the context as a consequence of the decision-making action. Some interviewees make a quick decision to show the consequences and then analyse them in order to continue or redefine actions;

- **What are the factors which determine the value of learning?** – The main factor is the judgment of the decision-making action. If the new reality conforms to the expected, satisfying the decision-maker in whatsoever way he senses it, then his social-actors' context, the knowable factors will remain, strengthening the interaction with them for the future, creating a durable relationship. Otherwise this strength will weaken and eventually become loose. It was interpreted that factors of success are related to the strength of the bond with the social-actors, the stronger the peer group or board staff, the closer the colleagues, the greater the success This question also raises the questions what is knowledge and how to measure it, i.e. do we measure (or just evaluate) the results of a learning process, the network structure of people and organizations that can make a judgement as to what is the best? It is possible to interpret an associated cost to the expertise necessary in the process: acquiring know-how, expenses with consultancy, expertise, etc. Quoting White *"how one defines 'expertise' is another matter altogether... We may have some degree of confidence in the expert's appraisal"* (White, 2006, pp.65). Consequently, *"assuming if the world is essentially deterministic; we do not search out its determinism at any cost. Information is costly. Bearing this in mind; limiting uncertainty may be preferable to certainty at a cost"* (White, 2006, pp.72). Following White, an organisation does not contain all the humans in the world. According to the interviewees, the value of learning can be found through the people, who stand as reliable and trustworthy for the information they provide and the supportive feeling they bring as humans, which contributes to finding solutions to solve problems and to the process of change all the interviewees advocate.

## 7.5. Recommendations

The following important recommendations were concluded based on the research results:

1. The results indicated that there are some systemic attributes in order to improve D-M under uncertainty. Therefore the author recommends facilitating systemic utilization by making more familiar decision-makers through increasing their exposure to them. These systemics are: brainstorming, communication and other facilities – human interchange facilities.

2. According to the research results the D-M differs from EUT since the former applies to a single decision-maker. Therefore the author recommends other ways where not only the decision-maker should answer but where the close group should also contribute to the context of D-M under uncertainty.

3. The main difference from other theories is based in the social-network of decision context, which influences the decision-maker's behaviour when facing uncertainty. This research's results point calculating decision knowledge which is based on factual data but also for human dialogue techniques, serving in the construction and reframing of the reality. In this context, risk behaviour becomes different from that of an individually isolated analysis, here there exists cooperation and not a defined goal, but one constructed under negotiated premises for what is the best, not the optimal or even rational for others outside of the participative process.

4. D-M in uncertain and complex situations is a balance between facts and the decision-maker's previous experiences. Under uncertainty the obtaining of facts is difficult, and the experience in uncertain and complex context is difficult to define in terms of its usefulness, because of the particularities and vagueness of the reality context under analysis. A decision-maker facing an uncertain and complex context, has four optional ways, as the author understood, to calculate decision knowledge in order to do the best:

- No experience: Facts and Emotional reads → Novelty decision

- No Facts: Experience and Emotional reads → Leadership/Risk decision

- No Emotions: Experience and Facts → Rationality decision

- No Calculating Knowledge and Social support: Emotional reads → Instinctive decision.

## 7.6. Limitations

The current research of D-M under uncertainty and complexity assumptions points to the development of theory grounded on the living experience of the interviewees who have offered their knowledge and experiences in D-M under uncertainty and complexity.

This research was conduced in a small set of business companies and professional activities so that the generalization of the findings to other sectors is too difficult because of different environments and context.

The resulting frameworks intend to be a basic type of theory, according to Gregor "*a theory for analyzing, describing and classifying dimensions and characteristics of individuals participants and situations, by summarizing the commonalities found in open interviews and observations*" (Gregor, 2006, pp.263). Supported by actor-network theory, an understanding of inanimate objects and material systems as co-agents of human intentional actors offers an extension to the basic theory, through ANT Network and the Enhancement Framework.

There are two main limitations to this research. The first relates to the interviews since it is extremely demanding on research resources, as some decision processes typically span periods of years; therefore the researcher is obliged to rely on the traces of completed decision-process in the minds of those people who carried it out. This research proceeded on the premise that what was captured really happened, but that not all that happened was necessarily important and useful. However, the process of theoretical sampling could provide the means to find the gaps of un-captured information, and the result is a continuous process of moving back and forward between data collection (interviews and observation) and repeated analysis.

The second limitation is related to the resulting Theory GTDM, which stands for a Theory of Explanation, although making testable predictions about the future was not of primary concern. Furthermore testing is needed in order to reshape concepts and tune processes. For this end, a heuristic exposition and future work is proposed, which follows.

## 7.7. Heuristic use of the Theory

This research shows that decision-making under uncertainty can be understood through a model centred on an interactional social web in order to construct knowledge of the undefined context. The author is convinced that dialogue and other interactional social constructs are the pathway to interpret, reframe, and re-construct uncertain contexts for decision-making. The author offers frameworks founded in a situational context, a decision process and a behavioural enhancement process.

However, this Grounded Theory of Decision Making under Uncertainty was constructed from a set of decision-maker participants, who provided their experiences and then, through the use of GTM and ANT, the researcher built the theory. The aim of this theory is to be a theory of Explanation, although it is also a process theory with some behavioural enhancements. Furthermore, to support these findings, the theory must be used as a process in uncertain and complex contexts. Consequently, the researcher aims to use it in practice, for which an implementation guideline is proposed at section 7.7-Heuristic use of the Theory (A schematic guideline is also included in appendix):

- Situational context (conceptual framework) – this framework offers a design to sense uncertainty in order to reach D-M.

  o For example, facing a context of uncertainty, the decision-maker will define a tacit position from where he answers the question "why" and what he "needs" to be better informed. Through these questions he will define an operational position to deal with the "unknown" searching information from "mechanicistic" forms (books, internet, asking others, brainstorming with others, doing analysis, etc.).

- Using Soft System Methodology (process framework or ANT network) to evaluate the decision process – this framework offers a dynamic perspective associated with SSM, developing a process of re-framing and changing the context for D-M, accommodating not a solution but a change;

  o During this process the decision-maker constructs new ideas based upon current and past knowledge supported by a community of actors in the decision context. However pleasure, working hard, family/partner and confidence count in bounding decision-makers under uncertainty.

Furthermore, referring to the participation of social-participants in the D-M context, to research an evaluation for the behavioural enhancements suggested – this study will offer a perspective for analysis of the impact on the decision-maker.

At some stage, the decision-maker has to make a decision which will have an impact on him as a consequence.

## 7.8. Future Research

It could be suggested that the limitations of this research, which were presented previously, could be considered as opportunities for future research. The final outcome of the research was to develop an explanation for D-M under uncertainty and complexity. Thus, this suggested explanation may be used to analyse and test the effective D-M under uncertainty and its impact across other and diverse sectors. Furthermore, researchers could successfully apply the designed frameworks within different fields and after data gathered they could compare it and find out if decision-makers have a similar behaviour. For example, this research could be applied in the Judicial System to make sure that the general nature of the research results. In addition, future research could be applied on the same initial business context, but it is recommended that the research takes more time and that the data sample size is increased in order to obtain more data information.

A research context for example could be to see how other categories should be developed and link within a context of small business decisions under a context of globalization – why it is so difficult to export goods. Also, this theory could be examined and verified by another method. In other words, the researcher has formed and presented GTDM and hypotheses from a specific context, namely under uncertainty and complexity and these can now be tested by another researcher in the same context or in other sectors or by using other methods.

The implication for academic research is that further investigation into the D-M under uncertainty and complexity is still needed. The influence from behavioural factors and experience organizational factors needs to be examined and tested in more detail. The influence of DSS on D-M needs to be examined and tested in more detail.

In other words the author suggests that his results be examined in future research:

*Question 1*: There is an Impact of Learning (new knowledge) on the decision-maker's professional composure.
- What are the measurements of the learning experience under uncertainty
    - o Collaborative discussion of experience between social-actors
    - o Classify social-actors about their skills

*Question 2*: There is a Calculating Decision Knowledge process under uncertainty.
- What are the Human skills needed for the interchange and producing information for the lack of knowing under uncertainty:
    o Non-human devices to get factual information
    o Interaction between social-actors in order to tune and adjust behaviours – socialize group

*Question 3*: There is a learning-story balancing emotional and factual reads under uncertainty
- How knowledgeable information arrives to the decision-maker
- What is enough: Factual Information or Emotional to be able to D-M
- There are feedback analysis for instinctive decisions

*Question 4*: There is an eternally vague context, represented by uncertainty
- How risk behaviour is assumed: individual or group
- How the reframing and reconstructing of the uncertain context is done
- There are established measurements

Finally, according to the research results, the Judgement of Decisions have been given less consideration. Hence the Judgement of Decisions applications and its developments in the uncertain context could be suggested also as future research.

# References

Ackoff, R. L. (1994). *The Democratic Organization*. New York: Oxford University Press.

Alasuutari, P. (1996). Theorizing in qualitative research: A cultural studies perspective. *Qualitative Inquiry*. 2, 371-384. Quoted in Charmaz (2006), pp.112.

Albas, C. and Albas, D. (1988) Emotion work and emotion rules: The case of exams. *Qualitative Sociology*, 11, 259-274. Quoted in Charmaz (2006), pp.111.

Allan, G. (2003). A critique of using grounded theory as a research method, *Electronic Journal of Business Research Methods*. 2(1) pp 1-10.

Allen, P. M. (1998). Evolving complexity in social science. In Altman, G. and Koch, W. A. (eds) (1998). *Systems: New Paradigms for the Human Sciences*. New York: Walter de Gruyter.

Alexander, C. (1996). The Origins of Pattern Theory – The future of the theory, and the generation of a living world. *ACM Conference on Object-Oriented Programs, Systems, Languages and Applications (OOPSLA'96). IEEE Software*, (September/October 1999),71-82.

Argyris, C. (1994) *On organizational learning*. Oxford: Cambridge,Massachusetts: Blackwell.

Arrow, Kenneth J. (Jan 1958) Utilities, Attitudes and Choices: A Review Note. *Econometrica*.1-23. Quoted in Mack, Ruth P. (1971) *Planning on uncertainty: decision making in business and government administration*. New York, Chichester: Wiley-Interscience, pp. 172.

Arthur, Brian W. (1999). Complexity and Economy. *Science*. 2 April, 284, 107-109.

Ashby, W.R. (1956). *Introduction to Cybernetics*. New York: John Wiley.

Aumann, Robert and Brandenburger, Adam (1995) Epistemic Conditions for Nash Equilibrium. *Econometrica* 63(5): 1161-1180.

Axelrod, R. (1984) *The Evolution of Cooperation*. Basic Books, New York.

Barnard, C.I. (1938) *The Functions of the Executive*. Harvard University Press: Cambridge, MA, Thirtieth Anniversary Edition. Quoted in Rowe and Boulgarides (1992), pp. 16.

Bateson, G. (1972). *Steps to an Ecology of Mind*. New York: Ballantine Books.

Bauman, Z. (2004) *Wasted Lives*. Polity. Quoted in Bryant (2006, pp.146).

Bazerman, Max H. (2006). *Judgment in managerial decision making*. (6 ed). Hoboken, N.J.: Wiley.

References

Beer, S. (1979). *The Heart of Enterprise*. Chichester: Wiley.

Bennett, S., McRobb, S. and Farmer, R. (2002). *Object-Oriented Systems Analysis and Design Using UML*. McGraw-Hill Companies, 2$^{nd}$ Ed.

Benbasat, Izak., Goldstein, David K. and Mead, Melissa (Sep., 1987) The Case Research Strategy in Studies of Information Systems, *MIS Quarterly*, Vol. 11, No. 3, pp. 369-386.

Bernoulli, Jacques (1713) *Ars Conjectandi*. Base. Quoted in: Chacko, George Kuttickal (1991) *Decision-making under uncertainty: an applied statistics approach*. Praeger, pp.20.

Bernstein, Peter (1996) *Against the gods: the remarkable story of risk*. New York. Chichester: Wiley.

Bijker, W. (1995) *Of Bicycles, Bakelites, and Bulbs: Toward a Theory of Socio-Technical Change*, MIT Press, Cambridge, Mass.

Biswas, Tapan (1997) *Decision making under uncertainty*. Basingstoke: Macmillan.

Blalock, M. (1991) Are There Any Constructive Alternative to Causal Modelling? *Sociological Methodology*, No 21, pp.325-335.

Bligh, John (Jan 2001) Learning from uncertainty: a change of culture. *Medical Education*. 35, 2.

Boland, R. J. Jr. (1985) Phenomenology: A Preferred Approach to Research in Information Systems, in *Research Methods in Information Systems*, E. Mumford, R. A. Hirschheim, G. Fitzgerald, and A. T. Wood-Harper (eds.), North-Holland, Amsterdam, pp. 193-201.

Boland, R. J. Jr. (1991) Information System Use as a Hermeneutic Process, in *Information Systems Research: Contemporary Approaches and Emergent Traditions*, H-E. Nissen, H. K. Klein, and R. A. Hirschheim (eds.), North-Holland, Amsterdam, pp. 439-464.

Bolloju, N. (2004). Improving the quality of Business Object models using collaboration patterns. *Communications of the ACM*, July, 47(7), 81-86.

Bordage, G. (1999) Why did I miss the diagnosis? Some cognitive explanations and educational implications. *Acad Med*, 72:1385-435.

Boulding, K. E. (1956). *General Systems Theory: The skeleton of science*. Management Science. Vol. 10, pp. 97-108.

Bryant, A. (2000). Chinese Encyclopaedias and Balinese Cockfights - Lessons for Business Process Change and Knowledge Management. *Proceedings of the 12th European Workshop on Knowledge Acquisition*, Modelling and Management.

Bryant, A. (2002) Re-grounding Grounded Theory. *The Journal of Information Technology Theory and Application*, 4(1), 2002, 25-42.

Bryant, A. (2006) *Thinking "Informatically" A New Understanding of Informations, Communications, and Technology*. Lewiston: N.Y.; Lampeter: Edwin Mellen Press.

# References

Bryman, A. (1993) *Quality and Quantity in Social Research*. London, Routledge.

Callon, M. (1999) Actor-network theory – The market test. In: Law, J. and Hassard, J. (eds) (1999) *Actor Network Theory and After*. Blackwell Publishers/The social Review. 181-195.

Casati, F., Shan, E., Dayal, U. and Shan, M-C. (2003). Business-oriented management of Web services. *Communications of The ACM*, October, 46(10), 55-60.

Chacko, George Kuttickal (1991) *Decision-making under uncertainty: an applied statistics approach*. Praeger.

Charmaz, K. (1983) Loss of self: a fundamental form of suffering in the chronically ill. *Sociology of Health and Illness* 5, 168–195.

Charmaz, K. (2003), Grounded theory: Objectivist and constructivist methods, in *Strategies of qualitative inquiry*, NK Denzin and YS Lincoln (eds.), 2$^{nd}$ ed, Sage, Thousand Oaks, CA.

Charmaz, K. (2006) *Constructing Grounded Theory: A Practical Guide Through Qualitative Analysis*. London: Sage Publications.

Chase, Valerie M., Hertwig, Ralph and Gigerenzer, Gerd (1998) Visions of rationality, *Trends in Cognitive Sciences*, 2, 6 (pp. 206-214).

Checkland, P. B. (1981). *Systems Thinking, Systems Practice*. Chichester: Wiley.

Checkland, P. B. (1983). OR and the systems movement: mapping and conflicts. *Journal of the Operational Research Society*. Vol. 34, p. 661.

Checkland, P. B. and Scholes, P. (1990). *Soft Systems Methodology in Action*. Chichester: Wiley.

Churchman, C. W. (1970). *The Systems Approach and its Enemies*. New York: Basic Books.

Clandinin, J. and Connelly, F. M. (1994) Personal experience methods. In Denzin, N. and Lincoln, Y. (eds) *Handbook of Qualitative Methods*. Thousand Oaks: Sage, pp. 415 Quoted in Shaw (1999), pp.49.

Cline, M. P. (1996). The Pros and Cons of Adopting and Applying Design Patterns in the Real World. *Communications of The ACM*, 39(10), 47-49.

Coplien, J. O. (1996). Introduction to Christopher Alexander. ACM Conference on Object-Oriented Programs, Systems, Languages and Applications (OOPSLA'96). In The Origin of Pattern Theory – The future of the theory, and the generation of a living world. *IEEE Software*, (September/October 1999), 71-72.

Cormack, D.S. (1991).*The research process*. Black Scientific: Oxford.

Crawford, Robert G. (Oct., 1973) Implications of Learning for Economic Models of Uncertainty. *International Economic Review*, Vol. 14, No. 3. ( pp. 587-600).

Dalbello, Marija, and Lisa Covi (2003), Tool or Sign? Negotiated Learning and Socialization Process in the Students' Perceptions of Technology in the Digital Library Classroom, *Information Technology, Education and Society* 4(2:2003), pp.

35-52.

Davenport, T. H. and Prusack, L. (1998). *Working Knowledge: How Organizations Manage What they Know.* Cambridge. MA: Harvard University Press.

Dayan, P and Yu, A.J. (2003) Uncertainty and learning. *IETE Journal of Research.* 49, 171-182.

de Finetti, B. (1974) *Theory of Probability – A Critical Introductory Treatment.* (2 vols). New York: Wiley. Quoted in: Biswas, Tapan (1997) *Decision making under uncertainty.* Basingstoke: Macmillan, pp. 61.

Deetz, S. (1996) Describing Differences in Approaches to Organization Science: Rethinking Burrell and Morgan and their Legacy, *Organization Science* (7:2), 1996, pp. 191-207.

Dubois, A. and Gadde, L-E. (2002) Systematic Combining - An abductive approach to case research, *Journal of Business Research,* Vol. 55, pp. 553-560. Quoted in Kovács and Spens, 2005, pp.139.

Einhorm, H. J. (1982) Learning from experience and suboptimal rules in decision making. In Kahneman, Slovic, and Tversky (eds.) (1982) *Judgment under uncertainty: Heuristics and biases.* New York: Cambridge University Press, pp. 268-283.

Eldabi, T., Irani, Z., Paul, R. and Love, P. (2002) Quantitative and Qualitative Decision Methods in Simulation Modelling. *Management Decision,* 40(1), pp. 64-73.

Evernden, R. and Evernden, E. (2003). Third-generation information architecture. *Communications of the ACM,* March, 46(3), 95-98.

Fawcett, J., and Downs, F. S. (1986) *The Relationship of Theory and Research,* Appleton-Century-Crofts, Norwalk, CT. Quoted in Gregor (2006), pp.623-4.

Fendt, J. and Sachs, W. (2007) Grounded Theory Method in Management Research: Users Perspective. *Organizational Research Methods.* Sage Publications.

Forrester, J. (1958). *Industrial Dynamics: a major break-through for decision-making.* Harvard Business Review. Vol. 36, n.4, pp.37-66.

Fowler, M. (1996). *Analysis Patterns: Reusable Object Models.* Addison-Wesley.

Frankel, D. S., Harmon, P., Mukerji, J., Odell, J., Owen, M., Rivitt, P., Rosen, M., and Soley, R. M. (Ed.) (2003). The Zachman Framework and the OMG's Model Driven Architecture. *Object Management Group, White paper,* Business Process Trends, Retrieved Jul/2004: http://www.omg.org/bp-corner/bp-files/MDA-Zachman-Framework.pdf.

Frey, H. C. and Patil, S. R. (2002) Identification and review of sensitivity analysis methods. *Risk analysis: an official publication of the Society for Risk Analysis,* 2002;22(3):553-78.

Gergen, H. J. (1985). The social constructionist movement in modern psychology. *American Psychologist.* Vol. 40, pp.266-75. Quoted in Robson(2002).

Gigerenzer, G. and Goldstein, D. G. (1996). Reasoning the fast and frugal way: Models of bounded rationality. *Psychological Review*, 103, 650-669.

Glaser, B. G and Strauss, A. L. (1967) *The Discovery of Grounded Theory: Strategies for Qualitative Research*. Aldine Publishing Company, NY.

Glaser, B. G. (1978). *Theoretical sensitivity: Advances in methodology of grounded theory*. Mill Valley, CA: Sociological Press.

Glaser, B.G. (1998) *Doing Grounded Theory: Issues and Discussion*. Mill Valley, CA: The Sociology Press.

Goodwin, R. M. (1951). Econometrics in business-style analysis. In Hansen, A. H. (ed.) (1951). *Business Cycles and National Income*. New York: W.W.Norton.

Gregor, Shirley (2006) The Nature of Theory in Information Systems. *MIS Quarterly*, 30(3): 611-642.

Guba, E. (1990) The alternative paradigm dialog. In Guba, E. (ed.) *The Paradigm Dialog*. Newbury Park: Sage quoted in Shaw, Ian (1999).

Habermas, J. (1984) *Theory of Communicative Action, Volume 1: Reason and the Rationalization of Society*, Heinemann, London, UK, quoted in Gregor (2006).

Hammersley, M. (1992). *What's wrong with ethnography?* London: Routledge.

Hayles N. K. (1999) *How Became Posthuman: Virtual Bodies in Cybernetics, Literature and Informatics*. University of Chicago Press.

Herzum, P. and Sims, O. (2000) *Business Component Factory : A Comprehensive Overview of Component-Based Development for the Enterprise*. OMG Press.

Holstein, J. and Gubrium, J. (1995) *The Active Interview*. Thousand Oaks: Sage. Quoted in Shaw (1999), pp. 147.

Hood, J. C. (1983) *Become a two-job family*. New York: Praeger. Quoted in Charmaz (2006).

Hurwicz, Leonid (1951) Optimal Criterion for Decision Making under Ignorance. *Cowles Commission Discussion Paper, Statistics*. 307. Quoted in: Biswas, Tapan (1997) *Decision making under uncertainty*. Basingstoke: Macmillan, pp. 189.

Hyde, K. (2000) Recognising Deductive Process in Qualitative Research. *Qualitative Market Research: An International Journal*, 3(2), pp.82-90.

Jackson, M. C. (2000). *Systems Approaches to Management*. New York: Kluwer.

Jevons, W. Stanley (1871). *The Theory of Political Economy*. London: Macmillan. Quoted in: Bernstein, Peter (1996) *Against the gods: the remarkable story of risk*. New York. Chichester: Wiley, pp.269.

Jung, Carl (1959) The Archetypes and the Collective Unconscious. *The Collected Works of C.G. Jung, V.9*. Princeton: Princeton University Press. Quoted in: Rowe, A.J. and Boulgarides, J.C. (1992) *Managerial decision making*. New York: Macmillan Publishing Company. pp.35.

Kahneman, Daniel and Tversky, Amos (1979) Prospect Theory: An Analysis of

Decision under Risk. *Econometrica.* 47 (2), 263-291.

Kahneman, Daniel and Tversky, Amos (1982) *Variants of uncertainty.* In Kahneman, Slovic, and Tversky (eds.) (1982) *Judgment under uncertainty: Heuristics and biases.* New York: Cambridge University Press. pp.509-520.

Kangas, K. (Ed.) (2003). *A Framework for Research into Business-IT Alignment: A Cognitive Emphasis.* Business Strategies for Information Technology Management. Idea Group Publishing.

Kaplan, B., and Maxwell, J. A. (1994) "Qualitative Research Methods for Evaluating Computer Information Systems," in *Evaluating Health Care Information Systems: Methods and Applications,* J. G. Anderson, C. E. Aydin, and S. J. Jay (eds.). Sage, housand Oaks, CA, 1994, pp. 45-68. Quoted in Klein and Myers (1999).

Keynes, John M. (1921) *A Treatise on Probability.* London: Macmillan.

Klein, Heinz K. and Myers, Michael D. (1999) A set of principles for conducting and evaluating interpretive field studies in information systems. *MIS Quarterly,* 23(1): 67-94.

Knight, Frank H. (1964) *Risk, Uncertainty and Profit.* New York: Century Press. Quoted in: Bernstein, Peter (1996) *Against the gods: the remarkable story of risk.* New York. Chichester: Wiley, pp. 219.

Kovács, G. and Spens, K. M. (2005) Abductive reasoning in logistics research, *International Journal of Physical Distribution and Logistics Management,* 35 (2), 132-144.

Kurtz, C.F. and Snowden, D.J. (2003) The New Dynamics of Strategy: Sense-Making in a Complex and Complicated World. *IBM Systems Journal.* Issue 42-3. E-Business Management.

Latour, B. (1991) Technology is Society Made Durable. In *A Sociology of Monsters: Essays on Power, Technology and Domination.* J.Law (ed.) (1991) Routledge, London, pp. 103-131. Quoted in Gregor (2006), pp. 624.

Law, J. (1992) Notes on the Theory of the Actor-Network: Ordering, Strategy and Heterogeneity. *Systems Practice.* 5: 379-393.

Law, J. and Hassard, J. (eds) (1999). *Actor Network Theory and After* (Oxford and Keele: Blackwell and the Sociological Review).

Layder, D. (1998) *Sociological Practice: Linking theory and social research.* London: Sage. Quoted in Charmaz (2006), pp.134.

Learning Theories Knowledgebase (2008, May). *Index of Learning Theories and Models at Learning-Theories.com.* Retrieved May 26th, 2008 from http://www.learning-theories.com

Lee, J., Siau, K., and Hong, S. (2003), Enterprise Integration with ERP and EAI. *Communications of the ACM,* February, 46(2), 54-60.

Levy, D. (1994). Chaos theory and strategic: theory, application and managerial implications. *Strategic Management Journal.* Vol. 15, pp.167-178.

References

Loomes, G. and Sugden, R. (1982) Regret Theory: An Alternative Theory of Rational Choice under Uncertainty. *Economic Journal*, 92, 805-32. Quoted in: Biswas, Tapan (1997) *Decision making under uncertainty*. Basingstoke: Macmillan, pp. 63.

Mack, Ruth Prince (1971) *Planning on uncertainty: decision making in business and government administration*. New York, Chichester: Wiley-Interscience.

Malcolm, E. (2004). Soft Systems Methodology. *Association of Chartered Certified Accountants*, January issue, Professional scheme, Accessed on-line Jun/2004: http://www.acca.org.uk/publications/studentaccountant/

Marion, R. (1999). *The Edge of Organization: Chaos and Complexity Theories of Formal Social Systems*. Thousand Oaks. CA: Sage Publications.

Martinsons, M. G., (2004). ERP in China: one package, two profiles. *Communications of the ACM*, July, 47(7), 65-68.

McMillan, John (1992) *Games, strategies and managers*. Oxford University Press.

Midgley, G. (2000). *Systemic Intervention: Philosophy, Methodology and Practice*. New York: Kluwer.

Miles, M., and Huberman, M. (1994). *Qualitative data analysis: A sourcebook of new methods* (2$^{nd}$ ed.) Newbury Park, CA: Sage.

Minchiello, V., Aroni, R., Timewell,E. & Alexander, L. (1990) *In- Depth Interviewing Researching People*. Melbourne, Longman Cheshire.

Mintzberg, H., Raisinghani, D. and Théorêt, A. (1976) The structure of "unstructured" decision processes. *Administrative Science Quarterly*, 21, 246-275.

Montgomery, H., and Svenson, O. (1989). *Process and structure in human decision making*. New York: Wiley. Quoted in Yates and Stone (1992), pp. 293.

Morley, D. (1995). Chaos 3.0. *Manufacturing Systems*. August, p.14.

Myers, M.D (2009) *Qualitative Research in Business & Management*. Sage Publications, London.

Neuman, W. L. (1991) *Social Research Methods*. Boston, MA, Allyn and Bacon.

Neuman, W. L. (2000) *Social Research Methods* (4$^{th}$ ed.), Allyn and Bacon, Boston. Quoted in Gregor (2006), pp.616.

Newell, A. and Simon, H. A. (1972) *Human Problem Solving*. Englewood Cliffs, NJ.; Prentice-Hall.

Newman, James R. (1988) The *World of Mathematics: A Small Library of the Literature of Mathematics from A'h-mosé the Scribe to Albert Einstein*. Redmond, Washington: Tempus Press, pp. 1333-1338. Quoted in: Bernstein, Peter (1996) *Against the gods: the remarkable story of risk*. New York. Chichester: Wiley, pp.223.

Norton, D. F. (1999) "Hume" in *The Cambridge Dictionary of Philosophy* (2$^{nd}$ ed.), R. Audi (ed.), Cambridge University Press, Cambridge, UK, pp. 398-403. Quoted in

References

Gregor (2006), pp.617.

Nuseibeh, B. and Easterbrook, S. (2000). Requirements engineering: a roadmap. *ACM Press, Proceedings of the conference on The future of Software engineering*, Limerick, Ireland, 35-46.

Orlikowski, W. J., and Baroudi, J. J. (1991) Studying Information Technology in Organizations: Research Approaches and Assumptions, *Information Systems Research*. (2:1), pp. 1-28 quoted in Klein and Myers (1999).

Parker, L. D., and Roffey, B. H. (1997). Back to the Drawing Boards: Revisiting Grounded Theory and the everyday Accountant's and Manager's Reality. *Accounting, Auditing & Accountability Journal*. Vol. 10, No. 2, pp. 212-247.

Patton, Q. (1991) *Qualitative Evaluations and Research Methods*, 2$^{nd}$ ed. New Bury Park, CA, Sage publications.

Peters, E. E. (1991). *Chaos and Order in The Capital Markets: A new View of Cycles, Prices and Market Volatility*. New York: John Wiley.

Philips, A. W. (1950). Mechanical Models in economic dynamics. *Econometrica*. Vol. 17, pp.283-305.

Pidd, Michael (2003*) Tools for Thinking - Modelling in Management Sci*ence. (2$^{nd}$ ed.) Chichester: Wiley.

Pitz, Gordon F. (1992) Risk Taking, design, and training, pp. 283-320. In Yates, J. Frank (ed) (1992) *Risk-Taking Behavior*. Chichester: John Wiley & Sons.

Popper, K. (1986) *Unended Quest an Intellectual Autobiography*. Fontana, Glasgow, quoted in Gregor (2006).

Ramsey, F. P. (1926) Truth and Probability, in Ramsey, F. P. *The Foundations of Mathematics and Other Essays*. London: Routledge, Kegan Paul; reprinted in H.Kyburg and H. Smokler (eds) (1964) *Subjective Probability*. London: Wiley. Quoted in: Biswas, Tapan (1997) *Decision making under uncertainty*. Basingstoke: Macmillan, pp.61.

Richardson G., and Ives, B. (2004). Systems Development Processes. *IEEE Computer Society*, 37(5), 84-86.

Robey, D., and Markus, M. L. (1998). Beyond rigor and relevance: Producing consumable research about information systems. *Information Resources Management Journal*, 11(1), 7–15.

Robson, C. (2002). *Real World Research – a Resource for Social Scientist and Practioner-Researchers*. 2$^{nd}$ ed. Blackwell Publishers.

Rowe, A.J. and Boulgarides, J.C. (1992) *Managerial decision making*. New York: Macmillan Publishing Company.

Ruane, Janet M. (2005) *Essentials of research methods: a guide to social science research*. Oxford: Blackwell.

Savage, Leonard J. (1951) The Theory of Statistical Decision. *Journal of the American Statistical Association*. 46, 363-91. Quoted in: Biswas, Tapan (1997) *Decision making under uncertainty.* Basingstoke: Macmillan, pp. 187.

Scott, D. (1996). Making judgements about educational research, In:, *Understanding educational research.* (Scott, D. and Usher, R. eds.). Routledge.

Shackle, G. L. S. (1961) *Decision, Order, and Time in Human Affairs.* Cambridge: The University Press. Quoted in: White, Douglas John (2006) *Decision Theory.* New Brunswick, N.J.: Aldine Transaction, pp.58.

Shackle, G. L. S. (1967) *The Years of High Theory: Invention and Tradition in Economics Though 1926-1939.* Cambridge: Cambridge University Press. Quoted in Gerrard, B. (2003) *Probability Keynesian uncertainty: what do we know?* In Jochen Runde & Sohei Mizuhara (eds) (2003). *The philosophy of Keynes's economics: probability, uncertainty and convention.* London: Routledge, pp. 239.

Shaw, Ian (1999) *Qualitative evaluation.* London: Sage Publications.

Suchman, L. A. (1987). *Plans and situated actions: The problem of human-machine communications.* Cambridge, UK: Cambridge University Press.

Silverman, David (2005) *Doing qualitative research: a practical handbook.* (2$^{nd}$ ed). London: Sage.

Simon, Herbert A. (1945) *Administrative behavior. A study of decision making processes in administrative organization.* New York: Free Press.

Simon, Herbert A. (1957) *Models of Man: Social and National.* New York: Wiley.

Simon, Herbert A. (1965). *The Shape of Automation.* New York: Harper and Row. Quoted in: Mintzberg, H., Raisinghani, D. and Théorêt, A. (1976) The structure of "unstructured" decision processes. *Administrative Science Quarterly,* 21, pp.253.

Simon, Herbert. A. (1982) *Models of bounded rationality.* Cambridge, MA: MIT Press.

Soh, C., Kien., S. and Tay-Yap, J. (2000). Cultural fits and misfits. Is ERP a universal solution? *Communications of the ACM,* April, 43(4), 47-51.

Sowa, J. F., and Zachman, J. A. (1992). Extending and formalizing the framework for information systems architecture. *IBM Systems Journal,* 31(3), 590-616.

Stacey, Ralph D. (2003) *Strategic Management and Organisational Dynamics – The Challenge of Complexity.* 4$^{th}$ ed. Prentice Hall Financial Times.

Stake, R.E. (1994) in *Handbook of Qualitative Research,* edited by Denzin N.K. and Lincoln Y.S. (1994), Sage London.

Steier, F. (1991). *Research and Reflexivity.* Thousand Oaks, CA: Sage. Quoted in Stacey, Ralph D. (2003) *Strategic Management and Organisational Dynamics - The Challenge of Complexity.* 4$^{th}$ ed. Prentice Hall Financial Times, pp. 9.

Strauss, A., and Corbin, J. (1990). *Basics of qualitative research: Grounded theory procedures and techniques.* Newbury Park, CA: Sage.

Strauss, A., and Corbin, J. (1994). Grounded theory methodology. In N. K. Denzin & Y. S. Lincoln (Eds.), *Handbook of qualitative research* (pp. 273-285). Thousand Oaks, CA: Sage.

# References

Strauss, A., and J. Corbin (1998) *Basics of Qualitative Research: Grounded Theory Procedures and Techniques*, 2$^{nd}$ edition, Sage, pp.12 quoted in Bryant (2002), pp.31.

Strauss, A. (1987) *Qualitative analysis for social scientists.* New York: Cambridge University Press.

Sveiby, K. E. (1997). *The New Organizational Wealth: Managing and Measuring Knowledge-Based Assets.* San Francisco: Berrett and Koehler.

Tatnall, A. and Gilding, A. (1999*) Actor-network theory and information systems research.* In proceeedings 10$^{th}$ Australasian Conference on Information Systems (ACIS), Wellington, Victoria University of Wellington.

Tesch, R. (1990) *Qualitative Research: Analysis Types and Software Tools.* New York, NY, The Falmer press.

Thaler, R. (2000) From Homo economicus to homo sapiens. *Journal of economics perpectives.* 14, 133-141. Quoted in: Bazerman, M. H. (2006) *Judgment in managerial decision making.* 6$^{th}$ ed. Hoboken, N.J. Wiley., p.7.

Turban, E. and Aronson, J. E. (2001). *Decision Support Systems and Intelligent Systems.* Prentice Hall International. 6$^{th}$ Ed.

Tustin, A. (1953). *The Mechanism of Economic Systems.* MA: Harvard University Press.

Tversky, A. and Kahneman, D. (1982). "Causal Schemas in judgments under uncertainty" In *Judgment under uncertainty: Heuristics and biases*, Kahneman, Slovic, and Tversky (Eds.), Cambridge University Press: New York, NY, 1982, pp. 103-126.

Tversky, Amos (1990) *The Psychology of Risk.* In Sharpe, William F. (1990) Investor *Wealth Measures and Expected Return.* pp.75. In Sharpe, William F., ed. (1990) *Quantifying the Market Risk Premium Phenomenon for Investment Decision Making.* Charlottesville, Virginia: The Institute of Chartered Financial Analysis, pp. 29-37. Quoted in: Bernstein, Peter (1996) *Against the gods: the remarkable story of risk.* New York. Chichester: Wiley, pp.274.

Tversky, Amos and Koehler, Derek J. (1994) Support Theory: A Nonextensional Representation of Subjective Probability. *Psychological Review.* 101, 4, 547-567. Quoted in: Bernstein, Peter (1996) *Against the gods: the remarkable story of risk.* New York. Chichester: Wiley, pp.279.

Vanhoenacker J., Bryant A. and Dedene G., (1999) Striving for 'Methodological Fit' in Business Process Change, *Knowledge and Process Management*, Vol. 6, Nr 1, pp. 24-36.

Venkatraman, N. (1989). The concept of fit in strategy research. *Academy of Management Research*, 14(3), 423–444.

Vogt, C. (2002). Intractable ERP: a comprehensive analysis of failed enterprise-resource-planning projects. *ACM Press, ACM SIGSOFT Software Engineering*, 27(2), 62-68.

Von Bertalanffy, Ludwig (1968) *General System Theory: Foundations, Development,*

*Applications*. New York: George Braziller. (also published 1971 by London: Allen Lane).

Von Foerster, H. (1984). On constructing reality *in* von Foerster, H. (ed.) *Observing Systems*. Seaside. CA: Intersystems.

Von Neumann, John and Morgenstern, Oskar (1944). *Theory of Games and Economic Behavior*. Princeton. New Jersey: Princeton University Press. Quoted in: Bernstein, Peter (1996) *Against the gods: the remarkable story of risk*. New York. Chichester: Wiley, pp.269.

Walker, D. and Myrick, F. (2006) Grounded Theory: An Exploration of Process and Procedure. *Qualitative Health Research*. (Apr 2006). 16 (4). 547-559. Sage Publications.

Weick, K. (1977). Organizational Design: organizations as self-organizing systems. *Organizational Dynamics*. Autumn, pp. 31-67.

Weick, K. E. (1984). Managerial thought in the context of action. In S. S. (Ed.), *The Executive Mind. San Francisco*, CA: Jossey-Bass.

Wenger, E. (1998). *Communities of Practice: Learning, Meaning and Identity*. New York: Cambridge University Press.

White, Douglas John (2006) *Decision Theory*. New Brunswick, N.J.: Aldine Transaction.

Wiener, N. (1948). *Cybernetics: Or Control and Communication in the Animal and the Machine*. MA: MIT Press.

Wilson, N. and McLean, S. (1994) *Questionnaire Design: A Practical Introduction*, University of Ulster Press, Co.Antrim.

Wright, George (1952) *Behavioral decision theory: an introduction*. Beverly Hills: Sage Publications. c1984.

Wright, T. and Crimp, M. (2000) *The Marketing Research Process*, 5th ed. Englewood Cliffs, Nj, Prentice- Hall.

Yates, J. Frank and Stone, Eric R. (1992) *The risk construct*. In Yates, J. Frank (ed) (1992) *Risk-Taking Behavior*. Chichester: John Wiley & Sons, pp. 1-26.

Yin, R. K. (1984) *Case study research: Design and methods*. Newbury Park, CA: Sage.

# Heuristic Sample Guideline Use

**Grounded Theory of Decision-Making under Uncertainty**

1) Picture an Uncertain Context – **Conceptual Framework**

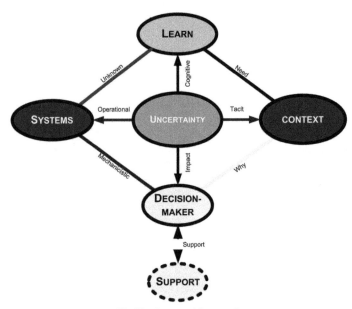

**Fig. 25** – Conceptual Framework

Use **Grounded Theory** – Open interviews within the group and auxiliary outsiders
a. Definition of Concepts
   - Who are **Decision-makers**?
   - How is interpreted uncertain **Context**?
   - What are the **Systems**? Human (techniques) and non-human devices
   - How is formed a social-network to solve problems? How they **Learn**?
   - Is there extra **Support**?

b. Definition of internal links
   - **Cognitive**: How many social-actors? Who are they? What skills they have? How they generate knowledge? How they communicate?
   - **Tacit**: What have been used tactics? How they have approach problems? How they reconstruct reality? What is a solution for

them?
- **Operational**: How they use systems? What they use as interaction for discussion and develop knowledge (*translations*)? Where they stand for facts? How they get factual information?
- **Impact on self**: How participative is decision-making? How is the chain of responsibility (*punctualizations*)? What is the image of the organization? What patterns of use they refer in decision-making (*inscriptions*)?

c. <u>Sensing Uncertainty – External Links</u>
- **Why** – Constructed meaning for defining a search for confront an uncertain context? Need: problem, solution, tender, desire, etc.
- **Mechanicistic** – inventory of previous experiences dealing with needs: innovation, change and uncertainty. Construct a set of knowledgeable environment use.
- **Unknown** – inventory of described situations for "we do not have", "we need to", "we do not know" and construct the opposite knowledgeable environments use.
- **Need** – How they feel need? Problem, solutions, tenders, desires, etc?

d. <u>Shape with complementary inventory of independent categories</u>:
- How they feel pleasure in the organization?
- They have constrains? About what? Do they show dual risk behaviour?
- How they dedicate to work?
- How confidents they are, in themselves and in others?
- How they work recognition? Do they have afraid? How they are responsible for their actions?

2) Drawing of flux ontology's – **ANT Network**

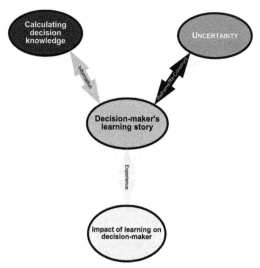

**Fig. 5. 26** – ANT Network

**SSM & Action-Research** – Construct ANT Concepts

a. Calculate Decision-Knowledge – Knowledge development
   - Definition of decision social-actors network
     - Human skills needed for the interchange and producing information for the lack of knowing[13]
     - Non-human devices to get factual information
   - Interaction between social-actors in order to tune and adjust behaviours – socialize group
   - Turn operational Systems in order to mecanicistic for the unknown


b. Uncertainty – evolutionary perspective of *need*
   (Recommended use of *Soft System Methodology*).
   - Reframe and reconstructed uncertain context
   - Define and establish measurements
   - Follow Soft System Methodology in dealing with Uncertain context

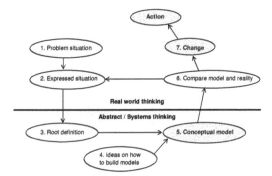

**Fig. 5. 27** - Checkland SSM stages


c. **Decision Learning Story** – Balance Emotional and Factual reads
   - How Information and Reality Change arrive to Decision-maker?
   - How meaning is being interpreted to decision-making?
   - Where is the balance? What is enough: Factual Information or Emotional? Are we able to decision-making?
   - Complement cycles with independent categories:
     - Do we need more recognition?
     - Do we have work hard?
     - Do we have pleasure?
     - Do we are confident?
     - Do we learn enough?
     - Do we have duality constrain risk behaviour?


d. **Impact of Learning on decision-maker (self)** – Learn experience
   - Observe results and discuss a judgment
     - Collaborative discussion of experience
     - Annotate amendments
     - Socialize and show feelings

---

[13] Brainstorming, Scenario Building, Colaborative Participation, whatever is adequate in that social-context group.

- Record experience
  - Analyse annotations taken and learn why some actions have been taken
  - Classify social-actors about their skills
  - Write a sample memo and record for future access
- Learn with experience and focus how and where it was balanced the decision:

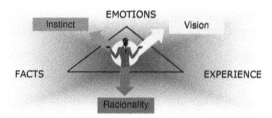

**Fig. 5. 28** – Enhancement Conceptual Framework

  - Fill complementary tables

| Factual Information | | |
|---|---|---|
| **Concept** | **Actants** | **Observation Note** |
| Social-Web | Who | |
| Resources | Operational | |
| | Tactics | |
| Process | Why | |
| | Need | |
| | What was unknown | |
| | What has been turn mecanicistic | |

| Emotional Information Reads | | |
|---|---|---|
| Emotions | Opinion for social actors | |
| | Other feelings observed | |
| | Fear | |
| | Un-Pleasure | |
| | Risk feeling | |
| | Appreciation | |
| | Being collaborative | |
| Experience | Factual Results | |
| | Impact of Results | |

www.ingramcontent.com/pod-product-compliance
Lightning Source LLC
LaVergne TN
LVHW042333060326
832902LV00006B/142